REVIEWS:

*This book is FANTASTIC!!! Not only is it written by a LEGEND but it's packed full of one on one interviews with some of the most influential doctors in the healthcare industry! You could spend months or years and thousands of dollars traveling around the country, attending seminars to acquire the information packed into The **DR. SUCCESS SPOTLIGHT BOOK**. Do yourself a favor, buy it now, binge read it and then you'll find yourself re-reading it just as I am!!!*

Dr. Cameron Roe
Anna, Texas

*It is with great enthusiasm that I write this testament to your new book. I have been in practice for almost 25 years. In the past few years I had lost a lot of my passion for our amazing healing art of Chiropractic. From the moment I met you and started reading your latest book **Dr. Success Spotlight Book**, my spirit has been reignited. Your passion and wisdom that you share is so inspiring. Since implementing just a few diamonds that you have written about, our excitement to serve has exploded. We have had some of the most fun and profitable days in a long time. I would recommend you to any Chiropractor who has lost the excitement that they first had in practice. By following your recipe and expertise there is only one way to go and that is to the top. When we get passionate about helping people again, our practice can't be stopped from growing, and your newest book is so filled with decades of this wisdom. Thank-you, Thank-you, Thank-you my friend. See you at the top!*

Dr. Sean McWilliams
Alpharetta, Georgia

WOW, I am awed by what you have done and are doing for the your-self, your family, and the profession of Chiropractic. I have known many people who have stood out in Chiropractic over the many decades I have been practicing, including Dr. Joe Stucky, Dr. Gonstead, Dr. Clay Thompson, Dr. Bill Harris, and so many more amazing doctors... but YOU ABSULUTELY stand above all those great doctors because you have done thing's I could never have imagined being possible! I am proud and humbled to know you and be a part of what you are creating beyond your legendary life. You have a light that never dims and have taken such a bite out of life that few will ever comprehend the depth of your being. You are in the process of pulling open my eyes to a world most doctors could not fathom as possible. You set a high bar to measure up to. WOW! WOW!! WOW!!!

Dr. Roy Ostenson
Appleton, Wisconsin

*The **Dr. Success Spotlight Book** is a compilation of some of the best in their respective fields, put together by a true genius, Dr. Perry Bard. I am constantly impressed by Dr. Bard and his ability to see and present things a little differently, like turning a prism to capture the most possible light. With this book, he once again allows us to "peak behind the curtain" and see how the greats do it. A must read for any doctor who wants to be the very best they can and achieve their full potential, especially in this day and age of health care in America.*

Dr. Frank Giampietro
Stuart, Florida

This book contains raw, honest, pertinent information from some of the greatest minds and All-Stars in our field. It truly is one of the best resources for any disc specialist. Dr. Bard makes the interviewees so relaxed with his questioning style that you feel like you are personally sitting down, face to face, with each doctor, and are being spoon fed all the information you will ever need to succeed in practice.

Dr. Carl Abramson
Nashville, Tennessee

Dr. Bard has put together some of the very best professionals in the chiropractic field with this book. I was able to learn something from each and everyone of them and put them into practice the next day at the office. I will have to read this book over and over just to absorb all of the nuggets of knowledge. Not only is there exceptional information about how to run a chiropractic office but how to run any type of business and life lessons as well. Dr. Bard has out done himself by putting all this information together in one book. Thank you, Dr. Bard!

Dr. Joseph Kirk
Effingham, Illinois

*Dr. Perry Bard's new book, **"Dr. Success Spotlight"**, provides revolutionary insight into what's working in today's most successful chiropractic practices. Getting the perspectives of multiple doctors highlights the fact that there's more than one way to build a profitable practice.*

Dr. Luke Henry
Greenville, South Carolina

*Dr. Bard has hit yet another Home-Run! His new book The **Dr. Success Spotlight Book** is a must read for everyone from a novice to a seasoned Practitioner. There are so many Gems, Golden nuggets, & take-a-ways throughout the book you don't want to stop reading, & once you finish all you want to do is re-read it as to make sure you didn't miss anything. Dr. Bard & his new book are game changers for the Chiropractic profession & I can't thank him enough for his time, commitment, & dedication to completing this book. I highly recommend The **Dr. Success Spotlight Book** and be ready to read it numerous times as you will not want to put it down. Thanks again Dr. Bard for seeing this Awesome book to publication & for all you do to better our lives. I truly can't thank you enough.*

Dr. Gary Biggs
Macon, Georgia

*I have had the opportunity to read Dr. Bard's book **"The Dr. Success Spotlight Book"** and have again learned from Dr. Bard!*

In reading the book, it becomes quickly apparent that even though we as health professionals have a common goal of optimal health for our patients', there are SEVERAL methods which we utilize in assisting them to reach that goal. I found each interaction with Dr. Bard and the Spotlight person had individual perspectives, even if the topic may be similar, just as different Chiropractors delivering an adjustment will be different even utilizing the same technique. It was very interesting to read about the diverse mechanisms/methods those in the book have developed in order for so many to benefit! Very interesting read, and it makes me challenge myself to do more as well. Very informative!

Dr. Stephen Johnson
Abilene, Texas
Truly inspiring!

So many of us getting the big idea and becoming stars! Simultaneously breaking the grip of insurance reliance! Even as a 35-year veteran, learned a ton of new and amazing things.

Thank You for your service to our profession.

Dr. Richard Geoghean
Wappingers Falls, New York

What an awesome read! Just like Dr. Perry Bard, these interviews are perfect, insightful, enlightening and entertaining. No one else could have written this book! Thank you, Dr. Bard.

Dr. Jeff Scheuermann
Slidell, Louisiana

This book is filled with the knowledge of some of the best doctors in the word. They freely share their proven systems and strategies that will help you help more patients, improve staff production, reduce stress and maximize your success.

Dr. Don Walsh
New Smyrna Beach, Florida

"The Dr. Success Spotlight Show Book" is a treasure trove of information. But it's not just information, it's full of thought-provoking gems that are life changing. When you read through the format and you contemplate the questions and then absorb the response of each successful participant interviewed by Dr. Bard…it is simply a mind-blowing experience. Reading through it all at once is like trying to drink from a fire hydrant. It is just so full of epiphany moments. This will be a book I will have to reread and reread and break down in smaller digestible pieces. A must read for any aspiring individual who wants to excel, especially if they are in the world of healthcare.

Dr. Steven Thain
Bellevue, Washington

This is a first! Ideas from so many successful doctors in one place that really work. Thank you, Dr. Bard, for bringing this expertise together and making your life mission one of helping others succeed.

I just wish I this book had been there when I first graduated from school. This is the part that we just didn't learn there! You have made practice enjoyable and rewarding again for so many!

Dr. Carey Girgis
Westerville, Ohio

This book is amazing. I listened to the interviewees during the show live however, As I read what they said I picked up more information second time around. This book is full of positives and great take-aways. I highly recommend reading it.

Dr. Mark Losagio
Bethlehem, Pennsylvania

Dr. Bard has put himself over the top with his new book **Dr. Success Spotlight***. The amazing part about this book is that every chapter has valuable information on improving your life and practice in all aspects! I couldn't put it down. A must read if you've been in practice a month or 40 years! Great job Dr. B!*

Dr. John Zilliox
Niagara Falls, New York

You know it's always strange to read about yourself and when I was given an early copy of this book I felt extremely honored for several reasons.

The first being that I've known Dr. Bard for over 35 years and during that time he's always been a man with a golden heart. Always wanting to improve and help his fellow man and women to better themselves and well he is just a pure GIVER. He's not a selfish person by any means or stretch of the imagination and he has an uncanny ability to break down the complicated to simple steps TO FOLLOW and get massive results . The second reason that I felt honored is that I was chapter 17 knowing that that's his lucky number and also his birthday. The third reason is being included amongst so many of my peers that have achieved incredible careers and achievements so to be placed in a book for all ages to read and history to enjoy, is a humbling accomplishment to receive...

I know that all who read this book will absorb this work of art will benefit tremendously as I have by reading it.

Long live the KING of NEW PATIENTS, "Dr. Perry Bard" ...with love and admiration.

Dr. William Moyal
Miami Beach, Florida

Must read book for the Ambitious Chiropractor!!

Dr. Benjamin Mitchell
Dacula, Georgia

Great success book and wonderful resource. Thanks for keeping us fired up and always pushing us to be out best.

Dr. Troy Dreiling
Vancouver, Washington

In Dr. Bard's book, **"The Doctor Success Spotlight"**, Dr. Bard very eloquently provides the reader with some great insights into some of the greatest minds within the chiropractic profession. No fluff here folks. Dr. Bard knows how to ask all the right questions and then sit back and listen as some of these great professionals share their own experiences and many of their tried and true success secrets. Following the interview, Dr. Bard is then able to decipher all the key takeaways in a manner to which he clearly articulates to his audience all of the "golden nuggets" that will help them to step up their own game and become the absolute best doctor they can be!

Dr. Kendell Mendonca
Tulare, California

Once again, Dr. Bard has proven his tactics of the interview skill set.

He has chosen to look not to the middle of the road but to the sidelines and pulled in the ideas from those who have that extra vision to be able to excel where many are afraid to wander.

He discovers the Secret Sauce and shares the pearls with the reader. Thank you, my Friend.

Dr. Marv R. Cagle
Greenville, South Carolina

Wow! I was looking forward to this book and now that I have it I am even more thrilled! Imagine having a personal conversation with dozens of the most innovative, successful and influential doctors in the chiropractic profession... that's what this is! Interviews with some of the doctors that I have looked forward to meeting and they openly discuss the things that are vitally important to them in their practice. I started my day this morning with one of the interviews and as I entered the room with my first patient, I could feel the boost of energy from the motivation and inspiration I received after reading it.

I have listened to many of the interviews and hearing the voices of the doctors give me an insight to who that person is. Now, having their message in print is even better! I am so glad you produced this and have made it available! Thanks to you as well as to the doctors that have shared so many secrets of their enormous success.

You say, "Success Leaves Clues," and here is a compilation of some of the best success clues I have ever seen. Thanks Dr. Bard

Dr. Mark Kestner
Murfreesboro, Tennessee

I have spent about 4 hours reading through this book and I thought it was absolutely outstanding. My favorite part was the bullet points listing the take-aways that you gave to the doctors to remember the most important points. As always, I do not know how you have taken the time to do this.

My parents cannot wait to get a copy of this book as Chiropractic is so strong in our family.

Every interview was so incredibly good I cannot even pick a favorite

You are an amazing interviewer I love how you asked just the right questions that every chiropractor wants to know the answer to.

I love the introduction where you mentioned you have one son in dental school and 1 in Chiropractic school. It was the best four hours I spent today.

Thank you so much for sharing you are awesome. I love you so much you are such an inspiration!

Dr. Richard Lohr
Decatur, Illinois

Effective communication is essential in every doctors office in the world today. Dr. Bard's revolutionary book will not only engage and inspire doctors at a visionary level, but through a series on interviews he also provides a host of pragmatic strategies that are easy to implement and applicable to doctors and their practices of all sizes and types. I have known Dr. Bard Personally and professionally for 32 years. His love of life, his family ethics, his dedication to our profession is nothing short of inspirational. Imagine a doctor averaging 20 New Patients a day in one Clinic. Imagine retiring at 40 years young. He didn't imagine it, he did it. I subsequently named him **THE NEW PATIENT KING.**

Dr. Bard breathes success as the common man breathes air. His famous statement "SUCCESS LEAVES CLUES", is outlined in every chapter of his latest book. It is a must for any doctor, any person looking for the Secrets of Success. The tools and insights Dr. Bard shares in his book have been instrumental in elevating doctors leadership and results throughout the world. It's required reading for any doctor or leader looking to play to his or her strengths and inspire others to win. If you want to make your mark as a leader, engage in thoughtful words and act on them, this book will show you how. Anyone committed to their own development as well as the success of their business 'can't not' read this important book, I loved it."

Dr. Eric Kaplan, DC,FIAMA
Author,
#1 Amazon Bestseller, *Awaken the Wellness Within*
#1 Amazon Bestseller, *The Five-Minute Motivator*

DR. SUCCESS SPOTLIGHT

DR. PERRY BARD

ISBN: 978-1-64184-053-8

"And during the moments that we have left we want to talk right down to earth in a language that everybody here can easily understand"

The Introduction of EVERY Dr. Success Spotlight Radio Show

To Laura,

Much like the perfect dish with the perfect recipe by the perfect chef in the perfect restaurant, this book in the pursuit of PERFECTION had many ingredients.

The most important of them were the most important people in my life.

Past and present.

It starts with my wife, Laura.

Never a day goes by when I look to the moon and stars and not say the word "Thank-you".

Some may call it luck, some may call it faith, some may say it was wishing, hoping and praying and all of that is true.

At the end of the day it was you, forever my dream girl on every level.

It was great 32 years ago and it only got better over time.

As a wife, as a friend, as a mother and more,

what more could I have ever dreamed of or wished for.

I am because of you and this book is the result.

To our boys, Justin and Devin.

I could have not written the scripts for your lives any better than you have each written for yourselves.

I am in awe of your spirit, your soul, your uniqueness, your drive, your passion, your talents, your humor and your love.

You have always had what we have always called, "another gear".

A special place that allows each of you to use your individual "super-power" to find a way.

A way to be, to become, to learn, to grow, to achieve, to overcome and yes, to win.

Your magnetic abilities to set the bar high and to dig deep to squeeze the juice out of the life experience is the stuff that dreams are made of.

As we always said, "your goals must excite you".

Even at times appear to seem unreachable, however that's the allure and the fun.

You will because of "your will".

From the playing field to Doctor school to the Game of Life, you are my heroes.

When reality exceeds even your wildest dreams, even your wildest fantasies, then that is the real magic.

Well, for your mom & I and everyone that has been fortunate enough to know you, the reality is your Star-power is omnipotent, forever present and

The BEST is truly yet to come.

BELIEVE........

I was very lucky from a very early age.

I chose the right parents.

Arline and Joel Bard.

Simply, no one ever better.

Maybe they chose me. What was important is they gave me everything I ever needed and more to exist, to grow, to thrive, to win.

What would you do if you went thru Life thinking that no matter what you did, it was all-right.

That you couldn't fail.

And yes, even a failure would be a learning experience and eventually turned into something good.

The epitome of F.C.B., (Faith Confidence & Belief) from a set of parents.

The ultimate and most precious gift they each taught me:

1-How to live by example.

2-How to laugh.

3-How to love.

4-How to appreciate.

5-How to give.

6-How to succeed.

7-How to deal with loss.

8-How to persist.

9-How to overcome.

10-How to find peace.

Eternally and beyond.....

ACKNOWLEDGMENTS

My life has been a movie.

Yes, award winning.

I was not the star.

The stars of the movie were everyone that I had the most special of relationships with.

Family and friends.

Some for a lifetime, some for a moment.

Some named, some not but you know who you are.

Love and eternal gratitude to:

Rachel McCrimmon, John Davis, Francis Katz, Anna Bard, Rita Gross, Leonard Bard, Lou & Sam Cruz & Uncle Moe.

Ronda Torres, Jana & Tim Gottschall, Joanne & Steve Pratt, Lisa & Bob Davis & Ron Cruz.

Tommy Clinton, Bill D'Addio, Ph.D., Dr. Jay Lombard.

Kenny Fahy, Chris Paulucci, Steve Taromina, Dr. Frank Getsen & Dr. Marc Frankel, Bobby Molinaro.

Dr. Russ Seger, Dr. Neil Cohen, Dr. Jordan Jordan, Dr. Mark Horowitz, Dr. Ara Anthony Avedisian & Dr. Anthony Ferro.

So, a crazy thing happened 32 years ago.

I met a Doctor named Eric Kaplan.

Little did I know we would share so much together.

Little did I know that we would do what many often wish for but never really seem to achieve.

That is to simply bring out the best in one another.

At the same time creating a proprietary, one-of-a kind operative system that would allow so many doctors to raise their game,

see more patients and help more patients.

To help the world 1 Disc at a time.

To help the world avoid toxic drugs, risky epidural injections and often unnecessary surgeries.

Teaching, helping, guiding Doctors from all over the world "add years to their patients lives & life to their patient's years,"

TOGETHER

As a partner, a friend, a confidant and more it's been the stuff that many have wished for, hoped for, desired and more.

The difference is we got to live it, share it, have it and achieve it.

This book is inspired by you and as I have always said "we have more to do".

Couldn't have done it with anyone better.

Much gratitude to our family of Concierge Coaches/DISC Centers of America Doctors.

The BEST at what you do and YES, it is awesome to be a representative of the #1 winning team of Chiropractors in the world.
We feel the same.

Much appreciation to Lacey for everything you do behind the scenes as well as Allison Holland who put her magic in to deliver the finished copy of what you are holding in your hands.

TABLE OF CONTENTS

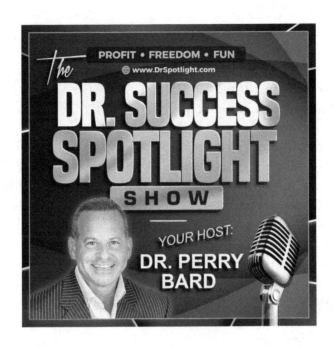

MEET THE AUTHOR

DR. PERRY M. BARD

-Resides in Highland Beach, Florida
-Undergraduate Studies at the State University of N.Y.- Farmingdale
-Graduate studies: Life Chiropractic College, Marietta Georgia, graduated 1986, Doctor of Chiropractic

Previous & Present Licensure:
-State of Florida
-State of Texas
-State of Georgia
-State of Tennessee
-State of Colorado

Certifications includes:
American College of Sports Medicine;
International College of Applied Kinesiology
Southeast Back Institute
National Board of Chiropractic Examiners
National Academy of Sports Medicine
Clinical Electromedical Research Academy
American College of Physicians
Board Member of The International Medical Advisory Board on Spinal Decompression
Post-Graduate Faculty Instructor - Parker University-Dallas, Texas / National University-Lombard, Illinois
Co-Chairman of The International DISC Education Association, (I.D.E.A.)
Board Member of The International Medical Advisory Board on Peripheral Neuropathy
State CEU Educator

Also Includes Physician for Members of:
Atlanta Braves
Chicago White Sox
Philadelphia Phillies
New York Mets
Baltimore Orioles
Chicago Cubs
Detroit Tigers
Cincinnati Reds
National / U.S.A. Bodybuilding Competitions
U.S.A. Powerlifting Association
Professional Golfers Association, (P.G.A.)
Screen Actors Guild, (S.A.G.)
Motion Picture Academy of Arts & Sciences - (The Academy Awards)
The Golden Globe Awards
Rock and Roll Hall of Fame

Former Bodybuilding Judge – National Physique Committee, (N.P.C.)

Current International Bodybuilding Judge – International Federation of Bodybuilding Physique America, (I.F.B.B.P.A.)

Co-Creator of:
DISC Centers of America
NEUROMed - Neuropathy & Joint Treatment Centers
Laser Pain Relief Centers
PRIMECare - Medical/Chiropractic/Therapy Centers
Palm Beach Slim – Doctor Supervised Weight Loss Centers
Palm Beach Massage Centers

Acknowledgements:
-Holds record of 20+ NEW paying patients per day for 4 consecutive years, (Single Clinic)
-Co-Pres. & C.E.O. of Concierge Coaches
-Owned 5 Multi-Million Dollar Clinics
-Brand Specialist – Decompression-Laser-Neuropathy-Weight Loss-Massage
-Chiropractic Marketing Savant
-Host: The Physicians Spotlight Radio Show
-Host: The Dr. Success Spotlight Radio Show
-Retired COMPLETELY at 40 Years Old, (only to return after 6 weeks of lying on the beach)

Dr. Bard also serves as a National Chiropractic Consultant to 100's of offices who are each dedicated to providing the highest standard of healthcare to countless individuals in their respective communities interested in attaining their individual & full health potential.

It's TIME for the Dr. Success Spotlight Radio Show

We started with a simple premise.
An UN-filtered, UN-rehearsed, UN-scripted, UN-cut, UN-edited "Q & A" session with some of the absolutely MOST successful doctors on the planet.
We ended with a CLEAR, CONGRUENT, CONCISE, COMPLETE and COMPREHENSIVE bullet-point list of "Plug and Play" action steps from these amazing doctors that all lead to 1 outcome…PURE SUCCESS!!!

There is an old saying,
"If you want better answers, then ask better questions".

That was our mission, our purpose, our desire, our focus and of course, our result.

The purpose was to empower Doctors by giving them the tools as outlined in this book from being the "Best Kept Secret" in their respective demographics to becoming the Doctor that every patient has searched for, desired and finally found.

The book is the culmination of 32 years+ of Success as a Chiropractor, Practice Owner, Investor, etc.
It was based on the direct result of the success of the Radio Show launched this year known as, **"The DR. SUCCESS SPOTLIGHT SHOW"**.

This Book started as a gift to our children.
1 in Dental School, 1 in Chiropractic School, right now.
It became a gift to the Chiropractic profession.

This book, (The Dr. Success Spotlight Book) provides the "Keys to the Kingdom".
It provides a TRUE "Inside-Out" look as to the neurology, the psychology, the physiology, the motivation and the persistence that the

BEST doctors in the country have that they have each individually utilized to achieve their own personal success.

This book provides you the reader a front-row ticket to be the "Fly-on-the-Wall" to allow you to discover the "How's & Why's" of practice success.

There is an old saying, "If you try to be everything to everybody, you will often end up being nothing to nobody".

Find your own groove.

Create your own magic.

Under-promise and way over-deliver.

That's how the game of practice, the game of success and the game of life is won.

I'll share a secret.

If I did not write this book, then I would have been 1st in line to buy this book as this is the book that EVERY person who craves more out of practice and more out of life wants.

Dedicated to people who breath success, this book is your oxygen.

The roots of this book go back.

Back to the days of early tube TV sets with only 3 networks.

Back to the days of growing up in Brooklyn, New York watching my Pop work as hard as anyone fixing these nostalgic sets.

If you asked him if he worked hard, he would tell you he never worked a day in his life as he loved fixing them.

The more challenging the better. He often said he was a "Doctor of Television Repair".

Long days, long nights, heavy TV sets up flights of stairs. No elevators, no heating, no help and 3 hernias as a bonus from lifting TV sets that no mortal man could lift alone.

Climbing ladders to roofs and taking his life in his hands all in search of providing clear reception to his customers who revered him, respected him and loved him.

He left it on the field and lived by example to provide for his family. That was where my work ethic came from and it was amongst the many gifts and life lesson's he shared as it was the "gift that keeps giving". All with 1 simple recurring theme.

That was this, "If you can work for yourself, do so as it will be the greatest thing going".

He lived by that code and was the 1st real "entrepreneur" I ever met.

He was a natural communicator and with passion and persistence he knew how to "close".

He had the ability to paint a picture and was able to key into someone's desire of "need & want".

In his time Television sets were a luxury, (even though we had 7 in our house).

He was able to communicate why they were a necessity.

He worked his ass off all to follow in the footsteps of his father in bringing his family from Brooklyn to South Florida, as he was able to retire at the prime age

of only 50 years old. His retirement lasted about 4 weeks when he found that he enjoyed his profession so much he returned and carried that thru till the time

it was time to depart. He was the greatest man I ever knew and if I am just 10% of him, then my mission has been completed.

He was and will always be my "Pop".

I went to high school in Brooklyn, New York.

The name of the high school was Lafayette.

Ask anyone from Bensonhurst and they'll tell you that was the school. It was generational.

From Larry King, to Paul Sorvino, to Rhea Pearlman, to Vic Damone, to Fred Wilpon to John Franco to Peter Max to Sandy Koufax, Lafayette high school symbolized Brooklyn at its best.

One day after a typical Brooklyn High School assembly with it's share of chairs thrown, screaming, ranting, raving and bedlam with students forcibly escorted out by security.

Truth be told, I might have been involved in the above referenced scenarios however the key word here is "might".

One day a guest speaker was brought in. In typical fashion no one paid any attention to her brief 10-minute lecture.

Her name was Lynn Rappaport and she was introducing a BRAND-NEW program known as the "INTERNSHIP High School Program of NYC".

She explained that if you have an interest in a vocation, that she could place you in that vocation for the last 6 months of your High school career.

She explained that you would get FULL CREDIT and actually have 2 High School diplomas. 1 from Lafayette HS and 1 from The NYC Internship program.

She explained to the general assembly that often students would work at printers, travel agents and accountants and she would place them there.

The entire assembly virtually ignored her with the exception of 1 student.

That student was me.

Then, just like out of a movie as she was leaving the auditorium I got up and ran to the back and asked her a simple question.

"Ms. Rappaport have you ever placed a student in a Recording Studio in NYC?"

She said not yet but if that's what I wanted she would go to bat for me.

That week she called me at home. She told me that she set up 3 interviews for me, 1 being in the largest voice-over studio in the heart of Manhattan on West 45th street and Avenue of the Americas.

It was called CUE Recording studio and as much as I wanted the Internship, they wanted me too.

A virtually impossible industry to break in to and here I was at 17 years old with an Internship that #1. Got me out of High School and gave me full academic credit, #2. Allowed me to learn about an amazing entertainment industry as the "fly-on-the-wall" in the heart of the action in the Big Apple and #3. Have freedom, fun and quirky subway rides into the city every day. At Cue Recording studio, every week we had some of the most interesting people in the world that openly and abundantly were extremely curious how this little 17-year old kid had the position of a lifetime. From Howard Cossell to Tony Randall to Don McClean to Lucy Arnez to Brooke Shields and so many more, they were all willing to share an "unplugged" side of them with me on a regular basis and share the ins & outs of the entertainment business. I learned the production side of voice-overs, commercials and radio shows and had some of New York Cities BEST recording engineers at arms-length. Little did I know that 40 years later, I would utilize the same techniques to create the Dr. Success Spotlight Radio Show and now Dr. Success Spotlight Book. Yes, experience comes in many forms and it all starts with 1 word, "AWARENESS".

which really is "A Heightened Sense of Heightened Senses".

We know that this book will raise your own individual AWARENESS and that is where the magic happens.

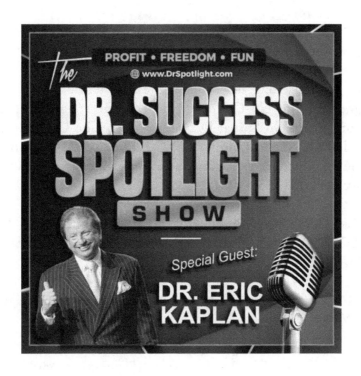

1

SOCIAL MEDIA SUCCESS – (DR. ERIC KAPLAN)

Read about: DR. ERIC KAPLAN & DISCOVER what has been the DRIVING force to become the MOST FOLLOWED Chiropractor in history in SOCIAL MEDIA, (Over 300,000 Twitter Followers) and HOW he has created some of the MOST lucrative practices in the country.

Dr. Eric Kaplan, (or as we often call him, DR. K) has helped create MORE Multi-Million Dollar Practices in "REAL-TIME" (meaning

Right Now) than any other Chiropractor on the planet. His resume is "unmatched".

A 4X - #1 Bestselling author, he is the President of DISC Centers of America, the Co-Chairman of the International Medical Advisory Board on Spinal Decompression, The Co-President of The I.D.E.A., (International DISC Education Association) and has the greatest GIFT to communicate seamlessly what we do as CHIROPRACTORS.

He is a MASTER communicator. He has become the **#1 MOST FOLLOWED CHIROPRACTOR** in the World, and in SOCIAL MEDIA.

Over 100's of 1,000's of followers who get a Twitter message from him **EVERY DAY.**

Dr. Bard:

Welcome to Dr. Success Spotlight Show! What an amazing way to kick this off and to welcome our most special guest. We're going to kick it off right here, right now with the one and only Dr. Eric Kaplan. Welcome to the show Dr. Kaplan. [1]

Dr. Kaplan:

Thanks, Dr. Bard. It's great to be here.

Dr. Bard:

The doctors that really know our history are really going to enjoy this. This is a show by doctors for doctors that reveals the best success recipes of what doctors are doing right now. It is absolutely uncut. It's unfiltered. It's really a behind the scenes look with how and why some of the absolute top doctors in the country are crushing it in practice. I mean, they are putting up numbers that are freaky and there's no better way to start. Then, my BFF, my partner, the president of Disc Centers of America, the co-chairman of the International Medical Advisory Board on Spinal Decompression and the co-president of the International Disc Education Association. I could literally do a whole show with your resume. There is something that our listeners are very curious about and that is how you became number one in the world, in social media? I opened up your twitter 10 minutes before the show started and I saw that you have and I hope everyone's sitting down for this OVER 301,000 followers in social media, which is freaky and crazy. So, we're going to jump right into the deep end of the pool and ask you, how did you get started in social media?

Dr. Kaplan:

*Well, I was a little lucky Dr. Bard. When I started in social media, it started from the publishing from the first book I wrote many years ago - **Lifestyle of the Fit & Famous** with the President of the United States, Donald Trump on the cover of the book. When I wrote that book, I went*

3

from city to city. But the world has changed, not just for the chiropractors but for the book business as well. Now, they realized with social media, they could do what we call book tours virtually almost in every state. They capture the essence of the theme of the book and rather than doing it in a bookstore in front of 100 people per se, you could do a virtual bookstore and you can be in front of thousands of people daily. One of my favorite people, a mentor, which you know very well once said, "success leaves clues." As I traveled on this journey, I realized that thru social media which my publisher got me started on, it was something that would benefit not only the sales of my book but my brand as well. My brand is showing people that there is an option for back surgery.

What I've learned as well as anything and one of the keys to social media, specifically on Twitter is to always work the process and always work the system. It's an ongoing process, but with our companies, Disc Centers of America, Laser Pain Relief Centers of America and Concierge Coaches, we found out by utilizing Facebook and Twitter that our doctors are able to acquire many, many new patients. That's something that's never been done before years ago as the yellow pages ended up to be a dying medium. We at Concierge Coaches have found a way to implement and utilize Facebook to get a quicker return on marketing for New Patients at a fraction of the cost.

Dr. Bard:

I think as you start to peel the layers back and you start to delve in to how you have literally over a hundred times more followers than even the second-place closest chiropractor in the world it became very powerful for you and your raving fans. It really started with your literary skills as a number 1 bestselling acclaimed author and with your affinity for putting out incredible content. One of the things that I think you've done so amazingly well is that you always keep it in real time, with regard to the way you've connected the dots of your life experiences and your personal success. For example, when you started authoring, I don't think a lot of doctors know this, but you actually authored for Sports Illustrated, which was really unique and brought in a whole new audience. Can you speak on that a little bit?

4

Dr. Kaplan:

Yes. I've always been a basketball fan as you know Dr. Bard. In college, we followed the Knicks, we followed the Yankees, we followed the Giants, but also as two sports fans in you and I we also understand the ability to monitor and track all sports. I found also through social media that athletes have a mechanism and a way of creating interest and what I did is I actually started writing for the New York Knickerbocker's blog and it was actually picked up by Sports Illustrated especially by people that write blogs out there. The medium I worked in then led to Sports Illustrated as they liked it and they started carrying my articles. I did the Bleacher Report and on all my mediums, I wouldn't post the links on my Twitter page. Some people liked what I was writing and some people didn't.

You can't be sensitive if you're going to be an author. What I like to ask chiropractors as I travel the country is "what's your unique selling advantage"? Meaning, every doctor out there today could start a blog and the blog could be as simple as we start with the letter A and we can talk about apples. We've got B and we can talk about bananas and if you can create a medium that teaches people what you know, how they can get rid of sinus infections, how they can build up their immune system and you could write a blog, then you can start simply by sending your blog to all your patients. Then you start to ask your patients to please email the blog to all of their circle. So, it's a matter of, working it, developing a plan and then working your plan.

Social media is a great way to approach connecting with others. So, when I was writing articles, little did I know that Sports Illustrated would eventually pick up the writings, but it started basically as a blog. So, my first thing is I went out there just start writing a blog. A blog replaces the old paper newsletter. It's more up to date. It's more thorough. People look up to that, they will view their doctors in a different light and there's a lot of content that a doctor could share with his patients. That's where I recommend that they begin.

5

Dr. Bard:

One of the things that I have to share is that I've known you now for over 31 years and I can honestly say, I've never seen you have more fun, more excitement, more dynamic, more pumped and more juiced in being able to now really pay it forward to whole new generations of Chiropractors. I think a lot of that stems from the simple fact that your son, Dr. Jason Kaplan is setting practice success records on a level that is fantastic. Who would have ever envisioned how fast he and his wife, Dr. Stephanie Kaplan would have moved to the front of the line. Can you just share how he's been able to accomplish that and how he's been able to do that also through social media?

Dr. Kaplan:

Some people say Dr. Bard that having me as a father is an advantage, but I'm sure if you spoke to both my sons privately, they can tell you it has its disadvantages too. What we try to do with our children is to share concept of simply that the enemy of great is good. I tried to tell my children that good just isn't good enough. I've always joked with my son as I always say that Jason is my favorite client but he's also my most difficult client, in the sense that, there are many things that he has to digest before he can implement. What I'm excited to say is even by using just 50 percent of what I told him, it's helped him 100 percent. But you know, Jason is not an isolated case.

You and I know since we've worked with hundreds of doctors throughout the United States, many of whom are the most successful Chiropractors in the country. For example, there's one doctor who's 73-years-old and was once retired. He was unhappy and was literally out of practice and came to our seminar and now, he's back in the universe and utilizing some of our Facebook marketing. He's bringing people into his office and he's closing spinal decompression cases and he and his wife are completely reinvigorated. So, this is not just for the young. It is for all doctors that want to have the greatest penetration at their target market for specific types of patients. We market specific to disc injuries, specific to weight loss, specific to neuropathy. You are going to bring in a person that's actually requested information from you on those categories. So, what you've done is instead of just soliciting people, you've changed the game where people are soliciting you, they're calling you. They want content and they want information and that's exciting. Jason has done this very well and Facebook has been a wonderful medium because it brings us targeted marketing on numerous leads. We are doing that in a very tailored and proprietary way and we happily share that with other Chiropractors who reach out to us.

We've long understood that your website has to be strong. You can't have a generic website that's the same as every other chiropractor and that says the same chiropractic stuff. Your website has to be specific. If someone looks up the word "disc", they do not necessarily end up going to a chiropractor. So, we, as in my son, have a very specific website that's strategically targeted for disc and branded with "Disc Centers of America". As a matter of fact, its www.wellingtondisccenter.com. That's how we target market. So, if people that are looking for disc related information, they can find it there. I'm proud to say that "Disc Centers of America" now holds more internet "Disc-Specific" real estate than any other group in the United States including disc injuries. We hold internet real estate online through Google, including Google searches, Bing, Yahoo and search engines. That's just one way to funnel people into your office and into your universe. My son, thanks you so much for all your help. We've just been very, very lucky to have great people within our team.

Dr. Bard:

I actually interviewed you on the radio Dr. Kaplan previously, about a year and a half ago and an amazing thing happened. What happened was for the doctors that were privy to that "special interview", the number one request that we received was how can I see exactly how you are doing it? In other words, are you willing to share it? Are you willing to show it? Are you willing to give examples?

That was the genesis and what came to fruition to something known as the Chiro Event Marketing and Patient Management Mastermind, which is at www.thechiroevent.com. Can you share Dr. Kaplan why this event really is the one event that allows them to see and learn about the actual tools that you're talking about?

Dr. Kaplan:

Sure. Well, I think one of the problems that Chiropractors have is that reimbursements have been going down on a state to state basis. They haven't focused on what they really need to focus on, which is building their practice correctly based upon the best cash-based model which we teach. I've been very blessed over the last month. I think we've been at the National University teaching the National Spinal Decompression Certificate program which set records.

We did a Spinal Decompression Training Master Class in Decatur, Illinois. Then, I went to South Carolina to teach CEU's. Dr. Bard, there are two types of doctors mentioned. There were those that are committed to moving forward and those that are stuck in the past. There are doctors that say, at the end of the day, I should have done this, I should've done that, and what I'm saying to you doctor is, we got to stop "shoulding" all over yourself. I think you need to get back into the game and that's why the Chiro Event Mastermind is so incredible. It's almost like a one-day M.B.A. It gives you the ability to take your practice to the next level. The problem is you're going to have to get off your butt and you're going to have to come down to Florida and prepare to change because I'll tell you exactly how and why we work with some of the most successful doctors in the country.

Dr. Bard, you were there and as you know, we have a doctor in Decatur, Illinois which now has 12 spinal decompression tables. I tell doctors that if you're doing decompression, how many tables do you have? If you have one table then you're not doing it. You're playing at it but you're not mastering it. My son has three tables. We have a doctor with five tables, another doctor with eight tables. I mean our doctors understand the best way to position themselves and how to position their practices and that's what you will learn at the Chiro Event.

The Chiro Event is not for the weak at heart. The Chiro Event is for a doctor that really wants to succeed, that understands that insurance is a declining industry and that they have to bring their A-Game into practice which we teach. That's what we do at the Chiro Event. We go over spinal decompression, we go over weight loss, we go over neuropathy, we go over joint care, we go over all of the mediums that lead people into your office. We isolate and work on marketing and implementation, meaning education with patients, utilizing the right product. We teach doctors how to be unique, how to be specific and how to take advantage of their uniqueness. How to implement that into their community and how to be the best at what they do.

Our doctors are not salesmen, Dr. Bard. Our doctors are educators. Our doctors are progressive doctors that know and spend time educating themselves through training, bootcamps, masterclasses and certifications. You see the secret to Concierge Coaches, if you've asked me what the real secret is I will tell you. Why are our doctors the greatest doctors and most successful in the country? It's a one-word answer, RESULTS. Our doctors get a specific result at Concierge Coaches and we warranty that in writing. I challenge any other coaching company in the country to do that. We do that with confidence.

How do they learn how to do that? Well, it starts with the Chiro Event and starts on the campus of Trump National. Trump understands many, many things. This is not about politics Dr. Bard. When patients came into my office, I never asked the patient if they're Republican or Democrat. I never asked if they're Jewish or Catholic. The bottom line is that we as doctors and need to be open to all mediums. President Donald Trump has built a great organization and when you come into his campus in Florida you get an opportunity to see that from the inside-out. You can watch that in a five-minute video at www.thechiroevent.com. The prestigious and exclusive Trump National club in Jupiter, Florida has become the official site of www.TheChiroEvent.com. I think you will see at The Chiro Event how you can become the "best of the best" in healthcare and how-to move your practice to the next level. We have helped so many people. I can't tell you how many Chiropractors that came to the event said that it was "life-changing".

So, if you're sitting there and saying, "what's new or how do I get more out of practice? Or 'how can I be the best that I can be'? It's very simple. Go to www.thechiroevent.com then, pick up the phone and come. The direct registration number is: 888-990-9660. Seats are very limited and every Chiro Event Mastermind has previously sold out, so call today for the date and availability.

Dr. Bard:

Although the actual number of followers that you have Dr. Kaplan in social media can be measured, what I believe could never, ever be measured is your heart. I believe that the Chiropractors and we will call them "the chosen ones" who would be so fortunate enough to grab a seat at THE CHIRO EVENT Mastermind would find that this was the "rocket ship" that actually served as the launching pad to allow them to reach the pinnacle in their own practice success. All they have to do is to visit: www.TheChiroEvent.com. Dr. Kaplan, you are truly the "Best of the Best"!!!

Until next time on the next episode of the Dr. Success Spotlight Show…. "Make it GREAT".

HERE ARE THE BULLET-POINT TAKEAWAYS:

#1 - By becoming an Author, he started the process. Once his publisher knew that his book had info that people wanted, they started building his audience.

#2 - Using Social Media for a VIRTUAL BOOK TOUR.

#3 - He connected his own "personal interests" and started sharing that and thus became a contributor to Sports Illustrated.

#4 - He figured out Blogging, (Example Topics) and believes in Repetition.

#5 - He connected Facebook to Twitter.

#6- He found that by teaching Chiropractors "How-To" become **non-insurance** dependent his cash-model presentation for Spinal Decompression, Laser Therapy & Neuropathy was embraced by the Chiropractic profession.

#7 - He shared this info with his son & daughter-in law who has used this latest info to **SKYROCKET** their practice 17 months in, to set records.

#8 - Who is Dr. Kaplan's FAVORITE client?

#9 - He decided to share the visual examples of his marketing at **www. TheChiroEvent.com**

#10 - He felt that he was so fortunate as a Chiropractor that he wanted to share this info and **"pay it forward"** for so many Chiropractors who simply needed the RIGHT advice to LIFT themselves to the place that they always wanted.

THE DR. SUCCESS SPOTLIGHT BOOK
Dr. Perry M. Bard

2

AUTHENTICITY SUCCESS –
(DR. FAB MANCINI)

Read about: DR. FAB MANCINI. Deep, Humble, Funny, Authentic, Real and MORE, Dr. Mancini "Lets it Loose" in this short but VERY powerful SHARE session of PURE GOLD. DISCOVER The 1 absolute success-defining lesson that he learned and shared privately on the show.

He also shares what I believe may be the SINGLE Greatest Mantra and at the end of the day, is really the defining statement as to WHO Dr. Fab Mancini is and WHAT he has always been about. You will LOVE this...

Dr. Bard:

Are you excited? I am beyond excited for this most special guest. I am your host, Dr. Perry Bard. Welcome to the Doctor Success Spotlight Show, and this will be pretty incredible. That's really an understatement. I have, really one of my heroes. Obviously not just a mentor for myself but for so many in our profession. I have with us here today, live face to face, one to one, eye to eye and heart to heart the one and only Dr. Fab Mancini with me. I have some goosebumps. I don't know if you can feel it. I want to welcome you to the show, Dr. Mancini.

Dr. Mancini:

Thank you, Perry, I'm so excited about being your guest today. More importantly, I'm so excited about this medium that you created to bring some real information where people can transform their lives.

Dr. Bard:

So, this is really a very special time for us in the profession. It's really such a special time for me personally. There's no greater testament, there's no greater joy, there's no greater success than to pass the torch down. So, my son is actually starting chiropractic college. Can you believe in eight weeks he will be going to the school that Dr. Mancini spearheaded and that being Parker Chiropractic College. When I say spearheaded, really what that means is he took the reins from the one and only, Dr. James Parker and made this an amazing, incredible, premier school to go to in becoming a chiropractor and more.

When we think of Dr. Mancini, everybody much like me, knows all his incredible successes. I think one of the things that I was always super curious about from Dr. Mancini and I get to ask him this face to face, is I'm very curious in terms of some of the challenges, maybe a little bit of some of the adversity that he may never have shared publicly or even privately. Simply because you don't reach the level in our profession that he's reached without figuring out a way to

14

really overcome challenges and battles. I'm so curious to ask you, Dr. Mancini, what was one of the most difficult times in your life and how did you overcome that in terms of eventually reaching the pinnacle of success?

Dr. Mancini:

Well, one of the things that I learned many years ago is that the circumstances or the challenges that we face never defined us. The only thing that defines us is how we respond to those challenges. I can probably have as many challenges as I've had successes but what has always made a difference is my response, so let me give you one. For instance, when I was in premed, I wanted to be a neurosurgeon and I have pretty much set up my path to go to medical school, become a neurosurgeon and revolutionize that world. I got into an accident.

The orthopedic surgeon in the hospital was a friend of mine. He says, instead of me giving you these painkillers and anti-inflammatories, you should go see my chiropractor. That was my referral to my first chiropractor. He changed my life. I then decided to interview 62 chiropractors because I felt to be a chiropractor, I needed to understand what it is. So, I went ahead and I did it. I went to Parker University. It used to be Parker College of Chiropractic and I enrolled. I got to the financial aid office and they told me that I did not qualify for financial aid. My parents had made money in the past. In those days, it was a little different than today and unfortunately, my dad made some bad investments and we lost almost everything we had. I called my mom and my dad and I said, "I'm going to go to chiropractor school" and my mother and father said, "listen, honey, we can't support you financially. Why don't you come home to Miami? Why don't you go to the University of Miami for a little bit, take some classes and give your dad and I a chance to recover financially"?

I did something that could've changed my destiny. I did not give up on my dream. I could have gone to Miami. What I did is I looked at all my worldly possessions and I had one thing that was worth something. Imagine at 20 years old or 21 years old, and that was my car. My parents had given me a brand-new Chevy Camaro that I called a "chick magnet" *because it was a beautiful sports car. It had 18 speakers and it was the only thing I owned. I began to go to different dealerships to see what I could get for it, so I can enroll in school. Financial aid told me that they could not give me any money for the first two trimesters but in the third trimester, I could borrow money to go to school. I want you to know that after two weeks the car was valued at the time at $17,000, the highest offer that I got was 4,800. The last day of registration, Friday, I went to one dealer that was not there the week before because he was on vacation. I told him my story, how I want to sell my car to go to school. He gave me $7,800. I took that check. I went to Parker.*

I paid for my trimester and I began my school. My roommate's father was so touched by what I did that he told me, and my parents not to worry about the rent for the first two trimesters that he will cover it. My parents sent me enough money to pay for food. I got a little bit of a job here and there too to get some extra money, but I want you to know that the best investment I made was the investment of selling my car that has multiplied into millions of dollars and the ability to impact so many millions of lives when I could have given my dream up.

So, my lesson here is don't ever let anything deter you from your goal, or from your dream. There's always a way that you can pursue that dream. If money is an issue and you don't have anything to sell, there are a lot of people out there that are looking for ways to invest and someone that wants to do something constructive. Even if they borrow or lend you the money and you can pay them back later. I want you to know that there's never been an excuse in my life where I said, I'm not going to do this because of what's happening because I remember that one lesson.

Don't let the circumstances in your life define you. So, whatever you find yourself dealing with right now, know that is only an opportunity to grow and that you don't grow in comfort. You grow in discomfort. So anytime I have a challenge and adversity heading my way, I always embrace it and welcome it and give thanks to G-d that this is going to be another opportunity when I can grow into the person that I was meant to be.

Dr. Bard:

So, I just took about 10 pages of mental notes just now on a host of different things that Dr. Mancini so eloquently shared. I'm going to tell you right at the very top of my list is the simple fact that a lot of people know you in a certain way and I love the fact that you're so blatantly open and frank and honest. I've known you for a number of years. You put this profession on your back and you had the fortitude and you had the love and really the foresight to know that as a D.C. (two letters behind your name) and a DR. (two letters in front of your name), that you could do some magical things in this world. I love the fact, more so now, Dr. Mancini than any other time in the history of this profession, is the road ahead being so bright for so many doctors, who IF (big word), IF they know who to surround themselves with and whom to listen to, how they can create a life and a lifestyle as a chiropractor, beyond their dreams.

What I'm so curious about right now, Dr. Mancini is this. If I've seen anything through the years, I've seen you do some incredible things. One of the things I've seen you do, is you've been able to reinvent yourself. Being able to reinvent yourself as not just a cliché. It is something that is real. It's dynamic. It's live. So, I am so curious right now to ask you this question in terms of how you've been able to so successfully reinvent yourself. As the days, the weeks, the months, the years have gone on, to stay in the forefront and to stay on your best A game right now, how did you do it?

Dr. Mancini:

Well, that's a great question, and one of the things that I also learned early on in my life is the fact that we were never meant to be the same. Change is inevitable in our lives. The problem is like Spencer Johnson wrote in the book, Who Moved my Cheese? Most of us want to resist that change because we don't see the potential of growth, abundance and happiness that comes with it. We tend to focus on what we will lose if that change actually comes. So, what you focus on is what you will attract as your outcome. So, I've chosen always to focus on the positive. So, the way that I've reinvented myself is this. My first portion of my 30-year career was spent as my first 10 years was as a chiropractor. I built a successful practice. The way that I did that was very simple. I identified the three most successful people that I knew. I went ahead and interviewed them. I went ahead and modeled them.

There was a guy in Sherman, Texas named, Dr. Rick Wren that I used to drive on Tuesday and Thursday and I worked in my office Monday, Wednesday, Friday, two hours there and two hours back because Dr. Rick Wren has seen over a hundred patients a day for over 25 years and I wanted to know what the magic was. So, I interviewed him. I modeled him and then I started implementing my own uniqueness into the formula because you can never really reach your full potential if you do it just the way other people do it. You want to learn from others, you want to model others and you always have to be authentic in the process. Otherwise, it won't last or it will not reach its destination.

The second thing is when I was called to be an educator. My mentor, Dr. Parker passed away and at 33 years old, I became the youngest president of a college or university in the United States. I freaked out for a year and a half. I kept saying, no, but you know what? When you're called to do something, understand that you're the person to do it. Eight or nine out of 10 people will tell you, you're too young to do it. You don't have enough education. You don't have enough maturity. You don't have enough experience. You don't have enough money. You don't know the right people but let me tell you an opportunity will never knock on your door unless you're the person to do it. Even if you see it as insurmountable, even if you see that nobody in your family has ever done it, even if you never met anybody that has ever done it, know that that opportunity is yours to sieze.

So, I decided to accept that after a year and a half of saying no. Of course, I gave my all to it and it was very successful. Then, I realized that my last seven years, I've been in entertainment. To be a host on television, the expert for Dr. Phil, The Doctors, many of the networks in Spanish and English and now negotiating my own talk show. Listen, I can hardly speak English. I don't know if you notice my accent, right? I make mistakes. I am not the most perfect person on television, but I'm authentic. I believe in my message and I know that even at my worst, I'm better than most. That's my mantra. "even at my worst I'm better than most". So, the key in reinventing yourself is to recognize that everything in your life has been a preparation for the next opportunity.

When that next opportunity comes, know that everything in your life will serve its purpose for you to succeed in that opportunity. Never question it. Never doubt it. Surround yourself with people that support that vision and you will always reinvent yourself successfully.

Dr. Bard:

I hope you are feeling the love, the passion, the heat and really the energy of somebody who knew how to take some hits and knew how to stand up the right way because he believed always in the truth. He believed in himself and he knew his talent and he knew that it wasn't perfect. It was not exactly maybe the way he initially envisioned, it but if you'll notice something, you'll notice one common thread amongst everybody that is interviewed on this show, and that is they are what we would call, "a student of the game". They refuse to rest on their laurels and that's why I am so excited for the future of this profession. If you take heed in the message.

If you take heed and you take one tool that Dr. Mancini shared with you here because he just gave me about 20 tools in the short time. We only have a short time together. I know, if I'm reading this, I want one thing. What I want is I want more. In other words, I want more Dr. Mancini, so Dr. Mancini would you be so kind, to share a little bit of your direct contact information. I know you have some incredible things in the pipeline in terms of content and videos and tools where they can get a more access to all the things that I've known you for and to be so powerful and so true.

Dr. Mancini:

Well, my personal email is Fab, F as in Frank, A-B at drfabmancini. com, so www. D-R F-A-B M-A-N-C-I-N-I dot com. My website is drfabmancini.com and in there you will see a lot of ways to stay in contact with me, but also many of the ways that I may be able to serve you and support you. You can follow me on YouTube, which is Dr. Fab Mancini. I put it up every week and motivation or two or three-minute video on how to get you thinking, how to get you moving in the right direction for the week.

You can follow me on Facebook which is Dr. Fab Mancini or you can follow me on Twitter, which is Dr. Fab Mancini or Instagram. So just know this, I am here to support in any way that you can but the one thing that I cannot do for you is to help you believe in yourself more. You can only do that and when you start putting yourself first and when you develop a vision and a mission and a life purpose that's bigger than you. That means that you're going to go out there and you're going to be thinking of ways to support others, and ways to bring value to others. That's at the highest level of your value.

The more value you create for the world, the more that you are valuable to the world. Then, remember also that in this journey, have fun. One of the things I love about Perry is the fact that he's always smiling. He's always having a good time. He's always creating ways to bring more value to you. In that part of the journey, wherever you find yourself is only a snapshot of the whole journey. Don't think that this is all there is because tomorrow is another opportunity for you to make something happen and to create the life of your dreams.

Dr. Bard:

Authentic, real, committed and absolute 100 percent pure love. His love emanates across the room every time I walk in, I see his incredible smile. It's magnetic and I want you to treat yourself. I highly encourage you to treat yourself by getting in his world any which way, shape, or form you can. I promise you, that if you get into Dr. Mancini's world, you will come away better.

HERE ARE THE BULLET-POINT TAKEAWAYS:

#1 - The Circumstances of the Situation never defines us. What defines us is how we respond to those challenges.

#2 - He started his journey wanting to become a Neurosurgeon after suffering an accident. An Orthopedic Surgeon referred him to his own Chiropractor.

#3 - He decided to interview 62 Chiropractors as he felt the calling to follow his heart and become a Chiropractor.

#4 - He initially was on the verge of not attending Chiropractic College as like so many he did not initially qualify for financial aid.

#5 - He was forced to sell his car. When someone heard his amazing story of wanting to sell his possessions to attend Chiropractic school, he was presented a check and this allowed him to enroll.

#6 - The best investment he ever made was the investment in himself by selling his car, becoming a Chiropractor and going on to make multiple millions of dollars by impacting so many lives.

#7 - Don't let anyone or anything deter you from your dreams. There is always a way. Challenges are an opportunity to grow.

#8 - Change is inevitable. Most people resist change. What you focus on is what your outcome will be.

You should learn from others but always be authentic and original to create your own magic.

#9 - An opportunity will never present at your doorstep unless you are the person who can handle it. It's your opportunity to seize.

#10 - Possibly the greatest mantra ever . . . *"EVEN at his WORST, he's BETTER than MOST"*.

3

TEAM BUILDING SUCCESS – (DR. RICH LOHR)

Read about: DR. RICHARD LOHR & DISCOVER how he created a 5-Star office that features 12 Spinal Decompression Tables. His office was the official site of the 1st-ever MASTERCLASS. Also, LEARN his "SPECIAL FORMULA" for creating the BEST staff & team ever, as well as his "unique" hiring policy.

Dr. Bard:

We have with us today, one of the absolute "best of the best", the one and only Dr. Richard Lohr from Decatur, Illinois. Welcome to the show Dr. Lohr.

Dr. Lohr:

Thank you so much for having me, Dr. Bard.

Dr. Bard:

What a treat this really is and for some of you who don't know the history or the background or in essence how this came about, I will share with you one number and that number is actually a magic number. That number is the number 12. The reason that number is magical is because Dr. Richard Lohr from Decatur, Illinois does not have three decompression tables, four decompression tables, five decompression tables but he actually has 12 nonsurgical spinal decompression tables and the coolest thing about that is they're all busy. All of the tables are filled Dr. Lohr, you didn't start out that way. In other words, how did you get to 12 tables? How did this start?

Dr. Lohr:

I bought a practice. A doctor passed away and there were eight doctors interested in it and they picked me because I could start right away and it turned out they had decompression tables and they had them in a back room and I thought to myself, those were traction tables, I'm a hands-on chiropractor. I believe in chiropractic that's what I do. So, I let them sit there for a year before I did anything with it and finally, I got on the table myself as I had a terrible sciatica in my right leg for years and after a couple of weeks getting on that table, my sciatica was gone. That was almost 10 years ago, and it never came back.

So, I developed this passion. So, I started converting all my chiropractic patients over to the decompression side. I tell my patients that all we need to do is that I have something here that I think is going to give longer, better results, as far as, when it comes to their disc and spinal condition So then, I was kind of bumping along and I was doing well with two tables but I was kind of stuck there and that's when I heard about the first Spinal Decompression certification class in Dallas and I knew of Dr. Kaplan and I knew of Dr. Bard from their past talks and the past things that they were involved in. So, it was a plane, train, and automobile thing. Our flights got canceled because there was a terrible snowstorm that 1st time. So, we got in the car and we drove over the 13 hours down to Dallas, so I could learn more about decompression. I was so hungry. I knew it worked but I didn't know why. I didn't know how to market it. I didn't know what to do. So, we drove down there and we got in Friday night. We had no sleep, virtually no sleep for 24 hours, so we were up.

You and Dr. Kaplan had a nice little beautiful executive room and they kind of showed us what was going to happen the next day at the decompression and they had food and drinks. Everybody was just kind of visiting around and I was on cloud nine. I'm finally going to learn about decompression. So, the next day, I was so excited and so I got back from that decompression training. All I did was I started implementing and I signed up with Dr. Perry and Dr. Eric for their management group, (www.ConciergeCoaches.com). The next thing you know, I'm going to boot camp. I'm going to the seminars that you guys give and going to the training, you guys are putting on. Next thing you know, I got to get a third table and it wasn't probably two or three months after I signed up that I had to get that third table. Next thing you know, I got two more, I had five now and we're knocking down the walls in the office. So, then we went to seven and then we had to move down the street because seven wasn't enough as patients were waiting. We couldn't get people in fast enough and so we moved down the street a year ago and it just went to 12 tables and we can still use a couple of more.

It's just been a great trip and I can't thank you and Dr. Kaplan enough; you guys brought me here. Especially being a part of DISC Centers of America, which is the number one most popular national brand of Spinal Decompression centers. I love being around other doctors who want to grow, who want to be the best and that's what I loved about both you and Dr. Kaplan. You always taught me how to be the best. Have the best equipment. Have the best training. Know your research. Have the best marketing. Don't skimp. Don't do anything halfway. You got to do it all. This was the first time, I had ever heard of that and I belonged to so many management companies and they sat down and they just grill you on the consultation over and over and over. What you had to script and what you had to memorize. It's not about that. It's really about being the best. That's really what it's all about, it really is.

Dr. Bard:

Well, it's easy for us to say that you, Dr. Lohr, really took this to heart. However, the reality is that part of your success, a major part is because you are so simply heart driven and for the doctors that were fortunate enough to attend something known as the Spinal Decompression MasterClass, they got that the second, and I mean the second that they walked into your drop-dead gorgeous office. We call that a "DDG clinic" and the DDG clinic stands for "drop-dead gorgeous".

It's an amazing thing. I'm going to tell you something that one of the doctors that attended the Spinal Decompression Masterclass in your office shared with me from that weekend. He said that, "the patient will write the check in the foyer in the reception area before they even meet you."

Dr. Lohr:

That's hilarious.

Dr. Bard:

One of the things I'd love to share is the simple fact that you're not a first-generation chiropractor. You are "tried and true" in the core principles of chiropractic. Can you share that a little bit in terms of your family background, in terms of how you kind of got started in this business?

Dr. Lohr:

Absolutely! My mother and my father were both single, both going to the same chiropractor. The chiropractor fixed them up. They both got such great results. They said, let's go to chiropractic school. So, they got married and they were 21 and 22 years old. Went right up into a chiropractic school and I was adjusted the day I was born. I never had shots or immunizations. We weren't allowed to have pop and sugar. I only have on special occasions, holidays, birthdays, those type of things. I'm so grateful for that kind of a start in life to be exposed to chiropractic at such a young age.

So, my younger brother is a chiropractor and my dad's brother too. He went off to chiropractic school after he saw the results that my dad was getting. So, there were four of us in the family. I've got sisters and brothers and nieces and nephews that were born in my parents' house and it was just the coolest thing you can ever imagine. Healthy all your life. I am so blessed that happened. I don't think I'd be even doing decompression today.

I wouldn't be a chiropractor if it wasn't for my father. He was so dedicated. He loved chiropractic and he passed that on to us. He's 86 and I talk to him every week and he says I really miss it. He misses being at the office and missed moving those bones. I just think that's such a cool thing that I was blessed with that early exposure.

Dr. Bard:

Don't think for a moment that I didn't enjoy that picture you sent me of you enjoying a celebratory cigar with your dad. I'm going to say that's the bonus picture of the lot. Thank you for sending me all those pictures. What I'm referring to is Dr. Lohr, much like myself is a photography fan. There's an old saying in that "we eat with our eyes first" and I think that's part of the visual appeal of the clinic that you created. It is in the fact amazingly visual and one of the cool things that you actually did was opening your doors for 1 special day of training for doctors. So many doctors for the past few months and few years have always inquired about how does a doctor even end up with that many tables? Obviously, you were able to do it based upon two simple words, which is "supply and demand".

You Dr. Lohr, figured it out a long time ago that if you create the demand, then it's just simply a matter of fulfilling the supply and thus how does that happen? So, what you did in your generosity, is you opened up your clinic for one special day for the Spinal Decompression Master Class. There had been so many rave reviews from this training. I don't even think that comes close to the incredible commentary and testimonials from what doctors had to say. That was just after the first hour remarkably. Can you share with us what you generously donated back to the profession known as the "Spinal Decompression MasterClass"?

Dr. Lohr:

Years ago, I would have given my left arm to go to because I had to learn decompression on my own until you guys came along. So, for years, I was stumbling along and I was just bumping along, stuck at two tables, not really growing. It was fun. I enjoyed it. I loved it but it just wasn't really going anywhere. I remember when I first joined Concierge Coaches, you introduced me to Dr. Girgis. He's got a huge heart. He's a lover. So, I went to visit Dr. Girgis in Ohio and he had five tables. I can't imagine having five tables. You and Dr. Kaplan said that my headspace needed to grow. You guys kept pushing me and I just didn't see the potential in me that you two saw at that time. I see it now.

You guys knew I needed that and so what the Master-Class does is for the doctors who attend when they walk in to our clinic, it makes your headspace just go, wow. I know exactly what that feeling is like. I was dying to go visit someplace and see it in action, see how they do that? Like you said, I was self-taught for years and not getting anywhere and everybody told me this saved me three years of trial and error. So many doctors came up and said, if I had to leave right now, I've more than got my money's worth. What it's doing is it saves the doctor's time and heartache, frustration and money of trying to learn it on their own. A doctor called me from Texas and said, "I saw this thing, I just want to get a cheap table" and I don't want to join anything. I said, "forget it, you won't get there. If you do it, it'll take you years and you'll have so many heartaches and make so many mistakes".

I refunded the patients the full amount in the beginning, and I tell you, I've learned just by what both you and Dr. Kaplan have taught me. We've developed systems and the most important thing are the staffs. Finally, after 33 years it's taken me this long to get a staff that I just love. Every one of them is just a starlet and quick story about that. When I bought this practice almost 10 years ago, I bought this from a widow and she said, "you're going to pay me every month until this is paid off, and I said, yeah". She said I would "have to keep her sister and my sister in law on staff". There's only those two, you just keep them, you can't fire them. So that was one of the biggest, stupidest things I ever did in my life, I said, okay as I felt sorry for her.

So, I kept those two on and one was there for 24 years, one for 12 years. Then I was being the invader. I was the interloper. We were never a team. I looked back at it as a four-year prison sentence because that staff had me held in prison. It was my own fault. That was a simply a very poor decision. If I have known you and Dr. Kaplan, you guys would say what? No way, don't you ever. Dr. Kaplan would say "Richie, don't you ever, ever agree to something like that". So, for four years, I did not grow. We didn't go anywhere. I had to wait until I paid her off, and then I could get rid of them. Then, I could bring in the right people and now the right staff. They're more like my daughters, like family. We just really respect each other. We have so much fun. We laugh all day and they patients come to me and they say we have a great staff. They've all been to the certification. They come to me and they say, Mary Jane Doe. She'd been in for about three weeks now. She's been a six on a pain scale. Is there anything that you want to change? She looked like she may be a little bit discouraged. Do you want to come and talk to her? Do you want to change anything? So, they come to me with the issue, so I don't have to spend all that time digging in with some of the patients for important content that may be affecting their healing.

They spent the day or so giving our patients the love there, hooking them up and they are so motivated. They all tell me, I love my job so much. I *would never leave you and that meant so much to me and everybody at the Master Class. I think that was the biggest compliment as doctors were saying that they wanted to take my staff home with them. Can I please have all of them? Where did you find girls like that? I have to tell you, we have never had anybody fill out an application for the last 10 years. We never advertised. We never put an ad out. We only hire people we knew. Patients and l like sons and daughters of patients and only people we knew. Laura who is amazing came actually came from Subway. I would go in there for lunch every day and I would peek in. If she was there, I'd go in and have lunch and sit down. I was watching how she was with the customers and how they'd get upset. She was always sweet, always loving, always caring, always patient. So, I looked up to her after I had been stalking her for a couple of weeks and I said, how'd you like to work Monday through Thursday? No evenings, no weekends. She goes, I would love it. I would do anything for a job like that. Another great staff member, I took from Casey's Pizza. Those are from a little small town. They were famous for their donuts and their pizza and they're all in small towns. All family owned and they're all over the Midwest. And I stole another gal from there she was with for seven years.*

I am always looking for the love and I wanted to see somebody here who wants to be number one and who's just going to love the patients. We can teach them everything else, but you can't teach them that. These are habits they either have or they don't. They're going to love these patients or they're not and I tell them that's the one requirement I have with you. I want you to love these patients more than anything else. I don't care if you make mistakes. We all make mistakes. I make mistakes however you've got to love those patients and they did and the patients sensed it.

My team is loyal and we're having so much fun here. I don't even want to leave. That's how important the staff is. They are my backbone. They make my life so much easier. They have freed up so much of my time that I am so grateful that I would strongly say, don't hire anybody off the street. Only people you know, like patients. Always somebody we know like that. Never anybody we don't know in a smaller town like this too. It is easier because everybody kind of knows everybody.

Dr. Bard:

You created an incredible championship team. They are all individual superstars but when you put them together, it's almost like a band that individually they could make great music. However, when you put them together, the quality and the depth and the detail of the music is so powerful and so strong. I believe the reason that was because right from the get-go you knew exactly who would work well on the team. In other words, and it is a membership only club, it really is. They're really almost like a sisterhood. They have to be able to be in sync because what we found during the Master Class was that your office specifically your team was basically communicating with you nonverbally, if that makes sense. In other words, they knew what you were anticipating. Talk about being on the same page and as a result, they really got what we always called, The Big Idea!!!

Dr. Lohr:

That's completely true.

Dr. Bard:

Now, for those of you reading this, if you want to meet Dr. Lohr, and you want to meet our other incredible doctors and you say, "I'd love to pick their brain and learn more and do more" there are opportunities and the opportunities are called the "National Spinal Decompression Certifications" in Dallas at Parker University and in Chicago at National University of Health Sciences. If you can't make that, there are other opportunities known as Concierge Coaches/DISC Centers of America boot camps and that's my ten second commercial for that. I have a feeling that there are a lot of doctors saying, you know what, I finally have the big idea. I got to learn more. That's the cool thing about what we do at The Chiro Event Marketing and Patient Management Mastermind, (www.thechiroevent.com). Dr. Lohr, you have done something dramatic. You've done something unique. You think differently. You act differently. You practice differently. You live differently. So, the lesson here doctors is very simple. Different is good.

HERE ARE THE BULLET-POINT TAKEAWAYS:

#1 - He bought a practice that initially had 2 Spinal decompression tables that were not being used at all. He started using them on himself & that helped him eliminate his personal challenges with Sciatica.

#2 - He attended the 1st ever National Spinal Decompression Certification held at Parker University. He attends all of them now as he constantly learns new ideas at each training.

#3 - He is not a 1st generation Chiropractor. His parents met at a Chiropractor's office. Went to Chiropractic College together and he was adjusted Day-1 with no shots, no vaccinations, no medicine. Just the Love of Chiropractic.

#4 - His clinic has major visual appeal and prepares the patient ahead of time before he meets them that they are in a 1st Class doctor office and they will receive 1st Class care.

#5 - By allowing DISC centers of America to hold their 1st Masterclass at his office it automatically expanded the headspace for attendees. They said it saved them 3-years of Trial & Error.

#6 - The Most important thing is his staff. They are "Starlets". He did not grow in practice for 4 years until he put together the right staff. They Love their job.

#7 - His staff comes to trainings at The National Spinal Decompression Certifications at Parker University & National University. He invests in them. Dr. Lohr also attends the Concierge Coaches/DISC Centers of America Training Bootcamps. Always investing in himself to learn more to provide a higher standard of care.

#8 - He never runs an employment ad. He only hires people he knows or can see in action in terms of dealing with people.

#9 - Any opportunity he has had to travel to learn from Dr. Kaplan he has taken advantage of and understands the power in taking the time necessary to surround himself with the right doctors and the right training.

#10 - His team communicates non-verbally and anticipates the needs of the patients as well as the needs of Dr. Lohr.

4

BLACK BELT ADJUSTING SUCCESS – (DR. MITCH MALLY)

Read about: DR. MITCH MALLY & DISCOVER how he became the "GO-TO" Authority in Educating Chiropractors who desire to BECOME a TRUE MASTER of their "HANDS-ON" TECHNIQUE Skills with a focal point on Extremity EXCELLENCE.

Learn how-to attract the most challenging Shoulder, Knee, Ankle, Elbow & Wrist Conditions by OWNING the True ART of CHIROPRACTIC. Also, LEARN his "ATTITUDE ADJUSTMENT" for creating the perfect INTENT to have the practice of your dreams.

Dr. Bard:

Today is a most, most special show. It's actually a very, very rare show. What makes this rare is the guest that we have, which is really someone that I have admired, someone I've looked up to, someone that I've really revered as do thousands, not hundreds, thousands of other chiropractors who feel the same exact way. It is such a special treat to have with us the one, the only Dr. Mitch Mally LIVE with us here on the Dr. Success Spotlight Show. Welcome to the show, Dr. Mally.

Dr. Mally:

It's a pleasure to be here. Thank you doctor.

Dr. Bard:

This is really such a special treat for a number of reasons. The real reason here is the simple fact that I have known you from afar and once I got a chance to really learn the truth, really learn the real golden nuggets as to what you have always been about in this profession is that you are Dr. Mally and I do not use this term lightly you are a true "Master". As a matter of fact, I don't think in my 31 years as a chiropractor, I've ever used that word in describing one of my peers.

The reason that I'm able to use the word, "Master" with you, Dr. Mally, is because as you know so well, that in our profession we have many whom are good, many whom are better, but there's rarefied air in really being the best and when I say the best, what I mean is Dr. Mally, you are known from far away and across the continents as really a master of technique with a specialization in the world of Extremity Adjusting. You are the real "Mr. Miyagi", if you will, in our profession. As to the level of certainty, the level of knowledge, but really the gift of teaching and sharing this incredible skillset with so many chiropractors across the country.

What I wanted to ask you, Dr. Mally is a number of things but let's just start at really the very, very top and that is this. I'm curious Dr.

Mally is there's always been a driving force in terms of your personal motivation to carry the torch for this profession with regard to teaching doctors how to be at the art of Chiropractic. What's been your driving factor for all these years?

Dr. Mally:

First, I want to thank you for the most amazing eulogy, I thought it was an interview. I'm going to put you into my legacy here and thank you for an incredible introduction. Where do I go from here? Number one, being a former injured athlete and aspiring to want to play pro-football or pro-baseball and my martial art career. I'll have to tell you, I was three courses shy going to med school to become an orthopedic surgeon or neurosurgeon and my two older brothers were a biochemist and an immunologist with a PhD and a masters. So, chiropractic was the furthest from a language accepted in our household. In fact, just the opposite. It was actually considered quackery in my household.

So, growing up with a research scientist and a medical background, to be honest, chiropractic was the furthest thing from anything I anticipated that I would do as a career. I was cutting people. I was assisting autopsies in Detroit. I've been involved in International Kidney Disease Research. I've seen tissues come into surgical pathology and the pathologist show me that it was cancerous. Then on the phone line tell the surgeon to do a radical mastectomy and in minutes we would have the entire breast in the lab. I mean, we're talking amazing medical pathology study. Also, being raised in Detroit, there wasn't a shortage of bodies when we're dealing with an autopsy. So, an opportunity to learn about acute trauma, spontaneous death, aneurysms and my four years of premed in that background laid an incredible foundation that allows me to flourish in today's world. To recognize a famous quote from Robert Greene, was that "the future belongs to those who learn more skill and combine them in creative way". When you look at the word of mastery versus mystery, your mystery creates wonder and wonder is the basis of man's desire to understand, that was Neil Armstrong.

When you come to mastery, it takes 20,000 hours to develop a level of mastery and let's be honest, how many people want to go beyond their chiropractic degree and their diploma when they graduate? Most of us, are just excited to make it through graduation and start practice. Well, as it is known to master means "to develop that skill that very few others will take the time" and what I call the three D's doc. You have to have the desire, the dedication and determination to want something so bad that you will go after it. It's kind of like the junior high school football player that wants to make it next year to the high school starting lineup varsity team. Well, if he rests on his laurels, he may not make it, in order to expound, he needs to be collaborative in developing a change within himself and his attitude to strive to do better than anybody else. So, I have my own cliché. If you're going to do that which everybody else does, do it better. If you're going to do that, which nobody else does, find it, do it, and master it. That my friend will generate the greatest outcomes that will create the practice of your dreams with revenue that will increase not only predicated on marketing and advertising but on the successful word of mouth of your happiest patients.

Dr. Bard:

So, I have one word and the word is three simple letters and those three letters are W-O-W. The reason that I'm able to say the word, WOW, Dr. Mally is the thing that I was so taken by you when I met you, was not only are you really the master of the physical sense in terms of helping, teaching, guiding, sharing, and really, really helping chiropractors reach a pinnacle, a level of confidence and a level of absolute pure skill. But one of the things that I noticed right away about you, and I think this is really such a gift, is that you are actually a master storyteller. You really have an interesting way about you to internalize where you've been, where you are and where you are going.

The reason that I love that about you is because you're doing the same thing for our profession by lifting them on a level that few, if any, have done before. So, my question to you is this in that your background is very interesting because obviously what you've done here is you've turned this into a competition and the competition is really amongst each individual doctor. In other words, helping the doctors do better, be better and really rise to a certain level that maybe they have never aspired to before. So, in terms of your background and in terms of your motivation, what are you doing right now to stay on the top of your game?

Dr. Mally:

That's a really, really good question. Number one, I am most definitely faith based, I'm philosophically based and I continue to work at my art. Many people call me "the sniper" in the profession and the 10th degree black belt guru and all the different names. The fascinating thing is as a sniper and I liken this for philosophy, for science, for art, for religion, for every walk of life, stay focused on that central theme of what is your desire and your greatest passion.

Mine is I cannot stand sickness and disease. I hate it with a passion but I love health and wellness beyond imagination. So, if I maintain my focus on sickness and disease, like a laser beam aim to a bullseye, this is why I have trained with the SWAT team as a sniper. I am a shooter and I've been a martial artist for 50 years. I was a pitcher, and a quarterback. I've always had an eye-hand coordination, but G-d gave me a gift of gab to support the hands on. I have to be very well read and researched. I have 18 residents that give me three articles per month out of 54 medical journals. Those abstracts are required as supporting documentation of everything that I teach. So, as I meet medical doctors and I'm in an integrative practice. I am in a surgical center. I have medical doctors and surgeons implementing interprofessional collaboration. They've learned to work together. The saying that I created was "why not prepare before repair".

We work together and we learned to respect one another's perspectives in healthcare. We have multiple disciplines. They're able to work more cost effectively and yet, more efficaciously as a team to help improve patient outcome. So again, my focus is not on income. My focus is on outcome. If one focuses on income it's because their outcomes are separate. If you focus on your outcome, your income will be great and you will be very happy knowing that you've given the patient the greatest respect and the greatest discipline that you can cherish, knowing what you did with the skills of your hands. Chiropractic means done by hand. Let's focus on our art, yet support it with evidence-based science and maintain a deep-rooted philosophy that we have the greatest healthcare profession on the planet. That my friend is what keeps me motivated and inspired.

The other day, I had an 85-year-old man with 15 years of neuropathy. He couldn't feel his feet. Been to chiropractors, neurologists, everybody else. I examined him and found where the entrapment neuropathies were in his feet, adjusted only his feet not even his spine. He came in the next visit, and he said, my G-d, I can feel the floor. The second visit, he came in this morning, he says, doctor you have changed my life, neuropathy for 15 years and I can feel the floor. I can feel my socks and my feet were burning and that my friend is the outcome that makes me come back to work for the very next patient.

Dr. Bard:

I love it and what I love about it is your fervor, your intensity, and the simple fact Dr. Mally that you obviously do not live in the gray. You live in the black, you live in the white and that's one of the things that I as do the thousands of chiropractors across the country, really love about you.

We are joined here on the live broadcast of the Dr. Success Spotlight Show with none other than the great sensei, the master, the really go-to guy in our profession from a hands-on perspective and much, much more, Dr. Mitch Mally. One of the things that I think is so refreshing about you doc and I know you hear this all the time, is you have such an incredible sense of humor. I think it's your sense of humor that has really allowed you to really shine bright in this profession. I will tell you something. What I was always very curious about with you is really two things. The first one, is how many frequent flyer miles you have doc because of the simple fact that if there's another doctor in the country that's teaching chiropractors on a state level and on a collegiate level more than you. I would love to meet them. It doesn't exist. So, one of the things that I think is so incredibly awesome about you is the ability that you have to instill in Chiropractors what we would call the C word.

The C word in this case doesn't stand for chiropractic. The C word stands for "confidence" and what you give chiropractors is a level of confidence that they aspire to. One of the things I'd love for you to share is your attention to detail and how you are now really empowering the chiropractors of tomorrow by working with some of the colleges here.

When we met you were so incredibly enthusiastic about when I shared with you that my son will be leaving in just a handful of weeks to start his journey in his life as a chiropractic student. So, he's pumped, he's juiced, he's energized, and he really couldn't be more excited. I think so much of that comes from you and you're doing that for students, not just the graduate level, but the postgraduate level as well. In other words, you're giving students the opportunity to have postgraduate level training while they are still in school. Can you share a little bit about how you are putting that together?

Dr. Mally:

Yes. From what I can share right now, I would tell our profession that they need to pay attention to their intention. When you say my sense of humor, there's truth in a sense that the underlying root of that humor is the validation of what it is that I'm joking about. So, for example, if you pay attention to your intention when you went into chiropractic college, why does it change when you graduate chiropractic college? Why did your focus change from wanting to be the very best that you can possibly be to what am I going to earn?

For example, the average student is going to graduate, I understand from my students about $250,000 in debt. So many people will say that W-O-W and I jokingly again with a sense of humor say why don't you turn that attention to intention and say, wow, this is the greatest investment I'm ever going to make in my life because it pays the best dividends. Your *house and your car as fancy as you want to have one day are not going to be paying you dividends. They're going to be externally giving you a sense of satisfaction. We all know that arrogance covers up insecurity. Well, when somebody has to have all the exciting, fancy things that they want to have one day. It's okay, if you earn it, you deserve it, and you want it simply just because. However, if you're using it to satisfy the underlying weakness that you're no better than the arrogant person trying to cover up an insecurity that's not good.*

Be whole, be inside, be internally beautiful, be internally between your ears successful. Pay attention to your intention to give and be a servant to others, to your community, to your family, to your friends and to your loved ones. Realize when you plant the seed, are we all looking to grow wheat or a fruitful tree? I would love the opportunity to meet your son and to show him and guide him, coach him, and mentor him to become one of the greatest chiropractors ever. If he shows that attention to intention, the desire, dedication and determination to be the sniper and not to be the rest of the infantry. Look, you can give a gun to everybody in the infantry, but why is there only one sniper to get the job done?

Who does every king, queen, and leader have protecting them, a street cop or the sniper who gets the job done? That's what you want to be in your community in becoming a leading expert in your community and the people will come to you because of your sincerity. They will learn to know you, like you, trust you because your focus is on your intention. Your attention is on your intention and that detail is what patients are paying you for. It will pay your bills and you will have the practice of your dreams.

Dr. Bard:

Dr. Mally, I can emphatically tell you as you know so well that I've done this now for 32 years. The best money, you will ever spend in your career is an investment in your skillset. It is an investment in your ability to help sick people get better by really investing in the art of removing interference and really balancing the body. Doctors know that when you study under the best, only good things can happen and to know when that tough knee walks through your door, when that tough shoulder walks through your door, when there's an ankle problem, or a wrist problem, and oh yes, even a spinal problem, you know exactly what to do. We're really so honored to have you Dr. Mally with us here. A star amongst stars.

Now, I don't know if you know this about Dr. Mally, but if you've ever seen him live one of the things you're going to be taken by immediately is his tailored and impeccable dress. One of the names they really should give you Dr. Mally "Dr. G.Q.". If you've ever seen him live, it's like an Esquire or G.Q. catalog live. He dresses for success. So, I have to ask you Dr. Mally is where do your suits come from. I kind of have a feeling they're custom because you're definitely a custom guy.

Dr. Mally:

I really thank you for that. Being the youngest of three boys growing up in a lower middle class. My father died at 49, and I was 18 years old. I always jokingly say from the lecture stage you can look at a multimillion-dollar foot store, like a running shoe store with millions of dollars in many, many different types of gym shoes. In my day, there were four gym shoes. There was the Jack Purcell, the Cat, the Converse All Stars and my brothers. So, I've found that one day be the youngest of three boys that I was finally be able to wear my own clothing.

So, I have a sense of humor about the GQ comment. The funniest part of the whole story and the truth be known. I now can afford the luxury of having my own clothes and I enjoy that because it's a sense of security knowing that my attention has always been on my intention. It wasn't what I wore. It wasn't being judged for anything that I had on me or around me because I didn't have. Now, that I can afford whatever, I still am unpretentious, but I will always dress for success. When I went to Palmer College, I used to wear a shirt and tie, have a briefcase and I would be a professional and people would look at you and make fun of you. But you know who has the last laugh? I'm still a professional, but I have an articulate tongue and I like to believe that more people, if they were believing themselves, look in the mirror, dress for success and say, "world, community, loved ones, friends, I am ready to serve you". I look the part, I act the part. Guess what? I am the part.

Dr. Bard:

Dr. Mally, I know how busy you are. Would you be so kind Dr. Mally as to share the easiest contact information for you for doctors who may have one or two questions?

Dr. Mally:

Well, sure, they're welcome to email me. I probably get about 200 emails a day. I will tell you that we look more at text messages these days. I may have gray hair, but I'm getting more, more millennial I guess with technology. So, my cell number that they can text to, indicating who they are and what their issue is and I can text a lot quicker in response time than I can email that could end up in a junk mail inadvertently being missed and I don't want to do that.

My cell number is 563-343-0394. I will not answer those calls, but I will respond to text messages. That is the fastest way to get to me. My office line is 563-823-5555, select 0 to get to you an operator. Leave a message and I can return a call. I return those calls over lunch hour or evening. Please make sure that I am answered when I do return a call to an office. Don't leave me on hold. Just ask your patients just a moment. I'll return in just a moment. I need to take this emergency call and I'd be happy to address it. If left on hold for too long, we'll just hang up and we wouldn't return the call. Finally, my email address is: mrmally@live. com. If there's doctors out there that want to purchase our DVDs and our training, they can do that. If they want to go to learn more, they can visit training.drmitchmally.com.

So, you've got ways to reach out to us. We do private, one-on-one, hands-on training like tomorrow, I'm flying to New Jersey and spending eight to 12 hours privately training two doctors on the 17 entrapments and how to take care of those 17 entrapments to the elbow, wrist, and hand. This is sniper training. If the readers want advanced skills for the elite entrepreneur from beginner, intermediate to advance. My training will take you to any level that you have a desire, a dedication and a determination and be ready because we're going to rock your world and you will in turn rock the world of those that you go back to and treat successfully.

Dr. Bard:

I think you've just rocked our world. I think you've just rocked countless chiropractors across the country who were privy to this information. A reflection of your commitment to excellence, a reflection of your commitment to the profession, a reflection of the love that you have for your colleagues and for your students and we are so appreciative that you took time out of your busy schedule to join us here today. We were gifted today with the presence of Dr. Mitch Mally. Master, legend, expert, and that is just a part of his special sauce.

HERE ARE THE BULLET-POINT TAKEAWAYS:

#1 - Originally from Detroit, he was a former high-level athlete in Football, Baseball & Martial Arts he was originally intending to become an M.D. as he grew up with research scientists and a medical background.

#2 - Mastery Defined: "to develop that skill that very few others will take the time to do so".

#3 - The 3D's - "The Desire, The Dedication & The Determination to want something so bad that you will go after it".

#4 - "If you are going to do that which everybody else does, do it better, if you are going to do that which nobody else does, find it, do it, & MASTER it."

#5 - Faith-Based, Philosophically-Based, he continues to work at his art as he is known as "The Sniper of The Profession".

#6 - He has 18 residents that supply him with 3 Medical Studies out of 54 Medical Journals each month with the latest research.

#7 - A collaborative physician he coined the phrase: "Why not PREPARE before REPAIR".

#8 - Focus on Outcome, not income as focus should be on your art that's supported by evidence-based science.

#9 - Pay ATTENTION to your INTENTION" and the root as to why you became a Chiropractor in the 1st place.

#10 - Invest in yourself for the best dividends and "Dress for Success".

5

CASH PRACTICE SUCCESS – (DR. MILES BODZIN)

Read about: **DR. MILES BODZIN & DISCOVER** how he created the **CASH PRACTICE** Program that has helped over 5000 Chiropractors free themselves from the **"Shackles of Insurance Dependence"**. Also, **LEARN his 4-STEP SYSTEM** for creating the BEST "turn-key" program to help Chiropractors INCREASE their collections.

Dr. Bard:

Today is a great day. If you're wondering why today, is such a great day, it is simply because I have with us a great guest. If you want to know how much I believe really in our next guest. I will tell you that he, as well as, his company were actually the first company that I ever gave a written endorsement to, completely 100 percent unsolicited, so many years ago.

It was simply because of one reason. The reason is simple and that is because I completely believed in what he was doing for chiropractors nationally and what he's doing for chiropractors now. I believed in it then, I believe more in it now than ever before. I want to welcome our very, very special guest here today to the Dr. Success Spotlight Show. I want to welcome, Dr. Miles Bodzin, president of the Cash Practice.

Dr. Bodzin:

Thank you very much, Perry. Great to be here. I really appreciate the kind words you just shared.

Dr. Bard:

You've been helping chiropractors figure out really what many believe to be, the biggest problem in practice for so many years, which is really making it easier for patients, to just basically say the word "yes". Yes, to treatment and yes, primarily to accepting the right financial packages to allow chiropractic to be reimbursed so much better.

You've been helping chiropractors avoid their dependence on insurance, and you've set them free. I think it's such an incredible thing that you've done this. At the same time, to some degree, you're still considered really one of the best-kept secrets in the profession. So, what I'd love to do here his have you share with Dr. Bodzin, what exactly is the Cash Practice?

Dr. Bodzin:

I would love to and let me also state by sharing earlier your statement about the testimonial letter or the endorsement you sent us, unsolicited, I concur with that. I remember it to this day. The letter you sent me had this little character you had on your letterhead. I was surprised in that you normally get testimonials or endorsement letters of someone that I've had some conversations with. So, this was something and this was just out of the blue and I'm like, wow, this is really cool. So, I do greatly appreciate that to this very day that was probably about 10 years ago that you sent that to us. I'm very proud of the fact that we've helped over 5,000 chiropractors now, free themselves from the shackles of insurance dependence and increase their cash collections. Most importantly, to help them serve their communities on a greater scale.

Ultimately, even though, our company is called, Cash Practice. We talk about the finances and helping patients to say, yes and help Chiropractors collect more money and not be dependent on insurance. Another milestone we recently hit. Our group of doctors collectively have just now reached a point where they've helped over half a million patients go onto affordable care plans. Even a bigger accomplishment I believe or another metric as a group is our members have just reached over $2,000,000,000 of processing that we've done for them. So, I'm extraordinarily proud of the amount of success among our doctors. Yes, it's true, we are one of the best-kept secrets. I still, to this day, will reflect back to my own days in practice and that my ultimate aim was not to market for new people at the time. It was to retain my patients and being a cash practice is just kind of a side effect of when you want to run a practice where you have high retention.

When I think back in the days or early in my days, I was struggling. My biggest struggle was not getting patients to follow through or having people drop out of care. That was a big, big frustration for me as it is for many chiropractors. It seems to be a trend these days that retention is becoming a higher and a more popular topic as I see and read through the chiropractic journals and the magazines. We see more articles and things being written about the subject matter of retention. That was always my gig, in how do I retain patients? Being in cash was just kind of a side effect of that. Being that, I had to get to a place, where if I'm going to retain people, not only did I have to get them to say yes to care, but I had to do it in a way that they felt good about it.

Number two is I had to make it so that they would continue to be with me for years to come. I'm proud to say that even though, I sold my practice a number of years ago to retire from practice to dedicate my time full time to run Cash Practice, many of those patients are still seeing the doctor who took over that practice merely because of the fact that the way we had set things up from the very beginning. So, to get back to your question as to tell a little bit more Cash Practice Systems, we're a software and training company that helps doctors. Basically, we say increase their cash collections and reduce their dependence on insurance. Really what we're doing is helping them learn how to retain patients. That's really what our gig is. If you use our systems, if you actually apply what we teach, and utilize it in its designed format.

Not only will you get more patients to say yes to care, but you will ultimately build a practice with extraordinarily high patient retention. One of the stats, I'm most proud of, is back in 2011, when I did retire from practice. Our stats showed that my PVA was 24 times than national average. We had a PVA of just over 300 visits. That wasn't just an accident that was a result of the systems that we learned in practice. I can't take credit for 100 percent of the systems that we do. I stand on the shoulder of giants and learn from lots of other people and apply those ideas and turn that into a software program that if doctors use the software and they use it the way it's designed, they too will have similar results.

For example, I can tell you example after example. There's Dr. Felicity, one of our doctors in St. Louis, who came on board with us and she's a great chiropractor. She knows clinically what she's doing, but she really kind of struggled with the whole process of getting patients to say yes to care, where her sign-up rate was a not very good at all. It was very, very low. Now, she goes on to say that nearly 100 percent of her patients sign up for care. She says 97 percent of her patients sign up for care. We're very proud about the fact that we're able to help these doctors get from a place of struggle and overcome that and not just, "Oh, I had a great month, or I had, you know, a great couple of months or whatever" but years and years and years later, they're still growing their practice. They're still continuing to add patients and not lose them.

Let me just clarify, we're not a coaching company as I talk about that we're helping and growing practices. A lot of times doctors confuse us and maybe that's why we're one of the best-kept secrets is we're not a coaching company. I don't want to create confusion out there. We're a software and training company that when you utilize us, we provide the software and tools. We do provide training for you, but we're not on the phone with you every week coaching you with that type of thing. Although, we do have an account success manager that when you join our program, there's someone at our company that works with you one on one to make sure that you're fully implementing the systems and holding your hand through the process.

To answer your question specifically, Cash Practice Systems a platform of four specific systems. Number one is our Cash Plan Calculator and that is the original program that we created 15 years ago and that's probably the one that you were exposed to back then. That is our program and it's gone through many revisions since then by the way. Of course, our software continues to be upgraded and improved over time. That's the program that allows you to create these financial plans that you're able to present to a patient so that it makes it easy for them to say, yes. It's a very professional compliant document. It calculates everything, provides your discounts and does everything you needed to do so that you have a professional agreement, for the patient to be able to sign up for it. The best analogy I can give you, is it is sort of like when you rent a car and you step up to the counter and they have you sign a document for renting the car. This is a similar type thing which produces a document that the patient signs for them to enroll in your services.

System two is our Auto-Debit System, which is our payment processing system. So, when you want to take that patient who says, yes, I'm signing up for 6 months of care or 12 months of care and you're going to be charging X number of dollars per month. Our system will automatically process those payments for you. Basically, any way you want to process payments, whether it's swipe payments, recurring payments, EMV chip terminals, mobile payments, bank AFTS. You want to collect payments online, you want to sell products. Whatever it is in dealing with payment processing, our software can handle for you. There's nothing it can't do and our rates are very, very competitive. I'll make mention of that as well. There's a lot of companies out there that provide recurring payments or payment processing. There's a million of them out there. What makes us unique? Is that when you're working with us, you're working with people who are very familiar to chiropractic, knows the challenges you're facing, knows the things you need to be dealing with. Because of our large volume, we're able to negotiate extraordinarily good rates.

Last but not least, is our payment processing is integrated with the other systems of our platform, so it is one comprehensive program. So, I mentioned the Cash Plan Calculator, which does the plans. The Auto-Debit System, which does the payment processing. Our third system is our Drip-Education Email Marketing System, which is an email-based patient education system or marketing system for those of you who are familiar with things like AWeber or MailChimp or Infusionsoft or those types of programs that's basically what our drip-education system does. It allows you to create landing pages and create marketing pages and allows you to capture leads online. It allows you to do email-based patient education. Basically, you can assign campaigns to people in various ways to assign the campaigns and then those campaigns obviously automatically will go out and send emails to those patients to educate them and market to them.

Then, our fourth system, which is the most recent system we added about five years ago or so. That is our Wellness Score. That is a tool for creating a patient's health report card. So, Dr. Bard, imagine you came in as my patient and as my report of findings, I share with you that based on all my examination and my subjective findings in my assessment tools and everything I examined on you, I determine your health is D plus or C minus, that helps me motivate you to want to get care. Then, over the course of care, I'm able to give you feedback during reevaluations, sharing with you how your health changed from D to C and C to C plus and C plus to B. It helps the patients to stay motivated under care. As we know, one of the reasons patients will drop out of care is because they just don't know how they're doing. With a report card, we found it as an extraordinarily effective way of showing the patient making progress.

So, in summary, we have a clinical system or Wellness Score demonstrating the need and the progress people are making. We have our two financial tools. The Cash Plan Calculator and the Auto-Debit System for presenting plans and processing payments. Then, we have our patient education system, the drip- education system. All four of those combined together is really what makes up the bulk of what Cash Practice Systems are. There're other things that includes as well, but I will keep it to those four-key systems right there.

Dr. Bard:

We call that bang for the buck. That's an incredible thing in terms of the comprehensive approach that you've put together. One of the things that I was so taken by you, so many years ago, which is so true to this day, is really how incredibly humble you are. One of the other things they learn about you and I don't know any other way to say this, except that I don't know if you had a crystal ball years ago. In terms of the direction, as to how the pendulum was swinging with regards to reimbursement to doctors, meaning as the model has changed, thank goodness in a most positive way for chiropractors around the world who are true specialists. Specialists in the world of spinal disc, through nonsurgical spinal decompression, specialists in the world of treating nerve conditions through peripheral neuropathy, treating joint conditions through the utilization of laser, doing weight loss programs, doing soft tissue therapy programs and so many other things that chiropractors can put under what we've always called the mall of services and these are cash-based programs.

What you've done, Dr. Bodzin is you've packaged this comprehensively. You've made this a seamless transition for doctors nationally to be able to make this user friendly, user friendly for them, user friendly for the patient, user friendly for their staff, and it is a team effort. One of the things I wanted to ask you was this. I was always super curious as to how you started in South Florida and then you ended up in Southern California. How does that happen?

Dr. Bodzin:

So, the way that happened that was really kind of out of my control for the most part. I was a young kid growing up in Miami Beach and in 1984 my parents decided to move to Southern California and I was still in high school. I was a senior in high school at the time. So, I came along with them to California in San Diego, and that's where my life got transplanted to. I have several older brothers. One that lives in the bay area since the '70s and the most immediate above me an older brother who moved to San Diego. A number of years prior or earlier, I think that was around '80, '81, somewhere around there. Anyway, my parents, when my dad retired, decided they wanted to come to California, since they have children out here and so I came along for the ride. So, that's how I ended up here. The one big move that was part of my life with my family, we came to a beautiful place like San Diego and I count my lucky stars that we did it. It's such a beautiful place to live.

Dr. Bard:

When I learned about the Cash Practice so many years ago, there was a four-letter word that you used. It's a great four-letter word, and it's actually one of my favorite four-letter words. It is the letters D-R-I-P and it spells, DRIP. The drip program was really genius and really what it did was it basically titrated education in the proper dosage and allowed patients to get educated properly. That was probably the first thing that I was taken by, when I first learned about your program. Can you share a little bit more Dr. Bodzin, about the merits of the drip program that you created?

Dr. Bodzin:

So, the drip education marketing system is an email system that started a number of years ago. It's been completely rewritten. It's a new platform if you used it in the past, it's completely been revamped and recreated from the ground up a number of years ago. The drip-education system was kind of one of these things that, was an Aha moment I had. I remember back in the mid-90s or so. This was back way before the Internet and the way a lot of marketing was done, if you remember the free reports that were sent out there where people that would call an 800 number and get a free report sent to them. That was a way to lead capture. Then after the lead was captured, you would send mailers to them over a period of time. That concept of sending people a series of pieces of mailings was a newer concept for me to learn at least back in those days from '95, '96 or so.

You remember those golden rod paper free reports that people would mail out for marketing purposes. I started collecting emails and this was back in again, '95, '96 or so. 1 out of 20 people had an email address. People don't even know what email was at the time, but we just started collecting email addresses from those who had them. My whole reason for it back then and I didn't have a crystal was my whole reason for it was I could send people these free reports and I can send people stuff for free through an email instead of having to spend money mailing this stuff out. I was a young kid getting started and I didn't have a lot of budget to work with.

So that was my whole reason for collecting email addresses back then. It was a free way of getting information out to them. It wasn't until later that as, it started doing well, not only can we use it for marketing purposes, but we can also use it for patient education. So, I started putting together 12 emails I want to send someone with pieces of content that I want to educate every patient on. What is a subluxation? The autonomic nervous system, the power of the body to heal, all of these kinds of concepts. Of course, as a Chiropractor, I wanted to teach everybody. I said, well, let me systematize that.

I'll share an interesting thing. I'm in the process of final production of a movie. We actually produced the movie that we are releasing it should be around October. So, it depends on when you read this, but the movie is called, "The Calling" and it's 30-minute movie. We produced it. We've got the script and had a production company that did it. It's inspired on my life, on the development of leaving the world of engineering and moving on to finding my calling as a chiropractor and eventually leading to where I am today. The movie is called, "The Calling" and we're building the website right now.

I'll give you the domain name for people who want to check it out www. thecallingmovie.com is the website. We're very proud of this story that we're releasing to share the message behind it. So, we talk about where these things come from. A lot of the story we tell is where did Cash Practice come from? Plus, the story of being inspired to become a chiropractor. Most of the things that are in the software, all of it comes from real world practice.

Dr. Bard:

I think one of the coolest things about it is the fact that I don't think it's coincidental, which begins with the letter C, that The Calling, which begins with the letter C, is really rooted in being a chiropractor first, which begins in the letter C. So obviously, I think you have CCC'd the day, if you will, pun intended. I got to tell you, I love the name of it.

One of the things I wanted to ask you about was this. I think in this business, if you've been around the block long enough and we've been around the block a little bit, much like yourself, that one of the biggest challenges, that chiropractors have is in the team that they surround themselves with. Meaning, the A-list team of support you've been able to put together in a five-star delivery system. I think when I look back now at the Cash Practice and I actually looked, before we spoke, I have to tell you, I was so taken by all your awards and all your acknowledgements and all the media outlets that actually picked this up.

Now you've had so many of the same team members with you from the infancy of the Cash Practice, which is really a statement to loyalty, to success, and to really putting together something that is magnetic, which comes from you. How have you been able to do that so successfully in terms of having such incredible team loyalty?

Dr. Bodzin:

Well, I'm glad you asked that question because it is one of the things I keep saying I'm most proud of which is the people that I work with. How do we do that? Well, I've been very fortunate that I've had the opportunity to meet some great people. One of my favorite things is this one quote that talks about leadership. I'm the leader of the company but the job of a leader, and I don't take credit for saying this. I read it somewhere else, but it resonates with me and that is, "the job of the leader is not just to create followers. So many leaders in our profession, I believe, fall into that category, where they become the guru or whatever it is, and they create a group of followers.

The job of a leader is to create other leaders in my opinion. That's what I've made my focus on is the people that work with me. My job is to turn them into leaders and people love that. I mean, if they're meant to be a leader, and that resonates for them. It's not a common environment for them to find. I remember Holly who's going on 16 years working with me, and, has become very well known in the industry. She was on the cover of a chiropractic assistant magazine a number of years ago and speaks at Parker and is a well-known figure now, Holly Jensen. I remember her saying to me a number of years ago saying, "there's times I'm speaking where I always say we instead of I", however she knows that it's an "I" statement, like it's something that I should be taking credit for. But by nature, I always say "we," I'm always giving the credit away to other people. She confronted me about that like why are you always saying "we" when it should be an "I." And I said, "Well that's just who I am". I don't take credit for things. I only take responsibility for things when things aren't right. But otherwise, my job is to give the credit away. So that's what I do.

Maybe that's one of the reasons I fly under the radar. Maybe that's one of the reasons why I'm one of the best-kept secrets. Because I'm not out there screaming from the rooftops, look at me, look at me, look at me. I'm busy working, I'm busy doing and busy helping other people grow. I'm very proud of the fact that, yeah, Holly's been with me from the very beginning because it's been 16 years. Amber Shepherd, who's been with me from the very beginning. We hired her when she was 18 years old. I don't say how old she is now, but she's been with me going on 11 or 12 years now. Then, we have Laura who's been with me, it's going to be 15 years this year, who runs our merchant services department. People with me from the very beginning. They're part of the story. When the movie I brought up before www.thecalling.com, in it, you're going to see all three of the people I just mentioned. You're going to see their characters being played by actors in that movie because they're such an integral part of it. I'm very proud of the fact of even the people we've hired in the last 10 years. We have people who are with us going on seven years, eight years of five years, lots and lots of loyalty.

We invest in our people. We treat them very, very well. Including all the basic things of pay and all of that kind of stuff and rewards and those kinds of things. But that only goes so far. What really, really creates a team that is super loyal is creating an atmosphere where number one is, it's a great place to work. For those of you who struggle with this, I have some friends who constantly have turnover. I could see from a mile away what's going on and the challenge we see in so many places of business when there's high turnover or they don't create that loyalty is there's a cancer in that business.

There's a cancer in that office, and the cancer is gossip. That cancer is office politics, that type of stuff. You must create a culture within your business and your practice where you don't tolerate that. The culture is, we are here on the team. We are here to help each other. We are not here to talk behind each other's backs. Then there's also the basic mechanics. We have regular staff meetings where the entire company meets once a week. I have 27 some employees and we'd get in a room for an hour and a half and have a staff meeting once a week. I remember we had some new employees that came on some time ago and they commented to Holly saying, I can't believe the CEO of the company is on our staff meetings, why is the CEO here? That's just because we as a team meet on a regular basis so we trained. All those types of things, but again, it comes from an attitude of I've taught this. Not only do I teach my leaders to be leaders, but our team leaders also teach their people and their departments to be leaders. So, we're all just stepping up and taking responsibility, and always, helping and sharing and working as a team and I'm making sure you're not doing the things that get in the way of that process and there's a lot of them.

The biggest one I can say is, is that you must make sure that your atmosphere is a safe atmosphere and a pleasure to work in. The killer of that, like I said, is the cancer that is office politics and gossip. So yeah, thank you for noticing that. I appreciate that.

If there's someone reading this and now saying, well, who do you hire? How do you find these people? Well, we recruit them. I would say the last couple of people, for example, we've hired, were just people that we met in public that were giving us extraordinarily great service. You could just tell the jobs they were in were not necessarily career jobs, but the service they were providing, you could tell they really cared. Then, we basically coach them, we solicit them, and we give them an opportunity to come interview with us. The last thing I'll mention in regarding that is that I found is where people, that you could see they're a diamond in the rough. I just mean they haven't been given the opportunity yet to shine. They haven't been given the opportunity to find their home yet. You could tell they have the characteristics, the personality, those character traits. I'll mention that we hire character.

We don't hire skill. Skills can be taught as long as they have basic skills. What we hire are character and we find that character has the opportunity to flourish in our environment.

Dr. Bard:

As they say, "The apple doesn't fall far from the tree" and it is there. Your team made it theirs because you've done that so perfectly by creating an atmosphere of inclusion and keeping it fun and keeping it real and keeping it exciting. You're what we call a "G.S.D." kind of guy. You're a G.S.D. doctor. For those who don't know what G.S.D. stands for, I'll make it simple for you. That is, getting stuff done. You, Dr. Bodzin know how to get stuff done. Notice how I cleaned that up?

Dr. Bodzin:

That's what I was thinking.

Dr. Bard:

I have one last question for you in closing and that is simple and that is when, The Calling comes out and you're walking the aisle and you're down the red carpet and you're at the Gruman's Chinese Theatre in Hollywood, California and you're holding up the awards and you're at the parties. Will you do me one favor? Will you remember me?

Dr. Bodzin:

Of course.

Dr. Bard:

Will you just make sure that you don't forget the little people and just will you promise to just remember me. Will you promise to do that?

Dr. Bodzin:

I promise. Listen, there's nobody I forget. I may forget someone's name because I'm terrible with names and Perry I've never forgotten your name by the way.

Dr. Bard:

Well, that's part of your magnetic ability to create a number one award-winning company that's made it so incredibly powerful. Dr. Bodzin would you be so kind to just share your contact information as well?

Dr. Bodzin:

I'd be happy to share that. So, the best thing to do is you can just go to www.cashpractice.com, our website. What I really encourage is once you're there, there's two things you can do. One is, you'll see there's a free eBook. That eBook is the secrets to increasing your cash collections without giving up insurance. That's an eBook that Ms. Holly Jensen and I wrote. Feel free to download that by entering your name and email and phone number.

If you want to speak to one of our representatives and basically get a consultation to learn a little bit more about us, you can do that too. You'll see there's a button on the website called, free consult. You can click on that and just schedule a time that's convenient for you, and one of our Cash Practice experts will connect with you and they'll answer your questions and see whether Cash Practice is something that's right for you.

There's no obligation to do that free consultation and we'd love to be of service to you. So of course, you can always call us directly at 877-343-8950. But what most people do is they just visit the website, click on that free consult button and book a time to speak with us.

HERE ARE THE BULLET-POINT TAKEAWAYS:

#1 - The roots of the need for him creating the Cash Practice Program was simple. Much like many D.C.'s his biggest struggle in his own practice were patients

not starting care or dropping out of care prematurely.

#2 - Enhancing P.V.A. and retention was key to him. His own personal P.V.A. was 24X the National average at the time when he retired from active practice in 2011 to focus full-time on The Cash Practice Program.

#3 - The Cash Practice Program is a Software & Training Program that helps doctors increase their cash collections & reduce their dependence on insurance.

#4 - He started as an Electrical Engineering major in school prior to becoming a Chiropractor which has served him well as the Cash Practice Program has processed over 2 Billion Dollars since its inception over 16 years ago.

#5 - The Cash Practice Program is made up of 4 Specific Systems:

A-The Cash Plan Calculator
B-The Auto-Debit System
C-The Drip Education system
D-The Wellness Score

#6 - He grew up in South Florida & relocated with his whole family when they all moved to San Diego which became the home base for the Cash Practice Program.

#7 - As the creator of 1 of the original patient education systems, the DRIP program was based upon the increase in the request for the FREE REPORTS that so many Chiropractors distribute. This helped automate the distribution of them and educate patients over time consistently.

#8 - He is in the process of releasing a movie titled: "The Calling"" that is a Personal Biopic of The Cash Practice Program. It will reveal the real story of The Cash Practice Program and how he went from Engineering to Chiropractor to Entrepreneur to The Cash Practice Program.

#9 - He never runs an employment ad. He recruits great people. He only hires people he knows or can see in action in terms of dealing with people. He looks for individuals that are "Diamonds in the Rough".

#10 - He invests in people and has created a loyal team by creating a great atmosphere and place to work. He's created culture of service and now with over 20 employees they meet every week to learn and to re-affirm their skills. He hires "character over skills".

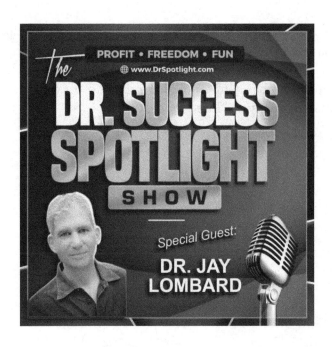

6

FUNCTIONAL MEDICINE SUCCESS – (DR. JAY LOMBARD, M.D.)

Read about: **DR. JAY LOMBARD, M.D.**- "EXCLUSIVE" & DISCOVER how he has created the BEST platform for CHIROPRACTORS who want to utilize Functional Medicine on the highest level. Also, LEARN his "SPECIAL FORMULA" for assessing patients correctly to provide a higher standard of care and how Neurology, Brain Health & Chiropractic are forever connected.

Dr. Lombard is based in New York City. He is a true **"Doctors-Doctor"**. Dr. Lombard has been featured on CBS, NBC, ABC, FOX & CNN and is often considered the **GO-TO Neurologist** for Doctors world-wide who are dealing with some of the most challenging Neurological cases. He is the Chief Medical Officer for a company he helped create known as GENOMIND. In the arena of "intractable neurologic diseases" including ALS., Parkinson's, MS & Alzheimer's. Dr. Lombard's unique approach based upon the most ground-breaking science, has been called by many as "Life-Changing".

Dr. Bard:

This will be different than anything you've probably or possibly imagined before. We are so fortunate to have with us one of the best of the best of the best, and I don't use those words lightly. We are so honored to have with us here today, Dr. Jay Lombard from the great state of New York. Welcome to the show Dr. Lombard.

Dr. Lombard:

Dr. Perry Bard, thank you.

Dr. Bard:

Let me give you just a very, very brief background on who we have with us here today. For those of you who don't know, Dr. Jay Lombard is actually not a chiropractor. He's a medical doctor. As a matter of fact, he is a neurologist by specialty but he's not your average neurologist, nor is he your average medical doctor. He's been featured everywhere. When I say everywhere, meaning he's been featured on CBS, NBC, ABC, Fox. He's been on CNN. He has an incredible foundation and incredible background. He's also the co-founder of a company known as Genomind, which does some of the most incredible work in genetic testing and more. He has some incredible medical appointments thru his career including to Cornell Weill Medical, New York Presbyterian Hospital, Albert Einstein College of Medicine. He has a resume that's really unmatched.

He's the author of not one, not two, not three, but three plus, plus number one books that have all been endorsed by some of the greatest medical minds in the world, including my favorite one, his new one, which we'll talk about on this show. It is his brand new, groundbreaking book, it is called, "Mind of G-d." What's so unique about, Dr. Lombard, is he is really the doctor's doctor, meaning, he is really a go-to specialist for doctors that have had some of the most challenging cases in the world. When I say challenging, not just from a musculoskeletal point of view, but really in the arena of Alzheimer's, in the arena of A.L.S., multiple sclerosis, Parkinson's, and obviously, such a big market in depression. He is the go-to doctor for all the other specialists that have had some really challenging cases come their way. He's had a who's-who list of celebrities and professional athletes and so many people of notoriety who really seek out Dr. Lombard for his amazing intuition and his incredible insight. One of the things that I really, really love about him is that he is, and I have to put this out there on the record. Just so you know he's been in my life for over 35 years, and there's not a day that goes by where I don't get up and say thank you for that. What I am so curious to ask him, and I am so curious to hear his answer is what is your definition, Dr. Lombard of an area that so many chiropractors have been really trying to create as a specialty for themselves which is the world of functional medicine. What is your definition as to really what functional medicine is?

Dr. Lombard:

That's a great question. First, I've been helping to start the Institute for Functional Medicine, with Dr. Catherine Willner who is a neurologist that people probably don't know about. She's based in Telluride, Colorado, who wrote a manual on a functional medicine approach to neurodegenerative diseases. That kind of set into motion, the idea that we could actually teach functional medicine to physicians whether they're MDs, DOs, chiropractors or Naturopaths. And I.F.M. has grown quite substantially since then. I just was recently back lecturing, after a several year hiatuses being with IFM on functional medicine's approach to depression, which is obviously a very pervasive problem in our society.

I think more than 50 percent of people in our country right now are probably on some type of psychotropic medication, whether prescribed, or not prescribed. So mental illnesses are a very, very big problem that we have and it touches obviously on chiropractic work because those patients are the same patients who are more likely to have chronic pain, subluxations, mechanical issues and psychological issues that occurred in the same body. So, to the first definition of Systems Biology is to understand is there's no disconnect between musculoskeletal understanding of the nervous system and its functionality and how that impacts the brain and how it impacts mood disorders. So, I'm glad to be talking to an audience of chiropractors because they are also addressing patients in a functional medicine way just as, alternative doctors, MDs and DOs are. So, Systems Biology is really a better word that I like to use to really explain what functional medicine means. Very simply, Systems Biology means the understanding of the interconnectedness of our organ systems. That's really the broadest definition I can give of functional medicine, is understanding the inter-action between the nervous system and the heart, between the GI tract and the brain, between the GI tract and the immune system. Of course, you know, as a neurologist, to me, it all comes back to understanding the brain, as being the convergence of the Systems Biology approach in functional medicine.

Dr. Bard:

So, this is really incredible in the sense that I believe for the tens of thousands of chiropractors that are reading this, you've actually just made history. The history, Dr. Lombard that you've just made is, and I know you got a lot of hair to stand up in the best possible way for chiropractors around the world is when you actually just used, for those of you paying attention, the "S" word. The "S" word remarkably is the word subluxation, which is in our realm, in our universe, is really the foundational component to what chiropractic has always been based on. This is an amazing thing, but you don't deal necessarily just on the philosophical level and not just the artistic level and not just the science level. You're really dealing on a higher plane. What I mean by that, is if you are by far the most intuitive doctor that I've ever met and that's not just my opinion. You've been called, part Sigmund Freud and part Sherlock Holmes, for your abil-ity to get down to the lowest common denominator, the true root of what's causing someone's disease. You're really the perfect amalgam of both. So, my question to you, Dr. Lombard is this. Where did that come from? How were you able personally to be able to reach a level of doctoring, to be able to get to the true root, the true cause of so many conditions that are such a challenge for not just patients, but for doctors alike?

Dr. Lombard:

The way that I do it is not through my own power. It's by letting myself to be open to the experience of the patient that's suffering and let them lead me to the answer for them. So, it's very difficult to do that, it requires, for all of us as physicians, and we all are guilty of tuning out at different times during the day because it's impossible not to, but it's really on a case by case basis. As being able to have the ability to put myself in that person's shoes in such a way that that illness becomes my disease. I think, well, if I had this disease, what would I do about it? That's been the way of discovering some of the insights that I've had about these different diseases.

Dr. Bard:

It's amazing in the sense that something really incredible just happened to us a few weeks ago. I shared this with a couple of doctors in our inner circle here of what I was so blown away by. What I was blown away by was this. Much like any other doctor out there that has to attend commonly what we call a CEU event or continuing education hours for all doctors, I happened to be at an event and what happened was one of the CEU classes happened to be on handling patients with dementia and with Alzheimer's. This is interesting because this is something that you would not necessarily imagine taking place at a chiropractic CEU event. The difference though, was mind-blowing and was that when I walked into the room, it was standing room only. They had to bring in abundant seats and they still couldn't sit all the Chiropractors who were there. It was the most attended lecture. So, my question to you, Dr. Lombard is why do you think now, more than ever, is there such a heightened awareness and consciousness on how to take care of patients with dementia and Alzheimer's?

Dr. Lombard:

I have two answers to the question. The first answer is, to why people care about it so much because they are directly being affected by it. As we get older, the aging brain is the single greatest risk factor for the development of dementia for ourselves, I mean all of us. So, we have parents in their 70's or 80's or 90's, a lot of people. Professional people are dealing with immediate family members who have Alzheimer's disease. So, there's a lot of interest in Alzheimer's at its root cause in a way that chiropractors intuitively understand an opportunity that they could have by learning about Alzheimer's disease and its pathophysiology contributing significantly to how one can actually prevent a patient from having dementia. So, let me talk a little bit about the biology of Alzheimer's disease and why, chiropractors should care about it, not just personally but professionally.

The reason is that there's a system in the brain called the glymphatic system, which is like a lymphatic system except it's specific to the brain. So, the brain has its own lymphatic system, just add a "G" to it, glymphatic. The glymphatic system is the system that allows the brain itself to remove the pathological proteins that exists in the brain. So amyloid and tau are protein aggregates that actually build up through the aging process. There's a lot of different theories on why those proteins build up. It's clearly a combination of genetics and epigenetics, meaning that people are more at risk of developing Alzheimer's earlier based upon these genes, things like ApoE4, CD33 and some other genes that we learn through a test called Mindful DNA. In addition to that, there's also environmental factors that also promote the acquisition of these pathological proteins.

So, the brain has to get rid of them and the way the brain gets rid of them is through the glymphatic system. I trained initially, as a DO, as an osteopathic physician, and then became a neurologist, but never left my DO roots. Particularly, because, in osteopathy, we have the cranial ability to palpate the rhythm of CSF flow. That pump is something that was being done for a hundred of years before they scientifically validated that the glymphatic system is what they're actually palpating. So, I think it's an exciting time for people who do manual body work to understand the connection of CSF flow. Particularly, disturbances in CSF flow and specifically disturbances in the glymphatic aspect of CSF flow and how it relates to manual therapy and even, words like subluxation because we know, that those systems are impaired in dementia patients leading to increased accumulation of protein. The best way is to think of the glymphatic system as the brain's toilet bowl, and if you don't flush that toilet bowl properly, those pathological proteins will produce cell death in the brain.

Dr. Bard:

You just had thousands plus, plus, plus of chiropractors salivate because for so many of them, they now know and now feel that obviously at the top of the ladder in the medical world in terms of respect, credibility, and reverence that they have a doctor here in you, Dr. Lombard that completely gets it.

You hit it right on the head when I was at that CEU event. They said, we have a feeling that the reason that this room is so incredibly busy right now is that there's so many doctors in the room right now is because of exactly what you just said. Number one, so many chiropractors having to deal with family members who are dealing with Alzheimer's and potentially dementia and the like. Including, the abundance of patients and patients' families. You've had rave reviews on your latest book which is at the very top of the bestseller list. This is the real deal, it is called, "Mind of G-d" and would you be so kind, Dr. Lombard to share the basis of "Mind of G-d."

Dr. Lombard:

The concept of the book is the convergence of understanding science and faith and how science and faith are not exclusive at all. I'm telling you that there is absolutely 100 percent convergence between science and faith and that's what the book is about.

Dr. Bard:

I love what you do because you have historically done something that so many doctors have had challenges with. Your ability to take something that's complicated and make it simple. That is one of your great attributes because you are a master communicator. Not just to the doctors but primarily to your patient base who travel far and wide to come and see you. It's vital and crucial because of the fact that there are so many chiropractors out there right now that want to do better. They want to help more. They want to do it right. They want to do it naturally. One of the things you've been known for, is actually the development of certain nutraceuticals, certain nutritional products that have helped chiropractors through the years and more. Can you share with them a little bit about the basis of some of the nutritional products that you actually created for them?

Dr. Lombard:

I can talk about what the compounds that are mostly doing the most beneficial things. What's interesting about that particular line of research and has to do with understanding how the immune system is over reactive in patients with neurological issues. So, it's not just Alzheimer's but a lot of disorders of the brain are actually due to inflammation of the brain. We sort of have learned that in a peripheral way, meaning that we're able to guess, if you will, that the brain is inflamed by looking at autopsies where there's more glial cells and other immune debris that point to abnormal immune system activity of the brain for almost every brain disorder.

We know that inflammation exists but the problem is we've always had that indirect assessment of brain inflammation. I think the greatest discovery that didn't occur by me, but occurred through a close colleague of mine at Yale, named Dr. Abreu, is that we can now actually essentially monitor the brain temperature externally because inflammation is essentially more heat. Think about a swollen ankle, what do you do? You put ice on it. If we didn't know exactly how inflamed the brain is, we don't know how to cool it off either. So, this discovery was actually in a press release about 15 years ago, that the Yale researchers have discovered a way of actually externally monitoring the brain temperature. That's very important because when you take a patient's temperature, you don't know their brain temperature because of the blood brain barrier.

So, the point is that this opens up a lot of opportunity for developing novel nutraceuticals that we can actually assess their ability clinically to decrease inflammation in the brain by their ability to lower brain temperature.

So, we're not just saying that these compounds are anti-inflammatory in the brain, we actually can validate that clinically. One of them actually is something that doesn't need to be validated clinically because we already know it does that, which is melatonin. So, melatonin is something that I think that probably every person over 65 or even younger than that should be on regardless of whether they're taking it to help them sleep or not. It is extremely neuroprotective. There're tons of research on its benefit clinically in patients with dementia. It's inexpensive and you can personally get it really from anywhere.

The second compound that I think also that has been well studied, as far as its preventative effects is ultra-low-dose lithium. We could talk about what an ultra-low-dose lithium means, because the problem is that when you say low-dose lithium to a conventional psychiatrist they think that dose is between 75 and 100 milligrams. When you say low-dose lithium to functional medicine doctors, they think of lithium orotate at a 5 to 10-milligram dose. The data on its effect, at least in one study that was done in Brazil. I don't have the exact paper, but they demonstrated that less than one milligram of lithium a day has been shown to help patients with cognition and their ability to preserve cognition, even people at risk of developing dementia. So, I wish I had that paper on hand to quote it directly because it's not my research. The point is that even lithium at levels of one milligram or less are neuroprotective in clinical studies. So, there's a lot of interest in using lithium as a non-pharmaceutical agent at these lower doses.

Dr. Bard:

There are so many things that I love about you, as they say, let me count the ways. One is the perfect alignment of science with your heightened sense and commitment to raising the standards of care for all doctors, chiropractors, medical doctors, osteopathic physicians, and more.

Dr. Bard:

This was really a hallowed ground show because of who the messenger was. Often, I speak about the message or the messenger. To me, they're both important, but at the end of the day, I'm always looking at where the message is coming from. I can guarantee you, that it'll come no better than our special guests here today, Dr. Jay Lombard. He is the best messenger. He is without question the most intuitive doctor I have ever met. He has helped countless people, countless patients from the worst-case scenarios. He is in my mind, "purely angelic".

HERE ARE THE BULLET-POINT TAKEAWAYS:

#1 - A classically training Medical Physician & Neurologist, he helped start the Institute of Functional Medicine.

#2 - A better definition of Functional Medicine is SYSTEMS BIOLOGY which is an understanding of the interconnection of organ systems, (i.e., How the Nervous System is connected to all other individual organ systems). This applies to Medical Doctors, Chiropractors, Osteopathic Physicians & Naturopaths alike.

#3 - Upwards of 50% of all individuals taking medications both prescribed & non-prescribed are in the arena of psycho-tropic drugs that often deal with depression. These patients are often chronic pain patients and are SUBLUXATED. Understanding brain health is the basis for this.

#4 - He has been called "part Sherlock Holmes & part Sigmund Freud" for his unique gift & innate ability to get to the root cause of the most serious and often un-diagnosed medical conditions. He feels that by putting himself in the patient's shoes & allowing him to make the patients illness his, he is able to create better insights for care.

#5 - There is a heightened awareness in the Chiropractic profession in dealing with patients suffering from Alzheimer's Disease & Dementia. Chiropractors are having to deal with this both personally & professionally and it is creating better opportunities for Chiropractors who have better knowledge & insights as to managing these patients.

#6 - The "Glymphatic System" (much like the Lymphatic System) helps the brain remove toxins & can be palpated, which is of specific interest to Chiropractors as this affects CSF Flow.

#7 - His NEW book "*Mind of God*" has had the highest reviews by some of the most respected media sources, physicians, teaching institutions and more. It is about the convergence of understanding

Science & Faith & how they are not mutually exclusive of each other but inter-connected.

#8 - His science & research helped create some of the most successful nutraceutical formulas (utilized by companies you know) & is based upon enhancing the immune system & helping reduce inflammation which can improve brain health.

#9 - He has contributed to NEW Research & Science based upon a ground-breaking Yale Study of the Brain & thus the ability to lower actual Brain temperature which can reduce inflammation. He cites Melatonin as one of the better Neuro-protective nutraceuticals.

#10 - He has been one of the Chiropractic Professions greatest allies and may still be the BEST-KEPT SECRET in both Chiropractic & Medicine alike.

7

MEDIA SUCCESS –
(DR. JASON DEITCH)

DR. JASON DEITCH & DISCOVER how he has helped more Chiropractors enjoy MEDIA SUCCESS than ever before. A master in Chiropractic Communications, learn how Dr. Deitch is teaching Chiropractors today to "Un-Market Their Practices" by following some NEW & CREATIVE ways to allow Chiropractors to master the skills of simple yet powerful communications and how-to create a thriving practice in today's market.

Dr. Bard:

There's an old saying that goes like this, "if something is good, it's going to stand the test of time." However, if something is great, it will adapt, it will change, and it will continue to prove why it remains at the top of its game. It is such a special treat and special honor to have with us somebody, who I know really defines that statement. We are so honored today to have with us, Dr. Jason Deitch, from Northern California. Welcome to the show, Dr. Deitch.

Dr. Deitch:

I appreciate it very much, Dr. Bard. It's a beautiful day out here in Northern California. Thank you so much for having me. It's a pleasure to be here.

Dr. Bard:

It's really an incredibly special treat for us and for all of our readers who know all about you. For the minority of our profession that doesn't know about you, I'll share a few things that I've always known about you. Before chiropractors actually ever even heard the word social media, with the emphasis on the word "media", you were Dr. Deitch, the first chiropractor to open the eyes of the profession to this incredibly, potentially great medium, with the emphasis on the word "potential". The reason that I say potential is because I believe across the board that some do it good, but some do it great. You've been the torch carrier for putting chiropractors and chiropractic as a whole to the front of the line when it comes to the media.

When I think of you Dr. Deitch and I think I told you this years ago, I said "you're an originator". You are actually the originator of this platform that became so popular for chiropractors and to do it on the largest scale. There's a couple of things that I wanted to ask you. Your opinion is so incredibly valuable to not just me, but to so many chiropractors. My question to you, Dr. Deitch, is how has Facebook and social media changed since you got started to where it's at right now?

Dr. Deitch:

Oh, that's a great question. If you're probably watching Cable News Network of sorts, you'll probably hear a lot of different opinions about that, especially these days, as we are discussing this in anticipation of the upcoming elections. How has it changed? Well, in many ways it's fulfilled one of its missions, which has always been from the very beginning to connect people. That's really been sort of the big idea that Mark Zuckerberg had from the very beginning. It was to get people connected around the world, even with different ideas, and from different cultures. Because the premise is very similar to in our profession, we both know that life is better when you're connected. I've always seen a very strong connection philosophically with what Facebook is intended to be, and I'll say, I guess with what chiropractic is intended to be, in that being connected is better.

I can go really deep for hours on the implications. For the most part, Social Media changed, in that people now readily accept it. It has become part of our culture, whether you like it or not. People are addicted to their mobile devices and are most of the times on a social network of sorts. Whether you like it or not, there's a good chance that if you're a grandparent, the only way you stay connected with your grandkids is probably through Facebook or whatever. It's become embedded into the fabric of our culture. I'm looking outside the window right now and a kid is riding his bike, texting on his device while he was riding his bike. It's just embedded in our culture. Literally, from the moment we wake up in the morning until the time we go to sleep, we are directly connected to our devices from morning until night.

That's not great news. I'm not necessarily proud of 'that's the way it is', but it is the way it is. I think the opportunity is there to use this tool as a force for good, instead of to some degree the way in which it's used as a tool for manipulation and influence on political issues. It's a tool we all look to for entertainment, connection, information, pictures and for most information we look for. We need to do a better job as professionals too, I think of it as someone hacked Facebook and made a concerted effort to flood it with positive messages of inspiration and unique messages of

81

what not only makes chiropractic great, but what makes you great, and what makes your practice unique. If I say, I'm a chiropractor to you, nobody knows what that really means. So, you don't know if I adjust or I don't adjust. If I use outside equipment or just my hands, whether I accept insurance or don't accept insurance. Whether I have a philosophical perspective that my job is to have you come in and get out as quickly as possible, or try to inspire and influence you to want to stay for a lifetime or none of those things by just saying, "Hi, I'm a chiropractor, let me talk about chiropractic" and is a medium that has changed. How has it changed? I ask again. It's become partly the culture of our fabric and it really has become the primary source for most practices; new patients these days when utilized correctly.

Dr. Bard:

So, this is really pivotal. It is a pivotal time in our profession. When I think about who really has been at the forefront of helping chiropractors communicate better, that's what you are known for. That's what you've done more eloquently, more successful, and really more proudly than any other chiropractor that I've come across. In sharing all that goodness with the rest of the world that didn't know how incredible you are, Dr. Deitch, what I'd love to ask you is simply exactly what you just mentioned, which is what I would call, 'the elephant in the room'. I think you know what 'the elephant in the room is', and I'm so curious right now to hear what you have to say about it. For those who don't know what the elephant in the room is when you talk about how many patients are under chiropractic care, either presently or previously, you'll hear numbers such as 8 percent or 12 percent or even 15 percent. I've been a chiropractor for 32 years now, and I have to tell you that when I'm in a social setting, I'm at a party for instance and I'm asked what I do as soon as I say, "I'm a chiropractor", the feedback I get is overwhelmingly ultra-positive, it's incredible. So, Dr. Deitch, where do you believe is the disconnect? In other words, if we're only hitting 8 percent, 12 percent, 15 percent of the market under care presently or previously, where in your opinion are we missing?

Dr. Deitch:

Well, that's a great question. I think we're living in a very interesting, perhaps, pivotal time as well, and that we have a choice to make here. In answering your question, what I think is perhaps a metaphor, my belief of the elephant in the room and the state of the profession and where the disconnect is. I want you to imagine for a moment that every attorney introduces themselves as an attorney;

I want you to imagine that anytime an attorney talked about what they did, they describe the law. Well, for example lawyers focus on contracts and we focus on law, we write briefs, we debate, we argue in front of a jury and we help people navigate legal issues. That's exactly true. That's what we do, correct? So, everything is all 100 percent being accurate, but I want you to imagine that you were brought up in a family that used attorneys specifically for estate planning and that was what you were used to, all the while. You had grown up in a family, in an environment and around friends, who were wealthy and always looked to attorneys to help them with their estate planning. More so, as far as you're concerned, you correlate attorneys with estate planners.

However, you move one day and you ask your attorney, "Do you know of an attorney in the town that I am moving in?" You go to the town that you're moving in to and look up attorneys and you end up with an attorney who's actually a criminal attorney. Now you walk in and you go, "Here are my papers" I need to change these addresses and I need to update some of the things in my estate plan and that attorney looks at you cross eyed. They decided to take your case on because they need more new clients, patients or whatever and because they are financially stressed out. I got a feeling if that continued to go on for a period of time, the whole thing would be a mess because clients would be walking into attorney's offices with an expectation of what they think and attorney does in return.

Then the attorney is going to be faced with the constant dilemma of "Do I tell them that I'm actually a high-profile divorce attorney with a very specific specialty, or do I accept a whole variety of different people so I can keep my doors open and all of that? I do different things and in different ways to the different types of people who come in, let's face it. They're willing to pay the bill and I need some people". To me, that's where the disconnect is. When-chiropractic is such a spectrum of specialties, the way attorneys can have an infinite amount of ways of expressing the law. I think that we are doing the profession a disservice, even worse is that we're doing the public a disservice by just keeping it at that level.

I'll make another metaphor. Imagine if every restaurant that you drove by simply had the sign of a restaurant. Now, you didn't know if you're going to McDonald's or to the French Laundry because they all just say restaurant, right? If you drive down the street, most chiropractors' offices just simply said, chiropractor, just as an attorney's office could say, attorney, a restaurant could say restaurant, a hair salon could just get a hair salon tag. There just isn't enough differentiation about what makes us unique. As a result, it keeps things extremely confusing and difficult for the public to know what they should be going to buy and bring home. I am going to a new area and I said to you, "Hey, I'm going down to Miami next week. Do you know a great chiropractor?" It's one of the most difficult questions for us to answer because typically when people ask us that question, they're saying some version of, I like what you're talking about, right? Whether that's quick care, I call it a fast fix for free. Come on in, we'll get you adjusted and we'll take your insurances with as little out-of-pocket expenses as possible. Give us a call when it hurts again.

That's one end of the spectrum versus the other end of the spectrum that says, "We don't talk about symptoms, we don't deal with insurance. We are here to reconnect mainly the spiritual and physical. Lay down and if you don't bring your credit card you're not accepted for care and the only type of care you're going to get is pay per service on a yearly basis, right? I'm being extreme to make the point. You don't know what you're getting, neither do you know who you're walking into and I know one of the most difficult questions we get is, "I like what you're talking about. Where can I get what you're saying?" It's where I live. I just think that's one of our challenges. I just don't think that we become, I'll say articulate enough. We live in a world where you just educate people about chiropractic, you're going to love it. But there are so many different ways of serving chiropractic that I think we're missing in the boat. So, it's sort of my simple overview of what I think is the disconnect in today's day and age.

Dr. Bard:

I've always loved one thing about you, and why you are one of my favorite chiropractors on the planet is because you have my ultimate respect. The reason you have my ultimate respect is because you've taken this as your mission. We're joined live here by Dr. Jason Deitch, from Northern California. You know, I'm throwing that northern thing in there a little bit. The reason that you have always been the "C" in chiropractic, but it is not just for chiropractic. To me, it was always about Credibility, it was about Congruence, it was about Confidence. One of the things that you've done is you've made it your life's mission to reinvent yourself and to help more chiropractors use that "C" word better and the "C" word is communicate.

You've helped chiropractors communicate better than anyone on the planet that I know of. I'm so curious to ask you something that I've always wondered about and I don't know if you know this, but my son actually lived in a place called Menlo Park, California. I got the chance to spend an entire summer there. When I was there, I learned that this is the home base of *Yahoo*, the home base of *AOL*, the home base of *Facebook*. It's exciting that they're all based there for a reason because they call that "Silicon Valley". I know it's not coincidental that you happened to be right in the heart of this incredible foundation for communicating. Why did you choose that area to live?

Dr. Deitch:

Well, that's a great question. I'll make a long story short. When I was graduating Life University, my criteria for where I wanted to be was I grew up in New York City, which as a chiropractor you can set up shop anywhere you want to is one of the reasons I thought that was a great thing to do. I wanted to be near a great city and I wanted it to be relatively close to great skiing. I guess two passions or things I envisioned. There are several different places in the country that did that too. The northeast was too cold, I've been there, done that, and it was time to move on. Salt Lake City was an option. Boulder or Denver, Colorado was an option. Some of them have better skiing and even worst cities, but what really made the decision for me was as I was graduating chiropractic school. I'll make a long story short. My father called me up one day and after trying to talk me out of becoming a chiropractor. He said, "Son, you don't know what people think of chiropractors". I said, "Dad, if you knew what I knew about what chiropractic really is, you'd see that this really is the potential future of all healthcare in America". He said, "I'm your dad and you're my son, you don't know what I know". I said, "I know that's true, but I'm the son and here's what I've discovered."

He was in his interest simply trying to save me from a massive mistake in his mind. He started getting adjusted, started attending some of the events that I've been involved with at school and so on. Fast forward, he calls me up one day and says, "I've decided I'm going to go to chiropractic school". So, at 55 years old, my father decided to do what he jokingly likes to say, 'follow in his son's footsteps and start chiropractic school'. So that ended up a third element to my choice, great city, great skiing and chiropractic school because the vision was that we would all have some sort of family practice and so on; that really solidified San Francisco. My dad went to Life West and I set up practice in Oakland.

The side story was that my dad hung up with me on the phone and he called my brother, who was playing professional basketball in Israel at that time. My brother had to suffer through all the family debates or conversations all around. My dad was thinking I was crazy and I was thinking this was a visionary, brilliant decision for my future. My dad said to my brother, "I'm going to go to chiropractic school." My brother said, "Can I go with you?" So, he left Israel, came back here, and the two of them went to chiropractic school together while I started the practice with my dad's wife, who was my office manager and we all lived in one house. So that was the decision as to why I came up here and that is also the epicenter of technology. The tech leadership is in many ways like the technology around the world. It was just that much more compelling and certainly has been a very fortunate decision, I'll say that.

Dr. Bard:

Your story is so original. I've had no clue. I love it that your father followed his son's footsteps, quite the opposite than we usually hear it. It's really interesting and that's why I'm so overjoyed to have you on the show because of the simple fact that I know there's a lot of chiropractors out there that had no idea of how you were rooted in the business, how you reached a level of heightened awareness, and to be able to help chiropractors reach a much higher level by just simply fulfilling their own potential.

The real reason we put the show together was a very interesting thing that actually happened to me so many years ago, where I had an opportunity to actually, be the "fly on the wall". You're not going to believe who I was on a fly on the wall for and maybe a doctor you know. He was a legend in this business and he gave me an opportunity to be the 'fly on the wall'. In other words, to see what the most successful chiropractors on the planet were doing and he was arguably one of the top 10. He might've been one of the top three most successful chiropractors in the world; his name was Dr. Lloyd Latch. Did you remember Dr. Latch?

Dr. Deitch:

Quite well. I was with his son and I would see Lloyd several times a year and he was right in San Francisco. His son's still there.

Dr. Bard:

It was an amazing thing years ago, and if you ever saw the movie, Basic Instinct, there's a story behind that for those who know. What Dr. Latch, actually did for me so many years ago was I actually called him out of the blue and I said, "Is there any way that I could just stop by your practice? I'm in south Florida, Palm Beach County. He's in San Francisco." And he said, "Are you serious?" And I said, "I would love to just meet you. I'd love to just hang out for like 10 minutes just to say hi." And he said," If you're serious when can you come?"

I said, "As soon as you'll take me." He said, "Get on a plane tomorrow," and I booked the plane within 24 hours.

I flew out there and it was one of the greatest days ever in my career of 32 years because it gave me the insight as to what one of the most successful chiropractors was doing at the time to run one of the most successful practices. What he did was he opened his heart; He opened his practice. It was completely different than anything I envisioned at the time. It was really the gift that kept giving after all these years. With everything you know, and you know a lot, and everything you've seen, and you've seen a lot, Dr. Deitch, if you were opening a practice now, on for example, a limited budget, what would you do to get your message out to the masses?

Dr. Deitch:

It's a great question. Without any doubt, I would 100 percent use a combination of real-life engagement, connecting with people, meeting people, being out and about not just sitting in my office, waiting for people to hopefully show up. But getting involved in the community through public speaking, through local organizations and groups would do a lot. We've got a new program coming out called, "Un-market your Practice". The reason we call it that is basically due to — I think, the unfortunate thinking most chiropractors have become addicted to, which is that you have to put out low price discount offers to strangers who know nothing about you to come into your office to get what they think chiropractic care is. Which in an overwhelming majority of cases, is different than what most chiropractors want them to think the chiropractic care is.

Most people think or hope they can come in, get cracked, leave, feel better and you'll take their insurance and they're on their way. Not that there's anything wrong with that, except for the fact that it sort of leaves out some of the benefits of longer-term care and the philosophy that we have, which I think are some of the best parts of what we have to offer. So, I'm a big fan. I think of myself as a practical pragmatist. So, I'm not saying that you have to starve and not help those people who are willing to come in and pay for your care. Now, what I am saying is that, we limit our communication to that, by thinking exclusively through the lens of marketing. So, I start the conversation of saying, "let's Un-market your Practice", which is to give people the opportunity to get to know you, get to know what makes you unique, get to know the benefits they can expect to experience by working with you specifically. Again, we all know, when I think through our history there are some offices that focus more on wellness and massage and lifestyle. Other offices that focus more on specificity, upper cervical technique, X-rays and seeing you in frequently. Other offices that are very specific to imaging and documentation for personal injury and extra service to be able to work with your attorney if you've been in some sort of accident.

They are all very different styles of care. I think that the main thing I would do to answer your question is number one, make sure I'm clear on this style of chiropractic I provide and I don't just mean what techniques. I mean, what is a fast-paced style or slow-paced style? Is this for families or just for a specific target audience? So, I would get very clear that we need to do better than just like all attorneys are not there to just help anybody find justice, right? Which is a very high level of appreciation. I get the idea that if you're a chiropractor anybody who presents with a spine, we can help. I get it. However, to be effective in business, you've got to make it easy for people to want to buy from you. So, we're not selling the concept of health. We're selling why you should come to me for an improvement in life because that could be an improvement in symptoms. It could also be an improvement in a particular sport, a golf score, it could be an improvement in a performance of some particular specific kind. So, we just need to know who our audience is, who we're speaking to, what language they speak, so to speak. I only know English, French or German. But as a metaphor, most of the world speaks different than chiropractic and chiropractic philosophy. We've got to do a better job at translating our personal, philosophical understanding of chiropractic and expression of it with people on the street so that we can be unique and different.

Going back to the metaphor earlier, we should be able to say, I'm a corporate tax attorney that works with companies of $100 million or more". That gives me a very specific understanding of the type of attorney you are and the type of client you work with. It's really easy for you to say, yes,

I'm one of those, or no, I'm not. Just saying I'm an attorney does not get people to yes, hop in and buy from you. We need to take lessons. Again, it applies across the board. I'm a doctor, okay, I went to a doctor, who is a psychiatrist and now I'm going to a doctor that's an oncologist, they're both doctors. We need to raise up the bars of our communication game so that we can be more articulate like who we are, who our audience is, the benefits they can expect to experience by working with us and through a series of getting out in our community and building a health tribe by understanding how to use Facebook and social media. It is essential also to know how to create a content posting strategy and how to get people to subscribe to our tribes. They see all of our daily inspirational posts so that earns us the right to share more about how they can have a better quality of life. Not just more about chiropractic, but more about how your target audience can have a better quality of life.

What role you play in it? And what role do people in your community play in it? So that you can really become a leader in your community and your health tribe in time becomes your number one source of referrals. I understand when you're just starting out a practice, anybody literally, who walks in the door is a good thing. When you're super busy in practice, or even moderately busy in practice, you have a different emotion about somebody who is I call "a deal seeker", maybe who found your coupon on Groupon and saw that they could get a massage on the first visit and an adjustment and X-rays and everything else for 25 bucks. There's a difference between the psychology of that person and somebody who was referred by a longtime lifestyle-oriented client who's gotten great results, referred a bunch of their friends and family, and here's yet another refer-ral by that person.

When you're factoring your time, your staff's time, your energy and the likelihood that somebody's going to start to care with you. In most cases, most of the time that referred person is going to be easier on your staff, less stressful for you and more likely to stick around than the deal shoppers. So, I'm not making decisions. I'm not passing judgment. You should only do one and not the other. You come up with whatever sort of percentages you want your portfolio, your patient traction to be in, but I'm always going to suggest making sure to include that you give people the opportunity to get to know you, to get to trust you, to get to learn from you, and get to understand the meaning in everything. Something they can expect by working with you before they ever sit down in your office. I'm going to say, Perry, this is sort of a perfect example of that.

You and I have learned a lot of value from each other online. We haven't spent a lot of physical time together and yet, I'm a big fan of yours and thankfully vice versa. For exactly the reason I'm describing, I've gotten to know you and you've gotten to know me. We follow each other. We see the exciting things that happen in each of our lives and watch the progress. We're impressed by each other's work. So, when I see you at a seminar, it's like we're longtime friends, even though we don't live in the same town. We haven't spent lots of meals and time or vacations together, and yet, we feel like we know each other and that's the same with lots of people. So, think of the celebrities we feel like we know because we've seen them on TV, or we watch them, or follow them on Facebook and Instagram.

That's to me the missing link here and it starts really with the doctor's perspective and it has everything in my opinion to do with rewiring, reframing, or re-understanding the context that marketing is great. My background is marketing. I love marketing, but professional services in my opinion, are held to a different standard than deal shoppers. When you go to buy a flight somewhere, assuming you're not stuck on a loyalty program or fly private, you're going to go to a search engine and you're likely going to look for the cheapest, closest option. You just want to buy. You're buying a commodity to get from point A to point B. You want to fly from West Palm to San Francisco. Unless you're flying private, you're going to a search engine to find the best deal. You are not concerned one bit, who the pilot is, who the service staffs are, who the flight attendants are going to be, and who the baggage handlers are going to be.

It doesn't even enter in your consciousness as part of your decision that's buying a commodity. My concern is that, we as a profession are present-ing like a commodity when in fact, we're specialists, experts and doctors. That the shift in my opinion I request for this profession. Starting with the person starting out, is that do they have enough self-esteem, enough understanding about the benefits of what they do/we do? They can see themselves and identify as an expert and appreciate the fact that when it comes especially to health services, or I'll say legal services, accounting services, etc. So, forgive me for being a bit facetious here, but most normal people do not look for the cheapest option. They look for the best option they can afford. We don't communicate to that market, as well as, we do from those that have convinced most in our profession that we need to come across as desperate. We need to decrease our fees. We need to put our personal philosophies somewhere aside and just simply give people what they want. Even though, that may not be what it is that we're passionate about delivering because theoretically, that's how we build the practice and make money.

My reason for why this is now more important than ever before is that my argument was really tough to convince people. When most people had really good insurance, because in those days the ends justify the means. You made enough money that you can justify whatever song and dance and show the justification you had along the way. They say, well, we got them in the office. They started care. I was able to bill top dollar for every code possible. It taught me two or three months of care and some of them stick around, but I'm making a good living. So, wink, wink, nod, nod it works. I can't argue with that because at the end of the day, people got mortgages to pay, schools to pay for, cars to pay for, trips to pay for and so on. I get it.

But in today's day and age, where more and more people have much higher deductibles, if they even have insurance coverage at all, and those copayments in some cases are equivalent to your actual out-of-pocket fee. That changes the equation significantly because now, people actually have to see the value and say yes to your care from the get-go because they're coming up with money out of their pocket from the get-go. That's a game changer for most chiropractors. We haven't changed our communication skills. We've just continued to get more and more frustrated that it's not like it used to be. We keep saying, well, I don't have time, I don't have energy or interest in doing something new like social media, because we spend our time, energy and money trying to get the old way to work in a new world. So, my continued mission in life is to try to bring some common sense or uncommon common sense to our profession. I think of myself as a contrarian. I've call myself "the daily disruptor" because I just want to give you full notice in advance that if we're going to have a conversation, it's more likely than not that I'm going to probably have a different kind of perspective on what most people think is normal. Just letting you know upfront, so we don't have to waste our time debating and arguing, if you're not looking for somebody to simply agree with you.

Dr. Bard:

That is why I was so incredibly excited to have you as a guest on this show because of the simple fact that you, Dr. Deitch are atypical. You are different. You have made it your life's mission to reinvent, to recreate, to re-strategize and to restructure yourself, your business model and the direction of this profession. As they say often that "if you try to be everything to everybody, often, you'll end up being nothing to nobody". This is a game of specialty, this is a game of setting yourself out to be the star of the show, to be the best "go-to" doctor, to be the doctor you would seek out individually through all your diligence to find the best. Everybody defines the best differently, but the one thing that they all share in common is the simple fact that they want to be proud of who they are seeing, and you've done such a spectacular job in our profession.

I've been such a big fan of yours for so long because of your innate ability to be able to help chiropractors cut through the noise and cut through the pressure and get to the lowest common denominator of success by positioning themselves correctly as a chiropractor in all their glory. Dr. Deitch, talk about if doctors are curious and they want to learn more as to how to position themselves correctly from a media perspective, from a communication perspective, how they can reach out to you, can you share that?

Dr. Deitch:

Of course. If you go to www.UnmarketyourPractice.com. I got a lot of free gifts. We got a training there and I've got the design starter kit that I give away for free. One of the things that have always frustrated me is you go to a seminar, they teach you all this stuff and that's awesome, but it's near impossible to implement or it costs a fortune, it just takes a lot of time and distraction. So, you're learning and it's great, but you never actually get it done and implement what needs to get done. So, I'm sort of putting both of those things together. I've got what others say is probably the coolest Facebook welcome video you've ever seen. It designed specifically for your cover image, the first thing that people see when they go to your practice's Facebook page. It is beautiful and it's effective.

It's designed so that people come to your practice's Facebook page and visually see how they cannot just click the like button. You can also subscribe or follow your practice's Facebook page. When you put this video up on your practice's Facebook page, you can download it for free at www. UnmarketyourPractice.com. You'll learn the protocol we're teaching that goes along with a step-by-step protocol, a technique of sort, instructions of exactly step by step on what to do. When you follow our protocol, you're going to find that 100 percent of the people who subscribe to your practice's Facebook page will receive 100 percent of your practice's Facebook posts. This is the complete 180 degree opposite argument or perception than "marketers" who tend to be down on Facebook unless you pay for advertising because only a small percentage of people that click the like button will end up seeing your practices posts. This solves that as 100 percent of the people you can get to not just click the like button, but also click following and see first.

Our promotional tools were giving to you for free to visually show people how and why to do that. One hundred percent of those people are people who receive 100 percent of the practices post. If you can follow a protocol, put a little bit of energy behind it, your practice can start going viral, which means being spread in your community for free authentically by people that actually are into it. You actually want to share it with their friends and family so that they can wake up inspired, following our protocol and learning more, not just about chiropractic, but about you and your expression of chiropractic.

This is a sustainable, ongoing basic program protocol that as you build the momentum, it keeps growing, getting easier. There's a saying and you know that it says, "Your net-worth is equivalent to your net-work." What we're talking about, is the influence, the power, and the income potential that you have when you're able to literally tap an app, click a mouse on your computer, or on your mobile device from anywhere in the world and have hundreds if not thousands, if not eventually millions of people see your information for free. That's the world we're living in. You see my kids watch YouTubers, who have literally millions of followers. They produce daily videos. They go out to millions of followers and these literally kids are making millions of dollars a year creating videos and building an audience. I'm telling you that's the way of the world we're in and it's going to continue to grow in that direction.

That's how we keep our name in front of people. That's how we get used to these tools to be referral generators and in many cases product sales generators that is easier, more cost effective and more productive in terms of income than ever before. That's the great news. It will simply start making our own transformations and I'll close by saying, "If we'll simply do what we wish the public would do, which is to be more open minded, be more willing and open to learning some new ideas, try things that may not be as traditional in the way it's always been done." I said to chiropractors that "Social media is to chiropractors what chiropractic is to the public. It's misunderstood and dramatically underutilized". Let's behave like we wish the public would behave and let's watch the world change when we change.

Dr. Bard:

There are so many great takeaways from what you just shared that should be in the forefront for every chiropractor when you simply said "100 percent". To be able to have that statistic, "100 percent success, 100 percent click on follow through", to me, stands out so bold, so proud, and it really is, Dr. Deitch. a reflection, very simply of you my friend who has always been a 100 percent doctor from the get go. You've put 100 percent of your love, your passion, your commitment, your energy, your focus in to this and at the end of the day, you've been one of chiropractors who has been one of the great givers to our great profession.

HERE ARE THE BULLET-POINT TAKEAWAYS:

#1 - How social media has fulfilled its initial mission of connecting people by providing entertainment, information, pictures and connections. Still not understood completely, "Social Media is to Chiropractic, as what Chiropractic is to the Public".

#2 - We must make a concerted effort to use the platform of social media to put out only positive messages.

#3 - What makes you as a "Chiropractor" unique & different. So many Chiropractors don't define who they are correctly by just saying that they are a "Chiropractor".

#4 - We have a choice to make as Chiropractors in terms of how we project ourselves and who we accept as patients.

#5 - We must become more articulate to penetrate more markets.

#6 - He grew up in NYC & relocated to Northern California to attend school and be both close to the city and his passion for skiing. Initially he was talked out of becoming a Chiropractor by his dad, who upon learning what a Chiropractor really is and does, he then decided to follow in his sons' footsteps and at 55 years old become a Chiropractor. Subsequently his brother chose the same path.

#7 - As the epicenter of technology and home to AOL, Yahoo, Facebook and more, (Silicon Valley) he knew he made the right decision to stay in Northern California which fueled his passion for communication and leading Chiropractors in that direction.

#8 - If he was opening a practice today on a limited budget, he would use a combination of real-life engagement and connecting with building his own health tribe of individuals who know, like & trust him.

#9 - The main thing you can do as a Chiropractor is to be very clear on the specific style of Chiropractic that you provide. You just need to know which audience you are speaking to in order to translate our own understanding of Chiropractic to others.

#10 - He created one of the coolest things for Chiropractors to allow them to upload videos to their Facebook page that follows a specific protocol to allow your subscribers to receive 100% of your Facebook posts and to make it VIRAL. By teaching doctors "Un-Market their Practice" he is creating new portals for doctors to thrive. He lives by the credo that "Your Net-Worth is equivalent to your Net-Work"

8

INSURANCE AND COMPLIANCE SUCCESS – (DR. MARTY KOTLAR)

Read about: DR. MARTY KOTLAR, (President of Target Coding) & **DISCOVER** how he has helped more Chiropractors "S.W.A.N." (Sleep Well at Night) than ever before by doing things the right way in a 3rd party payor system. An expert in Insurance Coding and Compliance. Learn how Dr. Kotlar is teaching Chiropractors today to MASTER the skills of Billing/Coding/Documentation/Compliance and how to stay on top of the latest Insurance changes for practice success.

Dr. Bard:

This is a special show in the sense that if you know me personally, you know that there is a subject that is so near and dear to my heart. I don't even know where to begin, but as they say, we're going to start at the very beginning because it's a very good place to start. Years ago, if you remember—and I don't want to date myself, there was a term that was utilized in our profession. It was known as "the goose that laid the golden egg". What "the goose that laid the golden egg" referenced was the third-party payer system. In other words, the utilization of insurance benefits and the applications of insurance with respect to how chiropractors were able to process insurance.

So, I am here to tell you that "the goose that laid the golden egg" is not the same goose, but I will tell you that this goose is alive and kicking. This goose is leaner, it's meaner. It is absolutely more efficient. I will tell you that when you play a game, and if you look at your practice as a game, you play to win. There are really two rules that you always have to live by. First you want to know the rules of the game. Second, you want to master those rules. This profound concept and understanding and how to do this correctly have had one doctor as their guide, their coach, their advisor for so many years, myself included. His name is Dr. Marty Kotlar. He is the president of Target Coding. It is such an honor to have you with us today. Welcome to the show, Dr. Kotlar.

Dr. Kotlar:

Thank you, Dr. Bard.

Dr. Bard:

This is a treat for me personally on so many levels. Primarily because of my relationship with the business of chiropractic, with insurance and with you for so many years. I know for a fact, that there's nobody on the planet that understands coding, basic C.P.T., diagnostic coding, I.C.D. and documentation, and that can teach doctors how to

100

do this better than anyone on the planet than you. You've done it in a very, very powerful way because you've taught chiropractors how to communicate what they do on the third-party payer system better than anyone. If you know anything about this show, the Dr. Success Spotlight Show, the thing that the doctors love about this show is we have no pretense. We dive right into the core questions. My question to you Dr. Kotlar coming right out of the gate, is in your opinion, how has the playing field changed for insurance reimbursement relative to what the doctors need to do in the present time to practice properly?

Dr. Kotlar:

Yes, it's definitely changed. For example, I remember when I practiced for many years before I started my consulting service. So, I remember being in practice and patients would come in and say, hey, Dr. Kotlar, I have back pain and pain radiating down my leg. I just simply diagnosed sciatica. I didn't do any orthopedic tests. I didn't do any neurological tests. That was something that you just did back in the day. It wasn't the appropriate thing to do, but you just did it. You took a lot of shortcuts many years ago because you got paid no matter what you did.

Nowadays, things have changed because you have to justify everything you're doing. Nowadays, if a patient comes in with back and leg pain, even if you have been in practice 20, 25 years and feel it that you got it figured out, you still have to do some orthopedic, neurological tests, chiropractic tests to justify what you're doing. So, to summarize it, what I'm saying here is you need to have a clinical rationale for what you're doing. I call it, "The what and the why." The what being your CPT codes, what you are doing. Those are your CPT codes. And why you're doing what you're doing are your diagnosis codes, and they have to match. They have to combine. They have to pair just like peanut butter and chocolate, or a red wine with meat. Your CPT codes and your diagnosis codes have to make sense. So those are the things that have changed over the years. You have to really justify what you're doing nowadays more than ever.

Dr. Bard:

What has always intrigued me about you is your background, and your background is unique because you, just like me, Dr. Kotlar, are a Brooklyn boy at heart. You decided years ago that there really was a massive hole in our profession that really needed to be filled properly. My question to you is, how did that evolve? In other words, how did you start, and then how did it evolve into what it became today in the form of the leading group that helps chiropractors communicate better in the third-party system? How did it start for you?

Dr. Kotlar:

Well, it started many years ago. During my first bunch of years in practice, I was chiro only and then I transitioned to an integrated practice. So, when I brought on other healthcare professionals like osteopaths, nutritionists and acupuncture, we did a lot of holistic services. I started writing articles for Chiropractic Economics. You see in my first bunch of years, about 12 years in practice, it was chiro only. It was straightforward. It was pretty simple, if you're just billing for chiropractic back then at least. So now, when we bring on a medical doctor, acupuncturist, osteopath, and physical therapist, we're doing a whole bunch of medical services with a holistic approach.

For example, if a patient needed a trigger point injection, we didn't use lidocaine. We used Traumeel, which was a homeopathic remedy. So, we tried to do everything natural even though we were doing some invasive procedures. So, my partners said, "Hey, we think that you would be the best to figure this out." I said, "Okay, I'll dig in." So, I started digging in and reading, and I had to bill for drawing blood, urinalysis and chest X-rays. A lot of the conventional medical staff and then one of my partners said, "Why don't you write an article to Chiropractic Economics, on proper billing codes in an integrated practice?" So that's how it all started for me. I started writing articles. Afterwards, I started getting calls from chiropractors all over the country asking me my advice, and how to assist them. And that's how I started consulting part time to chiropractors all over the country. Eventually, that led to me doing it full time. Later I went ahead and got my certification in compliance. I'm also a certified billing and coding specialist.

So, I take a little bit of the unconventional approach to helping doctors nowadays because most chiropractors are not certified coders. Most certified coders are not chiropractors, so I could take this unique approach. Being in the trenches for many years, and now, being an expert in billing and coding, I combined the two and it helped my doctors become very successful, and get them to be able to justify everything they're doing, so they could S.W.A.N. That's one of my favorite acronyms, "S.W.A.N." (Sleep Well at Night).

Dr. Bard:

I think I'm going to include that in my new mission statement. You've got to love this because I would attend Dr. Kotlar's lectures and literally be on the edge of my seat. The reason being because he, much like myself, would have such enthusiasm, such passion, such heart for new codes and the definition of new codes. So, he would explain to us, in essence, the changes because the playing field has changed, and the thing that has made Dr. Kotlar so incredibly unique is the fact that he has stayed at the front of the line in terms of keeping chiropractors positioned. That's a big word 'positioned' correctly for success in the future. Now, I think it's interesting because when I see you, Dr. Kotlar, I know for the fact you have at this phase of your life gotten massive frequent flyer miles. You probably teach more CEUs than anyone, but unlike other CEU courses, you really teach business. My question to you is this. If you could change anything about chiropractors in terms of how they look upon insurance reimbursement and their role today, what would you change about them?

Dr. Kotlar:

Well, a lot of people think of me as "the insurance guy and the coding guy". I don't consider myself the insurance guy. I don't think it's the proper title. If you want to give me a title, it needs to be "the compliance guy" because that's what has changed over the years. That's where my focus now is, as it relates to billing, coding, documentation, Medicare and HIPAA. So, I think if I had to take a look at one thing that has changed over the years that I have to make sure my clients understand is about making sure you're doing things right because that's what I hear all the time. Doctors come up to me and go, I just want to make sure I'm doing things right now.

So, I think one of the most challenging things for me is getting doctors to understand that they must comply with all their state laws and federal laws. That's something that's been a burden on some doctors because, for example, a few years ago, ICD-10 came around. For 25 years, we had an ICD-9. About three, four years ago, we got ICD-10. So that was a challenge for a lot of doctors. That was a lot more work. That was a lot more money. Many of the doctors had to spend money going to seminars to learn about ICD-10 coding and buy books and send their staff and many doctors go, "Man, I got to learn all this stuff and I'm not going to make more money, but I got to learn all this stuff." So that's one of the frustrating things that I hear from doctors about all the things they have to learn and all the things they have to do, but it doesn't necessarily bring them more money.

So that's the one thing that I've seen changed over the years, besides insurance reimbursement and managed care coming along. There are many laws, rules and regulations that the doctors need to follow, and they're really not that bad. Once you dig in and realize what needs to be done, it's not as bad as you may think, and that's what we do. We try and do all the heavy lifting for the doctor. So, they don't have to get bogged down in all the rules and regulations. We show them what they do. We give them the books. We give them the forms. We give them the manuals, and then it makes their life a lot easier.

Dr. Bard:

There is a small percentage of our profession that I would say, misconstrues their relationship with the insurance companies, when in reality what you've done so incredibly well, and your genius, Dr. Kotlar is to take that small negative of perception and turn it around.

You help them turn it into an incredible positive for these doctors thus empowering them, to put them in a real position of control. It reminds me so much of how I've always thought of you. I've always thought of you as not only a master communicator, but to me, you are, to a degree, a master translator. What I mean by that is, to me, no different than getting on a plane and going to this incredible foreign country, let's say France. Where you get to eat this delicious French food, have these French desserts and have this French wine, and you know people rant and rave about how much they love France, but I've got news for you. If you go to France and you don't know how to speak the language, you're going to have a challenging time. What you've done so well is you've taught chiropractors how to translate better.

In other words, what you've done here really well, better than anyone I've ever known, is you've literally set chiropractors free. You've given them a freedom that allows them to basically rise, and to be able to handle the reimbursement process correctly. To be able to sleep well not only at night, which is a beautiful gift, but also to really be in a position of leverage and control. I wanted to ask you a couple of things with respect to the scope of practice of chiropractors. I was very curious in the sense that, and I know you get this question a lot, but I'm curious now about the playing field of the different states. Case in point, I got a phone call yesterday from a doctor, who was asking me questions about the treatment of peripheral neuropathy. He was telling me about the state of Washington where he practiced and that he was limited in terms of his utilization of different modalities, in the electrical therapeutic realm. What's the biggest differences you're seeing now amongst the states with respect to what chiropractors are able to do incredibly well within their scope of practice?

Dr. Kotlar:

Well, every state's scope of practice is different. In some states, there are restrictions, while in some, you can do a lot of things that can make your life a lot easier. I'll give you one example. In the state of New York, where I practiced for many years, chiropractic assistants are not allowed to apply therapies. Chiropractic assistants in New York cannot even put a hot pack on a patient. Then if you go down to Florida, where I live now and work with a lot of doctors, the scope of practice is wonderful there. CAs can do just about every therapy in the state of Florida. Chiropractors can employ medical doctors and physical therapists. In other states, that's not allowed. So regardless of what state you practice in, to me, you need to work with what you got, and that's what we do at my company, irrespective of what state you're in. For example, back to New York, if you can't have CAs do the therapies, then you can employ massage therapists or other chiropractors.

The point I'm trying to make is, it doesn't matter what state you practice in, you got to make the best of what you have. As a chiropractor, you could always be successful regardless of the condition of practice. I don't know any chiropractor that does not have the ability to make a good living. You can bill for certain things in some states, you can't bill in others. I don't look at that as a negative. You got to go and do whatever you can do wherever you are. Nowadays, even if insurance doesn't pay for certain items, there are so many more cash services available that people are willing to pay for. It makes up for the insurance battles that we have. So, to me, it doesn't matter what state that you practice in, you could always be successful in chiropractic.

Dr. Bard:

I think you've hit the nail right on the head. The reason why is because you've been involved in so many practices. You've seen doctors flourish in both models with respect to an insurance-driven model and a cash-based model. It's really the amalgam, really the combination of the two, which you have to love. One of the coolest things that you do is you're able to look at what we would always call the "menu of services". One of the things I love greatly about chiropractic and being a chiropractor is the simple fact that we've got so many delicious choices on these "menus of services", and yes, not every menu is the same. Yes, obviously, the scope of practice will dictate and determine that, but there are so many incredible opportunities that allow doctors to not just have, for example, a PI-only practice, to not just have an insurance-driven practice, but to really have the greatest combination of such. Now, and I'm so curious right now, because you're constantly on the road, man, when you're not doing what you're doing on the road, which is helping chiropractors really rise to the very, very top and to take control of their business, take control of their practice, and literally take control of their life, what does Dr. Marty Kotlar love to do for fun now?

Dr. Kotlar:

Marty Kotlar does a lot of things for fun. First of all, I love biking. I ride my bike all the time. I go to the gym, I play tennis and I'm a huge baseball fan. My goal is to go to every baseball stadium in the country. I have about 20 under my belt and have a few more to go.

Dr. Bard:

I think I'm looking in the mirror. I knew it was much more than the Brooklyn thing. I've admired Dr. Kotlar from afar and close up for so long. If you know anything about the business of chiropractic, you know that you have to make it your mission to include him in your life in some way, shape or form. If our doctors have questions about anything that we've discussed today and more, how can they get in touch with you directly and what's the best way to contact you?

Dr. Kotlar:

Well, Dr. Bard, you said something earlier that is very important about the menu. When I bring on a client, one of the first things I do is to analyze their menu, and usually their menus are very limited. And that's one of the reasons why they contact me because they feel like they've ran out of things to do. They don't feel like they're providing as many services. So, one of the first things we do is we show them the Target Coding menu. The Target Coding menu is seven pages of services that could be provided. We go down the list of services, some doctors go, wow, I didn't realize I can do that. I didn't even know I can get paid for that. Tell me about that? And then we go down the list, and they say wait a second, I didn't know that was even within my scope of practice. How do I do that? How do I get paid for that?

I didn't know UnitedHealthcare pays for that. All of these revelations occur as we're going through the menu. So that's one of the things we do here at Target Coding; it's an analysis. The reason why we're so successful here at Target Coding is because of what I mentioned earlier, being in practice for many years, being in the trenches, knowing what it's like. And now, reading medical policies, working with hundreds of doctors and staff members every year and learning from them what's going on with their practice, and what their struggles are, and correcting them, and troubleshooting them makes us unique and different. Now, if anybody would like to get in touch with us, you may reach us via the website www. targetcoding.com. Feel free to email me directly at drkotlar@targetcoding. com and feel free to contact us at our toll-free number: 1-800-270-7044.

Dr. Bard:

If I was opening a practice today, the first phone call that I would make would be to Dr. Marty Kotlar from Target Coding. If you do that, I'll guarantee that you will basically set your practice growth ship in motion the right way, the best way, the most compliant way, the most diligent way and the most successful way.

HERE ARE THE BULLET-POINT TAKEAWAYS:

#1 - Today, you must justify everything that you do. You must have a "clinical rational" for what you are doing.

#2 - You must have the "What" & the "Why". The "what" is the C.P.T. Codes and the "Why" is your diagnostic codes (I.C.D.) and the must be paired properly.

#3 - He started in practice as Chiropractor and then eventually integrated his practice medically with a wholistic approach.

#4 - He is certified in Compliance and is a Billing & Coding Specialist. He then took his experience by being in the trenches as a practicing Chiropractor and taking an unconventional approach.

#5 - He takes tremendous pride in teaching his doctors to do things right.

#6 - Considered by many as "The Billing Guy" and "The Insurance Guy" in our profession however a more accurate description is as "The Compliance Guy".

#7 - His company "Target Coding", does more of the "heavy lifting" for the doctor in educating them about the proper rules, laws and regulations to run a more efficient and successful practice.

#8 - He has helped Chiropractors set themselves free by training and educating them in translating the insurance world successfully thus giving them better leverage and control.

#9 - Understanding the scope of practice within each individual state is really the key. There are so many cash-based services that patients will pay for removing the dependence upon insurance.

#10 - On a personal note his personal goal is to visit every baseball stadium in the country and he has only a few more to go to complete this bucket-list goal.

9

RE-INVENTION SUCCESS – (DR. BERNARD FURSHPAN)

Read about: DR. BERNARD FURSHPAN & DISCOVER how he has mastered the art of RE-INVENTION as a Chiropractor. Creator & Originator of some of the MOST POPULAR educational & promotional tools ever for the Chiropractic profession. An AMAZING ENTREPRENEUR, Dr. Furshpan has experienced a life well-lived and openly shares his exclusive success secrets in this ELECTRIC interview.

Dr. Bard:

Today is really going to be amazing. I'm going to tell you we have one of the most unique, one of the most special, one of the most creative guests ever on this show. It is such a pleasure and it's really such a privilege to have with us the one and only, Dr. Bernard Furshpan from the great state of New York. Welcome to the show Dr. Furshpan.

Dr. Furshpan:

Well, thanks for having me on the show, Dr. Bard. I really appreciate it.

Dr. Bard:

This is really a special treat, not just for us personally, and not just for our listeners, but for all the people in the future that have, found out about who you are, what you've always been about, what you are about, and really what you've always brought to the table. For those of you who don't know about Dr. Furshpan, I will share with you some inner secrets. The inner secrets started at the very top of the mountain. I don't know, if you are aware, but Dr. Furshpan created one of the most popular chiropractic products in the history of the profession in the form of not just a poster series, but educational tools that have allowed chiropractors to succeed, to communicate better, to explain, who they are and what they are about.

If you walked into any chiropractic office and you saw the famous Muppet picture poster and you saw the famous dinosaur picture poster and you saw the famous X-ray series viewbox films, which we're going to talk about on this show then, you know all about Dr. Furshpan. However, the theme of this show is not just about the materials that he created for our profession. The theme of this show is really about a subject that many of you are curious about, many of you have always wanted to know about, and many of you really wanted to find out who did it the best. I will tell you empathically that if you look in the dictionary under the definition of reinvention, you will see, Dr. Furshpan's picture. One of the most successful chiropractors in the history of the profession with one of the largest practices ever from the great state of New York. I'm so curious to ask you, Dr. Furshpan, first and foremost, how did you get started in creating some of the most popular tools for chiropractors ever?

Dr. Furshpan:

Well, first of all, thank you so much for the wonderful introduction. You read it very well what I sent you, (joke). I'd say honestly that's a good question. It started well before chiropractic. I was a cartoonist as an undergrad student, a premed student actually at Stony Brook University. I was also a cartoonist for the newspaper. I had this knack of knowing what people liked, what they thought was interesting and funny and entertaining and I brought that to the profession at the time when I graduated in 1980. There wasn't much in the way of marketing material. We basically used medical posters that showed graphic depictions of organs and blood and guts. There was only one chiropractic poster close to that. I recall at the time that it was, "subluxation causes death" and it was very morbid and very negative. I wanted to make it more digestible and that's when I created the first poster, "Subluxations get on your nerves". And I did that for my own practice. So, the things I did was to go from my own practice and I realized this stuff was working for me. At that time, I was seeing close to 800 patients a week and I said, "My marketing material is working." And you don't have to be the best chiropractor. But what happened is you become a very good chiropractor because you get a lot of stage time when you market yourself very well. You get busy and when you get busy you get good.

Dr. Bard:

What's incredible about you is you've always been such a visual person. You've been able to help so many chiropractors. You're famous personally and even in our profession because of the simple fact that you allowed chiropractors directly and indirectly to literally explode their practices. I'm going to tell you something, I'm in that group and the reason that I'm in that group is because, if you walked into every one of my treatment rooms, you were able to see something on a view box, which I thought was without question, the greatest gift of art to our profession, and it was your X-ray poster film series. Dr. Furshpan created, a series of X-ray films that allowed you to see normal versus abnormal.

Since, the mainstay of our profession is in teaching patients what the problem is, how it can be corrected naturally, noninvasively and thru Chiropractic care. This was the single greatest tool that in my opinion has ever been created for a chiropractor and that is in the form your symptom series. It included whiplash, headaches, back pain, scoliosis and more. You've painted visual pictures for the patient, and thus helping patients understand where they are and where they need to go. How did you come about Dr. Furshpan creating my favorite tool of yours, which was the number one seller for a company called Medical Arts Press because that's where, if you wanted it, you had to buy it? How did you come about creating this?

Dr. Furshpan:

It's was the respect for consumerism that's what it boiled down to. I'll give you some examples. Years ago, when I would fly you would've always asked the stewardess or the flight attendant how much longer until we land, right? But now, they respect the consumer, why keep it a secret? Why keep it a mystery? You see it on the screen. How much time? Where you are? With the satellite, they teach where you are located at the moment, where you're flying over, so there's no question whatsoever. People are living in a do-it-yourself society. People want to know what's going on. They want to know how to build something. They want to know how to book their own flights. They want to do things on their own, but they also want to educate themselves. So, this created an opportunity for me in understanding consumerism that they want to know what am I look-ing at when I look at an X-ray, what am I looking for and what are the lines that I'm looking at?

So, what I did was to take normal and abnormal X-rays and draw lines on them and then write words on it. So, you can actually see it on the X-ray, and I say, very clearly, this is where the disc is. A chiropractor may see the discs are between here, but they don't really visually understand what that means. So, I drew a disc in there with the nucleus pulposus shown to understand that it's like a ball bearing in between the joint. With that, they understand that this is how it moves into cervical or lumbar plexus. So, I realized that this is important to appreciate and respect our patients, who are consumers and educate them correctly so that they see what we see and they see that we understand what we're doing. Just the fact that we educate our patients, means that we're not threatened to tell them our mysteries, that we know what we're talking about and we have confidence in what we're doing.

Dr. Bard:

I am so overjoyed, so exuberant, so excited to have with us, Dr. Bernard Furshpan, from the great state of New York. Not far away being the Brooklyn boy that he is who know where all of this actually started. You are one of the greatest examples of a doctor who is at the core, incredibly and abundantly creative, but abundantly entrepreneurial. What I want to talk to you about, Dr. Furshpan is really your journey to 'now'. And the reason that I wanted to talk to you about that is that everything you've touched has been successful, not easy, but being incredibly persistent, you've figured out the "special sauce" as to how to navigate life a little bit better, and that's an understatement. Please share with us now, what you are doing in the evolution from the most successful chiropractor to where you are now and what you are doing?

Dr. Furshpan:

Well, that's a very good question. I'm glad you asked me that question because the core is to bring out the best in each of you, to bring out the best in oneself, and to bring out the best in others. That's what chiropractic does. It brings out the best in their health, that optimal health that they have. It therefore allows them to express their optimal health. But understanding the core of bringing out the best in others is the basis of all successful businesses and it's not about just how to make money. The question is what kind of a product can I create? It's all about understanding people. That's what it boils down to. Every business I've been involved with has to be concentrated and delved into the understanding of the human psyche, of their needs, of their ambitions, of the things that make them feel secure and making things that make them feel insecure and understanding the psychology and the mechanisms behind all of that.

Well, you need to succeed in any business that you get involved with. So that was the basic core. So, what happened was I worked seven days a week. I was probably one of the very few chiropractic offices in the U.S. that was open seven days a week. We treated a lot of patients. After 25 years in practice, I had an opportunity to move forward. During my practice though, I did have a TV show on cable. It was called, "To Your Health." I did that for 12 years and I was going around the country as a public speaker and as a keynote speaker at conventions, speaking about marketing and branding oneself and organizing a practice and also training thousands of chiropractic assistants in keeping the mystery out of running a chiropractic practice.

It was a very successful one. I decided to move forward in my marketing career. I had a marketing business. I worked for NASCAR. I did the next World Cup series pitch and that launched me into a whole another area and that was entertainment. So, I got involved in entertainment. I ended up moving the practice out of the facility that I was in and I rented out my building to another medical practice. I eventually weaned myself out so that I can move forward in my marketing career and ended up in the comedy business. Believe it or not, it's so wide open. It was wide open for me and I did very, very well in comedy. I also performed for about seven years. But besides the marketing, and the entertainment, I produce concerts at some of the largest and most respectable venues in the country and that got me into the whole other area. I ended up buying the Metropolitan Room, which is a jazz cabaret space in New York City.

My wife Joanne and I ran the venue for about seven years. It was probably the most successful cabaret jazz club in Manhattan. We were busy seven days a week, with about 20 shows a week and we were very happy, and we made a lot of friends. Again, that launched us into a whole other area. So, the thing is that it's almost like a road, but you've got to be open to accepting what happens on the road and just go with it. As long as you use that basic core concept that I was talking about, understanding people and being able to work with them and giving them what they want, you will succeed in everything you do. So, it doesn't really matter what genre, it doesn't matter what industry you're in, what matters is the love of being with people, working with people and having fun in what you're doing. So, I don't think I've ever worked a day in my life. It's all been fun and I'm still doing it. Now, I represent some great talents I booked theaters. I also travel with my wife and life is grand. She's also my patient right now. My wife is my only patient and she loves it. She gets all the benefits, the chiropractic benefits. She doesn't need insurance coverage. She doesn't pay me a copay and it's a wonderful life.

Dr. Bard:

Well, if life is who you know, thank goodness that she's married to you, which allows her to move to the front of the line. So, it's very interesting. I see a pattern here and the pattern is remarkable in the sense that it all begins with one letter. It begins with the letter "C". If you look at your life, Dr. Furshpan, from Chiropractic to Comedy to Concerts to Cabaret and they all share in common, the "C" letter which is at the Core of it, Communication. So, I'm going to call you the five C's doc, in the sense that you've done this so tactfully, so professionally and really so seamlessly. You've always been so incredibly magnetic. At the core, that's always been one of the things that have been so amazingly attractive about you.

There's a pattern here in that there is a comprehension which is another "C" word. You actually have a very unique comprehension as to why and how we are here. In other words, how we are able to squeeze more juice out of life. Now, it's interesting because I'm going use a four-letter word and the four-letter word is this. It is the word T-I-M-E and that spells time. What you've done, Dr. Furshpan, better than anyone is you've learned how to manage time better and really to have an "attitude of gratitude". In other words, to really get more out of this journey. How did that happen? How were you able to reach that level, but more importantly, being in a position to share that with everyone that's so lucky enough to know you?

Dr. Furshpan:

Thank you so much for the compliment. I have to give credit to the universe because we're just a creation of the universe and it's just a matter of standing back and just being in awe with what's going on and enjoying the very little details in life and the big things that happen. It's just a wonder to watch it's no accidents of that which goes on in front of you. Everything is just a beautiful creation that's constantly evolving. So, I started a meditation practice many, many years ago in the 80s. I also took a lot of success seminars and things of that nature. Then I created my own called "leaps and bounds" and I was training a lot of people on getting in-tune and getting in touch with oneself. What I also got very much involved in, and I have to include this also, is "quantum mechanics," which explains how everything works. There're four basic components in quantum mechanics and that's energy, space, time and matter.

If you understand how the four work together, you can really understand and forecast everything that happens. When you do that, it's a beautiful thing because you realize how creation uses these four ingredients to create everything. If you have some control over it, you can actually make things happen right before your very eyes. So, I've been writing this book called, "Wisdom in a Minute," and it's to help people see these basic four components and how they play a role. Mostly time; time is of the essence. When you understand how time works and the perception of time and how the perception of time changes, depending on the situation, you will have more control of your emotions and your direction. When you can therefore control your emotions, you become very successful because you will walk in a straight line.

Emotions is like hitting a guard rail. It really slows you down and handicaps you. Whether it's fear or overexcitement. Sometimes you can get overexcited about something and get very disappointed very quickly. So, it's about keeping an even keel of emotions and when you do that, your eyes are much more open and you're more intuitive to what's really

118

going on. You must be honest with yourself and with the people in front of you. Not being afraid to say what you need to say and do the things that you need to do. When you succeed, you will also influence others and affect others in a positive way therefore, leading by example. So that's been my goal, for me, to have my own understanding and conclusion of what this is all about, what life is all about, so that others can use me as an example.

The thing about gratefulness that you mentioned is that you can't tell people to be grateful. Now, I take a yoga class and sometimes the instructor will say, take a minute to just contemplate and then be grateful for the things you have. You can't tell somebody to be grateful. It's a space you have to be in and you have to get there. When you lose your health for example. You ended up in the hospital after a heart attack, you become grateful. From now on I'm going to exercise. I'm grateful for my body. I'm going to eat right. Then, after a couple of months, the person returns to their old routines. The thing is you need to lose something to become grateful. You don't miss water until the well runs dry. When somebody dies, let's say, an artist, you appreciate them. Then you lose a friend, you'll end up saying, "Oh my G-d" wishing you would have spent more time with them.

You become grateful for the things you lose. Why wait for them to be gone? Why wait for you to lose something to be grateful for when you can always appreciate it? You have to be in a space and realize the fragility of life and realize the fragility of the things you own and the things that you think you own, but the things that are around you that help you enjoy life. Thus, to create a life that you wanted, but realize that everything is fragile, that everything can go on a second. So, then you become more grateful when you see it from that perspective rather than being cocky enough to think that everything is forever and that you'll always have it.

Things come and go because the universe constantly changes. So, you have to appreciate that things are very fragile and that puts you in a space of great understanding. Everybody you meet that you are now grateful for their existence and what the impact they had on you is. Even if it's negative, you learned something from it. That's a lesson. So, everything that you experience now becomes a lesson and becomes part of your overall gratefulness for the things that you have and the things that you've learned and the roles that you play in life.

Dr. Bard:

It's incredible! Dr. Furshpan, one thing that jumps out again, another word that begins with the letter "C" and that word is the word Control. What you've done is you've lived by example. You've taught so many that are so fortunate enough to be in your circle, how to take control of their life, of their future, of their destiny, and really their world. You are at the core to me, Dr. Furshpan, a master storyteller. You've really learned how to frame life the right way. As a doctor, as an entrepreneur, as a giver, as a sharer, as a storyteller, and really even as an entertainer.

I think that's one of the amazing things about you. I wanted to ask you, for anyone who has the pleasure, the privilege, and really the excitement of being a friend of Dr. Furshpan in the social media world, case in point Facebook, then, you really get an opportunity to see somebody who is living the dream. So amazingly powerful and doing it so beautifully with your wife, Joanne. Traveling the world and has a love and an appreciation for your relationship on a level that I've never seen before. I'm curious to ask you, Dr. Furshpan, how did you meet your wife?

Dr. Furshpan:

That's funny. She says, online and I always finish it by saying online at the bank. We did meet online and most people are now going in that direction because there's more opportunity to meet people because people are people wherever you go. The fact is that you're limited with the routes that you take going to work, going to the supermarket, etc. There's only so many people you can meet. Obviously, this is an opportunity to meet a lot of people. I met a lot of people, and then when I met Joanne, my whole world turned upside down and my focus was strictly on her because I realized that she loves the things that I love, has the same life values and is respectful and was respectful for what I needed and how I lived and I was respectful to how she lived and what she needed and who she was. So, it was just mutual respect 100 percent across the board and it was mutual love for the same things.

It's just been great history between us. So, we were together for seven years and it feels like we've accomplished what a couple can do in 70 years. We've done so many things. We've been to so many different places, met so many different people. The business that I'm in is a very interesting business. So, I'm in the entertainment business right now and we meet a lot of celebrities, a lot of entertainers, and one of the things that Joanne loves is to dance. So, I'm very accommodating and I love to dance myself. So, if she wants to go dancing, I'll go dancing. We go dancing and we have a lot of fun dancing. She loved the show, "Dancing with the Stars." She always wanted to either meet the people there or be on that floor dancing or whatever it was.

So, we ended up going to that already three times and because we know some of the people, we have a number of contacts and connections with the show. It's just been a wonderful experience every time we go. Before the show airs, by the way, it's a live show, they allow the audience members to dance on the floor. So, Joanne and I were always the first ones on the floor dancing and it was a blessed moment. More interestingly, we've made so many great friends. The bottom line about whatever it is that you do, wherever you go in life, it's all about the friendships that you create because the quality of your life hinges on the quality of your relationships, bottom line. The better the quality of relationships you have with your family and your friends, and people that you know in business the better quality of life that you will have.

It's not about who's right or who's wrong. It's about just loving the fact that you're alive because this is very temporary. Remember the fragility that we talked about is essential. I'm going to just end off with one quick story. I had a wonderful patient in the very beginning of my career, who came in on time, paid on time and was wonderful. He also brought gifts to the staff. One day, he never showed up. It was so unlike him. So, we left him voicemail messages on his answering machine. At that time there were answering machines. It was nearly the 1980s. Three months later, his mother called up and told us that the day after we saw him, he was involved in a car accident and died. We had a staff meeting right after that because everybody was so upset about the news my staff was crying.

So, we gathered around and paid a little tribute to him. I asked my staff, "if you knew that the visit he had was the last visit of his life and you'll never ever see him again, how would you treat him?" They said, "We would hug him and we would never let him go, we will tell him how much we love him." That's my point in that you've got to treat everybody that way all the time because you never know if you're going to see them again. You'll never know if you're going to be gone or they going to be gone. Let's leave off on a positive note because every day should be like the first and last day of your life. That's my message.

Dr. Bard:

It is the greatest of all messages. We spoke about a four-letter word before. I'm also going to close with another four-letter word because when I think of Dr. Furshpan, I think of this four-letter word. I will spell it for you. It is L-O-V-E. It is that good. He is that good. He is humble. He is modest. He is a master master of relationships. If doctors are curious, Dr. Furshpan, and they want to have first access to your book when it comes out and they have questions, what's the best way to get in touch with you?

Dr. Furshpan:

Right now, they can go to www.wisdominaminute.com. I have some video clips there that explain a lot of what I talked about. There's no mystery. There's no secrets here. There are a lot of books that say the secrets of success. There are no secrets, it's all here. You can all access it and you can do it in a minute. That's when I say, wisdom in a minute. I'm not saying I'm going to give you wisdom in a minute. I'm saying you can reach wisdom in a minute. You can be your own guru. You can be your own rabbi. You can be your own priest. You can access the information, that's where the wisdom comes from very easily and that's what my book is about. Thank you so much.

Dr. Bard:

This was so much fun Dr. Furshpan and in closing, I'm going to use a word that I have a feeling a lot of you are going to have to Google. You're going to have to look it up when you think of Dr. Furshpan. Dr. Furshpan is at the core what we call a "mensch". Look it up, if you don't know what it means. He is the best of the best.

HERE ARE THE BULLET-POINT TAKEAWAYS:

#1 - He started as a Pre-Med student and a cartoonist. He always had a knack of knowing what people found interesting, funny and entertaining which he brought to Chiropractic.

#2 - He initially created these amazing educational and promotional tools for his practice in Long Island, New York

#3 - His respect for "consumerism" is what led him to creating the famous "X-Ray Film Series" showing normal vs. abnormal.

#4 - His artistic skills helped him modify the X-Ray Film Series he created that allowed doctors to explain what an X-ray reflects in simple terms to a patient.

#5 - He has taken the core principal as a Chiropractor of bringing out the best in health to now teaching individuals how to bring out the best in them personally.

#6 - Understanding people and the human psyche including people's needs and ambitions and what makes them secure is really the key.

#7 - When in practice he was one of the few Chiropractors in the country to be open 7 days a week for 25 years.

#8 - He's trained 1000's of Chiropractors & assistants in removing the mystery of running a successful practice.

#9 - He later became involved in the entertainment industry as a performer, producer, manager and more. As owner of The Metropolitan Room in the heart of N.Y.C. he established 1 of the most respected and successful Jazz & Cabaret centers in the country.

#10 - When you can control your emotions, you can control your life. This keeps you intuitive and allows you to master the concept of TIME by staying in a position of gratitude.

Listen now for details...

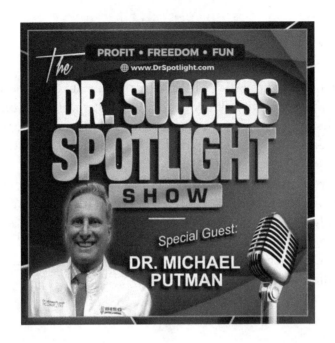

10

NEUROPATHY SUCCESS – (DR. MICHAEL PUTMAN)

Read about: DR. MICHAEL PUTMAN & DISCOVER how he has created a GO-TO NEUROPATHY Practice based upon Science, Research, Marketing, Communication and Packaging. A NEUROPATHY specialist in the pure sense, Dr. Putman shares his personal insights as to how he has created a NEUROPATHY practice that is a model built to out-perform all others.

Dr. Bard:

You're going to dig this one. Why? Well, because this is probably one of the most asked questions that we get with respect to the world of specialties. When we talk about the world of specialties, one of the specialties right now that is at the forefront of the line is the treatment of a condition known as PERIPHERAL NEUROPATHY.

Now, if you're curious and you're wondering and you're saying, why now, more than ever, then I will tell you empathically that there is a doctor who is leading the pack in his care for this condition and whom we are so fortunate to have with us here today from California. His name is Dr. Michael Putman. I want to first and foremost welcome you to the show, Dr. Putman.

Dr. Putman:

Oh, I'm happy to be here with you, Dr. Perry!

Dr. Bard:

This is a real treat for us. It's really a treat for all our listeners. Obviously when you look at the playing field as it exists today with respect to primarily the playing field of not just back pain, but more so, in the radicular component or in what we would call the neuropathy component, this field is wide open. This is because of the simple fact that so many of these patients are presenting with not just back pain, but the more common symptomatology of leg pain, burning, numbness, tingling, pins and needles and gait dysfunctions.

It is a brave new world for chiropractors, who have decided to make this theirs. In other words, they have made this market their market. We're so honored to have with us, Dr. Michael Putman today, for the simple fact that he decided that he was going to make this his market. So, my question to you, Dr. Putman, right out of the gate is why now, more than ever, do you believe that the playing field for the treatment of peripheral neuropathy is so ripe as we speak?

Dr. Putman:

Oh my gosh! Well, there's a number of reasons. One is that we discovered that the people that had this condition that it really changed or altered their life. It makes them feel that their whole life has gone away from them because it not only affects their balance and their gait, like you said, but also their sleep. It's part of an overall condition that it makes them sick and ruins their lives. And what's really frustrating for me and what really got me interested in it is the fact that there is no one doing treatment for them correctly. Basically, the only results that they get from taking bad drugs – such as gabapentin, Neurontin, Lyrica, etc. –is temporary relief in their symptoms, and what inevitably happens with them is that they end up taking more of these drugs and getting lesser results from them. This makes them end up in severe pain or on walkers and wheelchairs, with virtually no hope of survival.

To begin with, I became interested in the field during an interaction with a guy sitting next to me at a chiropractic seminar 5 or 6 years ago. I asked him what he did, and he responded, "Oh, I specialize in neuropathy. And I was like, "Oh, bummer!" I exclaimed because I had a background in it not only as a chiropractor but also as a functional medicine doctor. I've tried to help people like this before, but it's super frustrating. You could see why doctors resort to just giving them drugs to mask the pain. But he began to tell me about this device that they had come across, which you and I have discussed before. You called it "The Matrix". With a number of their patients experiencing a great deal of improvement.

I got excited about it and about anybody that wanted to improve the quality of their service. I started looking into it and researching it. During my investigation, I discovered that the equipment had some amazing effects in it. I started seeing the condition of a lot of these patients improving, and they were grateful that someone even tried to help them. It's really a win-win situation. There is no loss really, if you're honest and upfront with the patient because you helped them even a little bit. They are eternally grateful and super excited about what you've done.

127

Dr. Bard:

It is a unique demographic of patients who need this specialized care. One of the great things that you've done so well is you've really become a master communicator by making something that is convoluted, something that is extremely difficult for patients often to understand, to thus appear simple. And what you've done so well Dr. Putman is you've been able to specifically create your own systems in order to be able to educate patients better, to be able to help them overcome some of the fears, the anxieties, the issues and the concerns that you hit right on the head. And when I say right on the head, I mean the market that exists among neuropathy patients that are beholden to gabapentin and obviously Neurontin, Lyrica and Cymbalta. This is almost to some degree, a bit of a qualified market, or what we would call a filtered market. How would you say most patients find you with respect to treatment and being offered a much more viable option for the treatment of peripheral neuropathy at this phase of your career?

Dr. Putman:

I have done a lot of things over the years; I mean, I've taken out full page ads in my local paper, The Sacramento Bee, and driving people to dinner programs or lunch programs, where we put together a very simple program which can be educational, because people don't understand their condition. That's the first thing right out of the gate. All they know is that they have the condition called peripheral neuropathy. But they don't really know why they have it or what causes it. They might be diabetic and they got diabetic neuropathy, but they don't even understand why they would have neuropathy because of diabetes. So, the program I set up to educate people is, I think, the most significant aspect of my market-ing because it makes me an expert, right out of the gate. However, their perceived experts in neurology that they deal with are obviously their primary doctors yet nobody takes the time to explain to them why this condition exists.

And there may really be a way for them to gain control over it. Now they're not going to cure it. You should understand that's one of the things

I make sure that they know out of the gate. Hey, we're not here to cure Peripheral Neuropathy but we're here to teach you how to manage your life, to manage your condition, so that you can benefit with more function from your life, and be able to do the things you like to do. So, I've done a lot of the things that would really transfer from chiropractic types of models: I've done full page ads and little magazines, radio ads, and even Google ad words occasionally. Inevitably, they end up on my website because I live in a town where I practice in the suburb of Sacramento called Roseville. It's a pretty suburb, a more affluent area, I would say.

I have a website called Roseville Neuropathy Center. A lot of people end up there because they're just searching for neuropathy. Once they get on my website, they gain helpful information and in turn become more knowledgeable about their condition. So, in that sense, they come into my office prequalified, I think, because everything we do as you know, if they're paying cash for it, is to pay upfront usually. And then it becomes a need to really be honest with them and myself: can I help this person? This is because there are a lot of people out there that have these conditions. And I used to think that I would cater to everybody when I first started doing this. I just wish I could take everybody into the program because I know I can help them, even though some people are so sick that it's going to take a lifetime to get them better. And part of the art I think of practicing is to understand that and be able to communicate it to the patients, too. Because a lot of times, they will still go, "Hey, this is my only hope and can I get on board." And that way, you know, I feel like I'm acting out of integrity, I'm really acting out of goodwill, out of love, and out of just wanting to serve others. And that has always been my motivation.

Dr. Bard:

If you haven't caught the magic by now. Let me share with our listening audience that we have one of my favorites on the show with us here today, Dr. Michael Putman from Roseville, California, who you can obviously see the basic fire in his gut, the magic in his eyes and the reality of the simple fact that he knows in his "heart of hearts" that he is giving his patients their lives back. He is doing it with compassion, with integrity, with really heart-driven care, because as you can obviously see, to treat peripheral neuropathy patients, you have to understand their situation. You have to understand that they have fought many a battle. Many of them are fighting and dealing with systemic conditions that have now disintegrated or degenerated into a condition that you wouldn't wish for yourself and your worst enemy.

The worst part of it is it often gets progressively worse. So, as you could see what Dr. Putman has done so professionally and really so powerfully is the simple fact that he has put together a program that is unique, distinct and specific for the treatment of patients that are suffering from peripheral neuropathy. Dr. Putman is also known to have had tremendous success in the world of taking care of patients who also have a spinal disc condition. In other words, patients who suffered from herniated discs, bulging discs, sequestered discs, damaged discs, degenerative discs, and more because of your skill, your art, your training, your certification in the world of nonsurgical spinal decompression, you have been able to treat them successfully. So, my question to you is this: how much of a parallel do you see between treating spinal disc patients and peripheral neuropathy patients?

Dr. Putman:

They run right hand in hand. And a lot of these patients have both things going on. I've had many patients over the years that we've done both things to. We've done spinal decompression and treated their neuropathy symptoms, both at the same time, or one following the other. And the similarity is because a lot of true peripheral neuropathies are metabolic in nature. You have to deal with the person's ability to create energy in their body and heal itself at a metabolic level. Decompression is really focused on the neuropathy component from compression. From the disc compressing the nerve.

When somebody comes in, I want this patient to know that I know what the heck I'm talking about, that I'm not some fly by night guy that's just trying to make a buck on the latest fad. When a decompressed patient comes in, it's quite interesting to you because you are so educated so well in terms of teaching the national certification and in terms of the course that you just did in Dallas. Especially the ability to communicate what it is we do and why and what Spinal Decompression does include all the different components of what a disc problem is. But I want them to know that whether they sign up with me or not, they're leaving my office better than they came in. This is because they now know that they have a better understanding of the condition. And hopefully, they have some hope that they have options without going down the path of surgery and all the things that it leads to. So, in that regard, I think people are searching for, again, someone that's an expert, that can communicate effectively, and that they can trust.

Dr. Bard:

This is so crucial, so vital and so key in the bullet points that you have hit upon. And I think it's interesting, Dr. Putman, in the sense that, if you look in the dictionary under the word doctor, one of the definitions of the word doctor happens to be teacher. And I think that one of the incredible things that you've done so successfully is to be able to empower your patients, to be able to teach your patients how to take charge, and how to take control of a condition that really so many of them have lost hope in. The fact is you do not only give them their hope back but you do it based upon facts, based upon science and based upon the reality of the simple fact that you are a true specialist. I love the simple fact that you've gone above and beyond the call of duty. You have invested abundant time, energy and effort into sharpening your own saw, so to speak. One of the things I wanted to ask you is, with your background specifically in functional medicine, how much of a component is the nutritional aspect of taking care of peripheral neuropathy patients?

Dr. Putman:

Huge, huge. I wouldn't take somebody if they're not willing to do it because especially in this kind of condition, healing a nerve that's damaged from the inside requires two things. Peripheral nerves are always trying to heal themselves, always. That's the amazing thing about peripheral nerves as opposed to central nervous system. The central nervous system, if you rupture your spinal cord, it's not going to heal. Peripheral nerves have an immense capacity to heal. They're always trying to heal themselves. So, what I explain to my patients is that there is a reason there's something destroying their nerve from the inside. Yet their peripheral nerves are trying to heal, and yes, their body is trying to heal these peripheral nerves.

The only way that it stays the same or gets worse is because the thing that's destroying it is occurring at the same rate, or faster than your body can heal it. So, our goal always with peripheral neuropathy is twofold. One, we have this incredible unit that speeds up the healing processes of a nerve (The Matrix). And two, we want to slow down the things that are destroying it. That's the only way the nerves can heal. And again, it's always limited to how much they can heal. I don't know how much it's going to heal for you. I don't know what your body can do— All I know is they're the two major influences that can affect it. So, if somebody wants to come in and do the neuropathy treatment and they were diabetic and they wanted to keep eating, and what they eat is high carbs, you know crap, it's not going to help them. And I'm not going to allow them to come in and complain to my staff that it's not helping them. So, it's just being committed in knowing that there are huge inputs— a lot of times. I even do this with my disc patients, Dr. Bard. This is because a lot of them have chronic inflammatory problems going on, on top of this bulging disc or herniated disc. And that slows down their body's ability to heal. So, everybody that comes into my office is doing something to support the work that we do and it could be all the way from being a super strict diet, doing detoxification. They'll be cleaning the liver, getting on a modified ketogenic diet. Also taking some supplements for disc healing. But in all, we have to treat the person as a whole, and to disregard what they do outside of the office, I think, is a huge mistake.

Dr. Bard:

You are really to me Dr. Putman, the epitome of a doctor's doctor. If I had peripheral neuropathy or someone in my family had peripheral neuropathy, without blinking an eye, I would get on a plane and I would come see you because of the simple fact that I know that you are looking at your patients from a differential diagnosis perspective. You are not treating every patient the same way. I think that's always been a really kind of a landmine for chiropractors. And as a result, you are being, as matter of fact, upfront with them as possible. At the same time, you're really giving them often their last ray of hope to be able to get their life back. I wanted to ask you one more thing. You have put together really an incredible team behind you. I've actually been blessed and fortunate and lucky enough to meet part of your team. Would you share a little bit about how integral they are, how important, how key they are to your treatment of peripheral neuropathy, and how involved they are in the care plan as well?

Dr. Putman

Well, they're, like you said, integral, although I will go deeper in that. One thing is I also always love my staff. I love and care for them. They're super good, but I don't feel that nobody including me in my office is irreplaceable. That's the mistake I've made in the past because you want to spend a lot of time, energy and money training people and they're doing a fabulous job. But if they start to feel like they're irreplaceable, trouble soon follows. Everybody on my staff is phenomenal. I'm super proud of them because they care and they're educated and we all make every effort to have the same kind of dialogues with the patient. We don't want to be caught having or getting conflicting or contradictory information or anything like that, but they're a huge, huge component to it.

This really came out when I was just doing chiropractic because I didn't want to have 200 patients a day and it's no offense to you or anybody else who did. It's that just my body can't handle that. But I want to be at my maximum 50 of the highest quality of patients, and then I also wanted each patient to feel cared for, like they're part of the family. I recognize that that wasn't going to happen with me just doing that because I'm not a great small talk guy. It's just not my deal. I mean, I love people and I want to know, "Hey, how's your son John in college doing and stuff?" And that's great. But what I did see is that the staff has a lot more opportunity to embrace people and take them in as a family member.

That's really one of the things that I've always taught my staff. I modeled it after the show "Cheers". For example, when Norm walks in, everybody says, "Hey Norm, glad you're here." Listen to the cheers theme song. That's what I want my office to be like. We're always glad you came. We do a lot of different things in my office from decompression to neuropathy to what we call manual therapy, which is I have massage therapists that work on patients for a very short period of time, like 10 minutes whenever they come in. And every interaction that connects—I always get comments about people, "Hey, your staff is always so happy and it's always such a nice place to come to.

That's what I want. I don't want people to be dreading coming in because they're going to wait for a half an hour. It would be bad if the person at the front desk is not present and the staff that's working on them is uncaring or has something else or spending their time talking about their problems. That would be horrible. So, finding the people, it just takes a lot of effort as you will know, Dr. Bard, just to spend the time to create the culture. I'm a big, big proponent of building a culture because that's kind of sort of the tech world model and it applies to our office as to what we are here for. Why are we here? If you ever find yourself coming to the office to work and you're not happy, you're not satisfied, you're not enjoying your work, then leave, don't spend your life doing that.

It's not about me. It's about you, man, it's your life. If you don't like it, find something else, try something else because life's too short. This is a new way of spending more quality time at work. So, make sure you're happy doing it and changing lives. So that's the thing that I've always tried to build, and it takes constant effort to get all of this done. I mean, we all get into the habit of, like, just kind of becoming complacent and cruising along and like coasting and not thinking. People know when you're not present. So, my staff are always working on being present, and on being service oriented.

Dr. Bard:

How could one not want to be a patient in your office? When I listened to your words, I know for a fact that you know there's an old saying which says the apple doesn't fall far from the tree. Obviously, your staff have a heightened level of dedication and what it takes to take care of peripheral neuropathy patients because you've made an investment, a large investment in them, and you've made a large investment in yourself. I think that is the highest standard of attention to detail that any doctor, that any team can ever live by, because at the end of the day, these are tough cases. These are challenging cases, but you've been so incredibly successful with this. You continue to lead the pack. You are a specialist in the truest sense of peripheral neuropathy and it's been such a real, real honor to have you on our show.

The doctors love this show for one simple reason: we ask great questions. We get the best doctors in the country. And this is unedited, it's unfiltered, it is unrehearsed, and it is from the heart. And you could sense it in your voice, Dr. Putman, of the simple fact of how committed you are to your peripheral neuropathy patients. I want to thank you on behalf of our team here, and believe me when I tell you there is a team here, even though you hear just my voice. There is a team behind the Dr. Success Spotlight Show, and it is a team that is dedicated to allowing you doctors to be able to tap into this "front of the line" information of the best in the business, Truly and honestly, the best chiropractors walking the face of the earth that have decided to live by example, who are committed to excellence and are true specialists in every sense of the word, just like Dr. Putman. If you get a chance to meet him, he is a star, magnetic and attractive in so many ways.

I've had the opportunity on multiple occasions to be with Dr. Putman. That's where you start to see his star power and that's where you start to say to yourself, well, obviously, he gets those kinds of results in the peripheral neuropathy world because he's so incredibly focused and dedicated to his patients, which is really the core element of living in "present time consciousness". Being "one to one" with their patients and understanding that this is a magic moment for your patients and to be able to change their lives in the most positive way.

HERE ARE THE BULLET-POINT TAKEAWAYS:

#1 - Based in Roseville, California he learned early in his Neuropathy practice that these conditions are considered "Life Changing and Life Altering".

#2 - Medications at best dampen the symptoms and eventually stop working with patients eventually experiencing more pain, ending up in a wheelchair or a walker and often losing hope.

#3 - He learned that without the proper training and proper approach, most Chiropractors are frustrated and do not want to see Peripheral Neuropathy patients as it takes a higher commitment to training but the results validate it and the rewards are high.

#4 - Better technology has now allowed more Chiropractors to treat more Peripheral Neuropathy patients much more successfully.

#5 - These patients have a much higher level of appreciation once they start seeing results and the significant part of his Peripheral Neuropathy package is his amazing educational system that he created.

#6 - His Peripheral Neuropathy website helps pre-qualify patients and filter individuals to determine who are theist candidates for care.

#7 - He has seen a tremendous parallel between Spinal Disc patients that can be traced with Spinal Decompression and Peripheral Neuropathy patients.

#8 - Patients want a doctor who can communicate what they can do for the Peripheral Neuropathy patient and as a Doctor, why they are different in offering a more natural approach.

#9 - Peripheral nerves have a tremendous potential to heal and his treatment offers the opportunity to SPEED up that nerve healing process and SLOW down the nerve damaging process within their bodies.

#10 - Lifestyle management is key and he only accepts patients that make a full commitment to following his recommendations especially with nutritional support and metabolic care.

11

PATIENT "WOW" SUCCESS – (DR. CRAIG SPODAK, D.D.S.)

Read about: DR. CRAIG SPODAK D.D.S. & DISCOVER how he has established the PREMIER Dental center in the country. A 13,000 square feet facility that captures the "WOW" patient experience for all of their patients. A "GO-TO" 5-Star Dental Center for EVERYONE. From celebrities, to athletes, to entertainers and the South Florida community, Dr. Spodak has discovered how to create RAVING fans of his practice and provide a comprehensive TEAM approach to ultimate patient satisfaction.

Dr. Bard:

In the words of the great Mr. Rogers. "It's a beautiful day in the neighborhood". If you want to know, why today, it's such a beautiful day in the neighborhood it's simply because we have the honor, and the privilege to have with us a most, most special guest. We want to welcome to our show, Dr. Craig Spodak. Welcome to the Dr. Success Spotlight Show, Dr. Spodak.

Dr. Spodak:

Thank you. Good to be here with you, Perry. I'm really happy to be here.

Dr. Bard:

For those of you who are so curious as to why, I am so incredibly excited about having Dr. Spodak, as our featured guest. The reason is simple and that is, Dr. Spodak is a dentist. However, he is definitely not your average dentist. As a matter of fact, I don't even think the word average even exists in Dr. Spodak's vocabulary. What Dr. Spodak has done so incredibly well in the world of dentistry and really in the world of healthcare is really nothing short of remarkable.

He is a third-generation dentist and he's established the premier dental center in the country. If you think that's just hype, I can absolutely tell you that I will prove it to you here today. He, along with his father, Dr. Myles Spodak who is a Brooklyn boy at heart built the #1 go-to dental facility. It has a "who's-who" of patients, who travel far and wide to see Dr. Spodak and his incredible team, which I'm going to talk about. He has put together a 13,000 square foot facility that I could sum up really in one word, in three simple letters, and those letters are the letters W-O-W.

He and his team have really created the ultimate patient experience and really the ultimate wow experience. For those of you, who are curious as to why I'm so excited about having, Dr. Spodak, as our featured guest the real reason why is he's done something so dramatic and so different. You only get one chance to make a great first impression and he has owned this. So, my question to you, Dr. Spodak coming right out of the gate, jumping right into the deep end of the pool here is, where did your motivation come from in creating the ultimate wow patient experience?

Dr. Spodak:

I appreciate all these kind words. So, thank you, Perry. You've always been super kind and supportive of me and what you say is very much appreciated. It means a lot to me, so thank you. So where did that come from? Dentistry is a very large industry, maybe it's $140 billion industry, so it's a very, very large industry. At the end of the day I don't believe dentistry is a form of healthcare, although we'd argue that it is a health-care segment. I truly believe it's more akin to retail because your teeth are basically optional. I mean, I'm a dentist, I have a high regard for teeth, and I would be miserable, if I even had to lose one tooth. However, you can live a proper full life without teeth, so everything around dentistry is discretionary. So, I really think of the dental segment as a branch of retail versus just the rest of healthcare.

The only thing medically necessary is an extraction of a diseased tooth but beyond that, everything else is a discretionary purchase. So, I took a lot of examples from retail when I was designing the facility. I wanted it to feel different. I know a lot of people are scared when they come to the dentist. So, I wanted to touch on all the different senses. From 85 percent of our space being day lit, to the colors that we used, to the music playing in the parking lot. I just wanted people to reframe their dental experience so that they could say it could be different and that's what I did. I set out to be inspired by other forms of retail, the Apple Store, Starbucks, etc.

When I first went to my first Starbucks in 1994, they had their special menu. I couldn't even order a regular cup of coffee. I ordered a Frappuccino, these words I'd never have heard before. So, it was a very different experience and I wanted to borrow that and put it into dentistry because restaurants and retail businesses spend a lot of money on helping their customers feel safe and secure and valued. What better environment to do that then in dentistry, where people are routinely coming and sometimes scared. So, I thought if it works for restaurants, hotels, and retail, then it will work for dentistry, so that was the source of inspiration.

Dr. Bard:

There are really so many parallels between the practice of dentistry and the practice of chiropractic, who happens to be our core audience, who follow us in mass. At the same time, there's really some distinct differences. I think the most common parallel obviously is and you knew this right from the beginning, is you have the ability to change somebody's life in such a positive way. There's an old saying in that we live in a visual world. As I say, "we eat with our eyes first" and I think that's one of the things that you dominated in the simple fact that obviously, when they walk into your facility that it is unlike anything that has existed that I've ever seen. In dentistry, this is just unmatched. One of the things, I think you've done so incredibly well is the lighting in your facility. In other words, when you walk into your place it is alive, it's electric, it's energetic. I know that comes from your team. I know that comes from your staff, which I want to ask you about, but can you talk a little bit about the lighting of Spodak Dental?

Dr. Spodak:

So, like I mentioned before, 85 percent of our space is day lit. There's disconnect between the way spaces are built and used. So, windows are expensive. So, if you're a chiropractor or a pizza parlor or a dentist, you're probably going to find a strip mall or other medical space that is kind of designed as a vanilla box and you have to put your practice in there. Glass is expensive and a single square box is also expensive as well. So, we're forced to take on spaces that are not really readily designed for the environment that we wish to practice in.

I mean, if you bought a pet canary, and you wanted to take care of your canary the pet store would tell you to put the canary by the window. My last building that I worked in with my dad, there was one piece of glass in the entire 4,000 square feet. I would not know if it was 3:00 PM, 7:00 PM rain, sun, we'd have no idea. That does something to your limbic system, being in an environment like that. We have studies that show us that being exposed to daylight is better for us. In fact, there was a hospital study that was done recently, where they figured out that people that went into the ICU after surgeries, if they had a window in their recovery room, they tended to get less postoperative infections, and recovered more quickly. They figured out that the only difference between them was the glass, the window. So just exposure to the daylight is healthy and it's good for you and we're very proud that we have that. In addition, it affects purchasing decisions as well. So, there's some studies that show that daylight affects purchasing decisions. These are just interesting things to study and I was a big student of these principles in the building.

Dr. Bard:

Well, you've put it into motion and it is such an experience that I could speak on personally with respect to it is not just the visual experience. It's an auditory experience. It's a kinesthetic experience. It really is quite the experience. There's an old saying in that "success being in the details". I can absolutely tell you that one of the things that sets you apart right out of the get go, is you could have built this incredible facility and you could have really, really put everything together the way you did. I think what is amazing is you could have rested on your laurels. You could have gone into kind of a "hands off" doctor approach and instead it's really quite the opposite. You are completely hands-on in this practice in having the ability to really, guide the ship.

One of the things to me that stands out incredibly well about your practice is your ability to treat every patient no matter, if they're professional athlete, an entertainer, an artist, or a celebrity as well as every single one of your patients. All of your patients are given such a five-star patient experience which is unmatched. I have never seen anything like that. One of the things that I would love for you to speak on, is the thing to me that shines the brightest in your office, which is your incredible, all-star team or hall of fame team, that you

141

put together. Where does the motivation come from to put together this type of team that's really hitting on all cylinders?

Dr. Spodak:

Well, you touched on something earlier. You said, if you put the building together that's really slick and you don't deliver on a value proposition to your patient, you're not going to do well. The culture of the consumer and our patients are different now than there has ever been. So not only do they expect to come to you, if you're a chiropractor and get adjusted and all that, but they want an experience. So, it's not too good enough that you're going to be able to get them, perhaps feeling better. There're other people in your community that can do the same thing. They want something different. So, they want an experience. Thus, part of it is your facility and your team. Your team is actually the biggest part of your experience in my opinion.

I mean it's fortunate for you guys in chiropractic. You can readily tell if you feel better or not. So, you go and you have a pain, and you may get a work up and you go through a series of treatments and you start feeling better. In dentistry, is patients don't necessarily know if you're helping them or not, so as long as you don't hurt them and you do the work to their standard, they don't know if it's good work or bad work. They just don't know. They know it doesn't hurt. So, in dentistry, we have to give the patient something to perceive as higher value. One of the things that was very important to me is my team. If you build the box and fill it with a bunch of people that have no alignment on values and principles and don't treat the patients well, you won't do well. Gary Vaynerchuk is a person that I really emulated to in some ways and he has a great thing to say about marketing. He says, "the cheapest and best marketing strategy of all is to care". So, no one will love your practice unless your team loves it first. I don't care what branch of healthcare you are in. It's the same thing in a restaurant, by the way, if you ever go to a restaurant and you ask the waitress, what do you like, the fish tacos or do you like the steak? She looks at you dead in the eye and she says, she's never eaten here in my life. I mean, you're never going to order on that restaurant or the converse of that is don't get the steak because the fish tacos are really good and the chef actually catches the fish himself and they have the whole story around it.

So, for me, it's not the customer is always right or the patient is always right. I actually flipped it around and the team has got to be put first in my opinion. So, if your team is first, if they feel loved, connected and cared for that is the key. So, I have worked with several dentists. I've done some consulting and some lecturing, where they're really nice to the patients and they're really rude to the team and it's not sustainable. So, I think it's really incumbent upon us as the business owners and the leaders of the practice to grow people and to help them feel nurtured and cared for and that's how the patients will feel it as well. So, we put a big focus on that, spend inordinate amount of time on training the team and investing in the team and doing things for the team and allowing programs for the team to reward each other. We have peer-to-peer recognition programs, where teams can hand out money to other team members. So, it's pretty cool, we have a very intricate process there.

Dr. Bard:

What I love is the parallel that you've made here and one of the secrets here, is taking the what is the complicated and making it simple. I think that is one of your incredible talents and what's made you so magnetic and you've done this incredibly well. You do this eye to eye, you do it face to face, you do one to one, you really do it heart to heart with each of your patients. You really do it with your demographic. The thing that made you stand out without question, above and beyond all of your peers that I've ever seen is really one thing and that is your ability to "change perception". I think, so many patients perceive dentistry as they do chiropractic really on a singular, really almost on a myopic level. To some degree, even with a biased approach. They have an opinion which maybe set in stone, so it's going to be hard to move that opinion. I think what you've done here is you've directly challenged that. How have you been able to change the perception of dentistry so well?

143

Dr. Spodak:

Well, I think that's all we hope to do. I mean, Starbucks changed the perception of coffee, Howard Schultz, the iconic CEO of Starbucks decided that coffee was going be something different. He traveled to Europe, and he saw these really cool cafés, where people are sitting and spending an hour and a half talking and he called it the third place, not work, not home, but a separate place where you could go. When he pitched this idea to everyone back in the late 80s, no one would fund him, because at the time, the average cup of coffee was 35 cents that looked like a place like the coffee, out of a Seinfeld episode. Similar to a diner, which wasn't really nice. At the time retail was thinking, how do we get people in and out faster? McDonald's was proud to tell you that over 2 billion were served, like that was some sort of badge of honor that we get them in and out, so quickly that we have to attach the chairs to the table so that you don't sit in the restaurant. You get your burger, you eat, you get the hell out as quick as possible. Starbucks flipped that around and said, we want people to sit here because maybe if you sit for a while, you might actually buy a Michael Buble CD or buy a croissant or whatever. They figured that if we can get to stay in the space longer and feel comfortable there, they'll do better. At the time, no one had proved that metric.

So, I'm not the first by any stretch to redefine the perception of our industry and I appreciate those kind words, but others were doing it as well at the same time. A lot of your colleagues, Perry, are doing it with chiropractic as well. I think you have to just set out with a vision. I think most people fail to plan. They don't have much intentionality around their business. They just kind of do it day by day by day. They have no vision for where they're going. The unfortunate thing about having no vision for where you're going is you're going to get there and you're going to get to a place that you don't want to be at. So, no matter what, we're all working towards something. There's the business that you're in and the business that you're becoming. I think it's important that you have some form of set vision point for what you're trying to create. So, I was very intentional about mine and I actually did what I called a "descriptive vision".

So back in 2008, I had three or four people working with me. I sat down and I wrote out this really elaborate vision of what it's going to look like, and feel like. So, things like, I pull up to my office, and it inspires me where I work and this is how I feel and this is what my office looks like and these are the people that are walking in and how that feels. So, I spent a lot of time, intentional time and I think most people just don't. It's not really a failure to execute so much as a failure to plan. They do it as a secondary thought. I was just a little bit more intentional about it, and I think there's a need to recreate that periodically too. So, I did that 10 years ago, but I've done one recently for the next three years as well because things are always changing. You guys have new equipment. We do too, new modalities. There's probably less need for office space and maybe there's mobile chiropractic or those types of people going for house visits, who knows? One thing, we can see is that businesses are getting disrupted so darn fast now. Who would have thought five, seven years ago that I could go car free for three months and be fine with Uber? Or they didn't have to go to the bank to deposit a check but I can't remember the last time, I went to the bank or now you and I have Amazon Prime from Whole Foods from where we live. So, I ordered a yogurt to my house. I got it there in an hour. I don't have to go to Whole Foods anymore, it's crazy.

Dr. Bard:

What's crazy is the simple fact that you have really made this yours completely. I have to tell our readers that I have the unique ability to talk about you and really talk about Spodak Dental in kind of a unique sense because not only is my wife, a patient of yours but so is our older son, who as we speak, is in dental school right now, thanks to you as well. Our youngest son, who yesterday just started his first day of chiropractic school is a patient of yours too. As well as myself, who of all patients happens to be the toughest of tough patients in the sense that I am the most skeptical and I am looking at everything. I am looking at dentistry, the same way I look at chiropractic. That is there's always good, there's better, and then there's the best and then there's even a higher level. When we think about what people aspire too often, when they, describe their dentist or describe their chiropractor and you'll hear words that start to sound like average, which is really "the best of the worst and the worst of the best". Who the heck wants to be average? I will tell you that if you, Dr. Spodak were a chiropractor, you'd be such a freaky good chiropractor, it would be scary. If this dental thing doesn't pan out the way you thought, I'm telling you as a chiropractor, it would've been ridiculously great. I'm only kidding. You are really hitting it on all cylinders. I would love you to speak a little bit about what you have done because you've done this better than anyone I've seen, on how you've handled social media with respect to the positioning of Spodak Dental in the social media world. Can you share a little bit about how you've done that so well?

Dr. Spodak:

Thank you. So, the first thing, I want to point out is don't have any fear around social media. Social media is essentially just word of mouth. So historically, if a patient went to go see you and left your office, and they felt great, they just got an adjustment, they're feeling aligned and they're feeling great and they happened to bump into a friend and the friend says, "what are you doing over here"? I just went to my chiropractor, Dr. Bard. He's amazing. Oh wow, let me get his number. So that's how it's supposed to happen. Now, we have to check in, so if you can in some way incentivize or encourage a patient in your practice to check in or post that they're at your office that's key. That's basically the same thing as I'm walking out your office and meeting with 600 friends at the same time and getting on a megaphone, and just saying, I just left Dr. Bard's office and I had an adjustment and I feel great. Because what happens is when they post that on their timeline and anybody who likes it or comments on it, that will be shared as well and it's very viral. So social media is not this daunting thing. It's just word of mouth on steroids. People will be talking about you, so don't be scared if you're more in the age range of Dr. Bard and myself. If you employ someone in your office, let's say under the age of 35 or 40, they're actually on social media all day long while you're paying them, just not your social media there. So, you can make them the social media guru or the social media champion and let them handle your page.

One of the things, I want to point out about with social media is this is not a place to put advertising out. It's not a place to say, come in for the $100 evaluation, x-rays, and spinal analysis. It's not that, because that's a spammy, pushy type of advertising. You're pushing out a message as offensive and it shows up in people's newsfeeds and your friends unlike your page. So really what you want to do is you want to build engagement. You want to get conversations going and towards social media. It's not just about posting something. If you're posting a bunch of crap and no one's liking it, you're not really posting anything of value. You want to have a conversation, so keep it a video or a visual and ask questions. So, things like, what do you think of this, does this look good or do you like this better? We want to wish Cindy, a happy five-year anniversary with our practice, anything celebrating people, humanizing the practice, and building engagement and building your conversation. The metric for social media is not how many posts you put out, but how many people are interacting with the posts you put out.

Dr. Bard:

So, here's my proposal to you. My proposal to you is you may want to consider changing the name of Spodak Dental to "The Spodak Dental Party". The reason I say that doc is because not only is it a party with respect to the environment that you've created for your team, which is above and beyond the greatest team of dentists. I mean, it's just ridiculous how incredible they are. We could do a whole show just on them, but the simple fact is that you've really changed, not just the perception, but almost the rules to a degree, about how patients seek out doctors and especially, how far they're willing to travel. You've made it so user friendly for patients to travel across state lines, across international lines, to really make this the ultimate dental experience, where patients now, can travel far and wide to come and see you. Same as true for a number of our doctors, our chiropractors, who are specialists in the world of disc, in the world of nerve, in the world of joint care, they have these experiences now, and now you've done the same thing in dentistry. So, if a patient is curious about making an appointment with you, but even, more so, what I would encourage all our doctors who are reading this that if they want to have the ultimate dental experience for themselves to either drive or fly in, to come to Spodak Dental, what's the easiest way to get in touch with your office?

Dr. Spodak:

Just our website, www.spodakdental.com or you can Google us. That was really kind of you, Perry, that's so nice. I appreciate those kind words and I know you mean them, so that's even more special for me to hear that. So, thank you.

Dr. Bard:

Well to me, you, your family and your team have gone above and beyond, the call of duty and you are the gift that keeps giving. You've made this such an incredible experience for everybody, who are so fortunate enough to know you, to become a patient in your office, to go through this experience, to meet your doctors, to meet your team, and to simply do one thing, and that one simple thing is to come away better. As they say, "good, better, best, never let it rest, until your good is better and your better is the best".

HERE ARE THE BULLET-POINT TAKEAWAYS:

#1 - Dentistry is a 140-Billion-dollar industry. Dr. Spodak, a 3rd-generation Dentist has taken the best of retail and integrated many of the details that set certain retail businesses apart from the rest. Apple & Starbucks being two of them as an example.

#2 - Touching on all the senses was a big part of helping patients overcome anxiety in creating a welcoming, harmonious, center for patient care.

#3 - One of the key components to the ultimate patient experience is the lighting that exists in his center. With 85% of it being day lit he references studies that show how lighting affects healing as well as decision making.

#4 - Team values and principles as well as attention to individual patient needs is a key component to his clinic success. Putting his team first is vital.

#5 - It all starts with the vision that you have for the practice and then including everyone in to the same vision.

#6 - The vision should include as much detail as possible from the time you would drive up to your clinic and what that feels like at every step of the patient experience.

#7 - He has excelled in the use of social media by creating incentives with his patients to get involved & to share their experiences as he feels it's like having a megaphone to promote your practice.

#8 - The metric for social media success is not the amount of posts you put out, but how many people are interacting with the posts you put out.

#9 - He feels that social media is just word of mouth on steroids. Patients under 40 years old are constantly on it so you can employ them to make them your social media guru. You want to not pro-mote ads on it but instead create conversations, thus humanizing the practice and building engagement.

#10 - He makes tremendous parallels between Dentistry & Chiropractic and how to make it a "WOW" experience across the board.

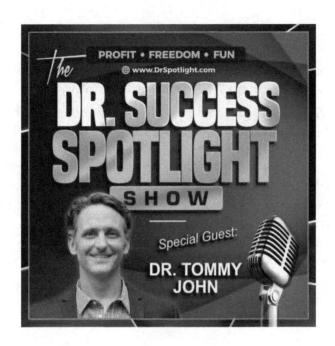

12

"CHIRO-BASEBALL" SUCCESS – (DR. TOMMY JOHN)

Read about: DR. TOMMY JOHN & DISCOVER how he has helped countless athletes and baseball players minimize risk and potentially AVOID THE SURGERY named after his father, the Hall of Fame caliber baseball player, "Tommy John". Learn how he has created a renowned and ultra-successful TRAINING CENTER in Southern California. The author of "Minimize Injury/Maximize Performance" Dr. John shares EXACTLY what he does as a Chiropractor to position himself as the torch-carrier for helping young athletes and their families stay healthy.

Dr. Bard:

On today's show is a subject that is so very near and so very dear to my heart for a number of reasons which you will learn about. As many of you know, there's actually two things that I have always been so amazingly passionate about. One obviously, is chiropractic that's pretty obvious, but the second happens to be something that many of you don't know which is the game of baseball. Now, on today's show, we have such an incredible guest, as we get a chance to discover together some game changing strategies for ultimate patient care, for radically improved patient outcomes, and for success on abundant levels. It is absolutely my sincere honor and my privilege to welcome to the Dr. Success Spotlight Show, the one and the only, Dr. Tommy John. Welcome to the show, Dr. John.

Dr. John:

Thank you very much Dr. Perry. I appreciate the opportunity.

Dr. Bard:

Now, for those of you that may not know, Dr. John is actually based in Southern California and his teachings, his patient care, his outreach, and more have spanned not just nationally, but internationally as well, and that's not by luck. Now, for those of you who may not know, if the name happens to sound familiar when we speak of Tommy John, it is, and that is, Dr. Tommy John is the son of absolutely, one of my all-time favorite baseball players, Tommy John, who had such an incredible career with the LA Dodgers and NY Yankees. He is without a doubt, a hall of fame, caliber player. He is a hall of fame person. If you've ever listened to him speak, he's really the type of player you would absolutely make a movie about his life, in terms of what he has given to so many, and thankfully he still does.

He also became the namesake of a surgical procedure that so many of our doctors happen to see patients for, and who actually are either scheduled to have this procedure or have had this procedure, and that the "Tommy John Surgery". There is a major pendulum swing right now in the area of sports medicine and it starts with education. I think what you will see here today, is what Dr. Tommy John has done is he has written a book on this which actually is a groundbreaking book that has created more buzz, more talk, more change than has been seen in such a long time regarding this topic and so much more. The name of the book is, *"Minimize Injury, Maximize Performance"*. It is *A Sports Parent's Survival Guide*. As we always say here, on the on the Dr. Success Spotlight Show, we don't pull punches, we ask tough questions, and we don't tread lightly, especially on a subject so serious here, so right out of the gate, Dr. John, what I am dying to ask you, is why now, more than ever, why is the timing of your book so crucial right now?

Dr. John:

What we're seeing is an epidemic. Not just in baseball with the Tommy John Surgery happening at the highest level, but no sport is safe. Concussions are up 500 percent, ACL surgeries in 6 to 18-year-olds are up 60 percent in the last 20 years. Dr. Andrews who's a renowned orthopedic surgeon, over 40 percent of his entire practice is on children. So, what we're seeing is the nature of what's going on, all the attention is brought to who we watch on TV, who are making millions upon millions of dollars getting this surgery at a radical pace. If we just take Tommy John Surgery alone, over 57 percent of them are happening in 15 to 19-year-olds. So, it's not even happening at the professional level, which is where my dad having gone through what he did in 1974, was so proud of his name being attached to something that a professional can extend his career with, to provide for his family. That's an amazing feat. That's something that we're all proud of as a family but now that the name is attached to something happening in kids more than adults, that's something we're sick and tired of, and what this book has to say just going on at the youth level.

Dr. Bard:

This is so interesting because of the simple fact that this is really become, I'm going to use a big word on this show. It's a word we've never used ever in the history of the Dr. Success Spotlight Show, but this has really become an "epidemic". For those of you who are not familiar with the Tommy John Surgical Procedure I'll explain it. It really is a surgery that was named after a procedure which is otherwise known as an "ulnar collateral ligament reconstruction". Sometimes when you hear the name "Tommy John Surgery", I think often what it does is it minimizes the seriousness, the damage, and the potential long-term effects of this.

Now, what you've done, Dr. John is dramatic and what you've done is really groundbreaking, in the fact that, what you've done in your book is you have encompassed this in a nutshell. You give some incredible statistics with respect to the number of Tommy John Surgeries in 2014, surpassing the entire period between 1990 through 2000. Now, that's a 10-year span. Now, only 20 percent in your book as reference, ever make it back to their previous level of performance and between 25 and 30 percent of those athletes, who have had the procedure find themselves no longer able to play baseball. You cannot help watch the MLB Network, watch ESPN, watch Fox Sports, and not hear about this. You are now the torch carrier, for changing this and this has made such a dramatic turn in terms of where this is going. So, my question to you is where does it start in terms of attacking this problem right from the get go?

Dr. John:

It's got to be in the home, and that's what in the book has done. It puts the power back into the hands of the parents because they're the ones signing the kids up for year-round sports. They're the ones paying for the extra clinics and camps and showcases and off-season travel teams, and all this extra stuff that just adds pressure emotionally and physically to this growing, developing human that can't handle it. It's got to go back to the parents making the decisions and it's all for the good of the kid. Now, I'm up against the Goliath. I might as well take on the pharmaceutical industry, if we're going to talk about it. The youth sports industry is over $15 billion a year and growing.

154

It's out of control. So that being said, they're very clever, in their market-ing and their advertising to the parent in a "fear of missing out" kind of mentality and they're very clever at it. You have well-intended parents wanting just the best of their child. No doubt. Nobody wants to hurt their child. So, what they're doing, they're being preyed upon, and I've got people coming in all the time stating they're going to be left behind. I'm like, "listen to me, this is not how an athlete develops". This is not how a human athlete, whether they play sports or not develops. There is a way to go about it. We have to start young. The imprint of everything we are as an adult, is built upon the foundation that happens in our youth, and we need to target their first.

Dr. Bard:

So, if you're not familiar with why, Dr. Tommy John has really been a star, I have a new name for Dr. John. He probably was called this before, but I believe he absolutely he is "the chosen one". The reason why I believe he's "the chosen one" is because we are so fortunate as chiropractors. Now, I don't know if a lot of you know, but my grandfather actually worked for the Brooklyn Dodgers. So, there's a long history in my family from not just what our children would eventually do in the sport, but family history as well. When I became familiar with the name "Tommy John". One of the things that, if you remember his career when talking about Dr. Tommy John's father, was what happened initially, after the procedure. Dr. John how has the pendulum swung because initially, it didn't start that way. It was done as a reparative procedure to try to hopefully, get a little more mileage out of one of the best arms in baseball.

Dr. John:

Of course, it was literally one of those things that my dad was not going to be told, no. My dad's like, "what do you got in your bag of tricks Dr. Jobe"? Dr. Jobe was like," I've got this one thing I can do, but it's never been done before". My dad's like, "fine. Is there any chance at all"? "Sure, there's like maybe "one in 100 chance you'll come back, and ever throw again". My dad goes, "done, let's take it". So that's all he wanted was the chance, and Dr. Jobe actually gave him the opportunity. He said, "this might fall apart, your arm might just completely fall apart when you go to throw again". And he goes, "then you'll do it again"? And he goes, "all right", but it might happen again. He goes, "you'll do it one more time, you will perform the surgery three times", and then if not, he had Hoyt Wilhelm set up to teach him the knuckle ball, if he couldn't sustain a fastball. So, there was no stopping my father at the time in 1974, and then not being done. Interesting enough, the next season after my dad had his surgery in 1975, the radar gun entered baseball and then they all of a sudden, tried to put an objective number to talent. Kind of what we do in medicine. Now, all of a sudden, you've got people trying to pitch to a gun, and not pitch to get out. I think we've seen that as perverted as it can be now, where it's stats and s metrics and science, and its technology and then we're going to measure it and their spin rates, and this and this. There's no art and philosophy anymore in baseball, in the pitching sense.

My dad came back, pitched and had to figure it out. The goal of the pitcher the major leagues was to adapt. If that doesn't sound familiar to us as chiropractors, the goal of human body is to adapt. So, he's put into a game and he has to adapt. Does that mean he throws his best up? He just gives whatever he can to put his team in a position to win and he did it 288 total times over 26 years. With the majority of those coming in the 14 years after the surgery. Never missing a start because of his elbow. He never missed the start because of his elbow in 14 years, so something that man did was right. Nowadays, you hit the nail on the head. We are not afraid of surgeries anymore. We aren't afraid of surgeries just in general because of how they're talked about. Everyone has got one, everyone has got them scheduled. Everyone is measuring their lives on how many surgeries or medications they're on, instead of like what events or what traveling or life activities they've done.

So now we have this "Tommy John Surgery", and the protocol will save me, where I think one of the blessings of it was my dad had nothing to fall back on. They were following him, and this is one of the most profound things ever said in medicine and I'll never ever forget it. Dr. Jobe as the doctor, the medical professional says, to the patient, "TJ, we don't know what's about to happen, we are going to follow you and you are going to listen to your body". How about that? That's one of the most successful surgeries in the history of sports that if we could apply that everywhere, my gosh, what would happen in medicine and health and lifestyle, fitness and everything else that we've got but that's what he had to do. He had to listen to his innate and if he did this and it didn't feel good, he did something else. What he found was if he threw every single day, he felt great. If he used ice, he felt like crap, so he put heat on it. He had something in his car that he would grip all the time while driving. He was doing things. It was 24/7 all the time thinking of how to improve himself so that he could put himself in the best position to win a baseball game and that's what he did. Historically, that's what we've seen as the most successful "Tommy John Surgery" of all time was the first one.

Dr. Bard:

I actually said something in the beginning and I'm going to repeat it for the first time ever, but a little bit different. I mentioned before in the beginning of the show that if there was ever a movie, or there was ever an athlete, or there was ever a story that where they should make a movie about an athlete, about an individual, it should be Dr. John's father, Tommy John with 288 professional MLB wins. On the hall of fame life that he has led, but the real story here is this. If there's a movie that should be made, it's really the movie about, Dr. Tommy John, and the reason is simple. The reason is because this is one of the greatest stories. This is a Rocky-like story as a chiropractor and I would love for you to share just a little bit, Dr. John, about how you started and your evolution to the point, where you are at right now, in creating one of the greatest training centers, one of the greatest facilities, literally a laboratory for the best. I have to say this, a little tongue and cheek, "cutting edge", if you know what I mean, because it's the complete opposite of surgery in Southern California. I would love for you to share your rise, your evolution, your maturation from player to student to doctor to leader?

Dr. John:

So, I was a multisport athlete all through high school and I wasn't good until my senior year. I wasn't excelling in baseball to the point that my dad never pushed me. He wasn't going to push me because I wasn't good. I didn't express anything that was pushable. All of a sudden, my senior year, I got good and that's when I reduced down to one sport. I quit basketball and I was going to play baseball at the next level. I ended up setting my goals and I became the Gatorade State Player of the Year in 1996 in the state of Minnesota, as an 86 mile an hour, 5'11" right-hander, middle infield pitcher. I got a division one scholarship at Furman University and my goal was to play in the Cape Cod League. Now, the Cape Cod League, is the highest level of amateur baseball in the summer that collegiate athletes play in the summertime. I've seen them play when I was 12 years old and I had set that goal for myself. After my freshman year, I was runner-up freshman of the year. I played second base and I pitched, I was a dual position player at that time, which is unheard of now. I ended up getting invited to the Cape Cod League to play. Just before I got invited there, I had a tired, achy shoulder in the league. I was pitching in that summer after my freshman year to be proactive and get ahead of the game. I went in for an MRI. Well, when you get an MRI in the joint like that, they have to do an arthrogram, which is a dye injection. That dye injection got infected. I had a deep capsule infection, 103 fever and my shoulders swelled up. I was vomiting. It was scary, and it was life threatening. They went in, flushed the shoulder out, the infection ate away my capsule and now I'm at the rehab center. While I'm in the hospital bed the Cape Cod League called me, and I never forget it because I bawled my eyes out because I had achieved the dream that I set forth at 13 years old. I'm lying in the hospital bed and I can't provide anything, and it bothered me to no end.

So now, I go into the rehab approach and I'm asking questions and they didn't like me because I asked so many questions. I always wanted to know why, I wanted to pull things apart. Why do people get injured and other people don't? What's the commonality between why everyone is on the same protocol for the same injury when we're all individuals? This is interesting to me and the therapist didn't like that because they couldn't answer it. The physical therapy model is upside down on its head and so they're going at symptom care rather than getting at the source. Even then, without even any chiropractic background, the big idea was just there's a cause and what is it? Why are we treating all these other things? So then ended up graduating Furman with a bachelor's and a master's in Health and Exercise Science. I was so dead set on playing professionally that I earned my way onto pitch professionally at the independent league. So, I pitched professionally for two years, hanging them up after that when baseball wasn't fun anymore.

Then I got into Sports Performance and Rehab. So, here's how my day played out. I would personally train people in the morning from 5:00 AM to about 11:00. I had a two-hour break in the day. Then I would come back and train NFL, NHL, NBA, high school or young youth athletes for their particular sport while also working with rehab scenarios like an 86-year-old, with osteoporosis and a diabetic, plantar fasciitis, herniated discs, you named the soft tissue injury, I was working with it. At nighttime, I would do skill specific lessons, and I performed over 11,000 baseball lessons in that 8-year, period of time. So, I've seen every edge of performance in sports and everything and I wanted it all. Well, our rehab and training system needed to be preceded by a chiropractic visit and I had never heard of that before. But what I did notice, our chiropractors that we had in our facility in Illinois could only come one day a week and he would come on Fridays and all our people would go see him on Friday, and then we'd get them on Saturday and Sunday and move forward for the next week. What I noticed because I was very, very, aware of changes no matter how minute, was that after they were adjusted, if they needed the adjustment, they performed better. Their electrical system was different, their patterning was different, their strength, their ability to communicate, their recovery, their training, everything changed. And I was like, "wait a second, what are you doing in that office"? I want to know what you're doing. The guy couldn't break it down for me. Again, very frustrating when you have somebody that wants to know why and has questions and he couldn't articulate an answer.

I wanted to cut everybody out of it. I'm not going to be the middleman to anything. I want to have it all and so I ended up going back to chiropractic school at 32 years old. I shut down my baseball business. I put my house up for rent. I went to Life and I spent the next 4 years getting my doctorate and I fell backwards into a profession that we all know is one of the biggest, greatest ones on the planet, dealing with the greatest system of all systems. I literally had no clue that it was so much bigger than soft tissue injuries. So, I had the rehab and the training and all that stuff setup. I just needed this element, but now, what I found out was that I could help mental health, digestive, endocrine, I mean, you name it. Anybody on the spectrum of dysfunction, I could help them to start the care with a chiropractic visit. So now, that's what I've got set up in my office at San Diego. Anybody who walks through the door, whether it's just a human athlete looking to perform in life regardless of what that is. I'm just here to remove what's preventing them from being their best self.

Dr. Bard:

This is really one of the greatest stories of reinvention. Dr. John, you are so incredibly humble, you're incredibly modest, you're a master communicator, and you, Dr. John you've taken the lead role here, to become the torch carrier for this change. I'm going to call this change, "the four P's". The four P's to me, stands for number one, you are Proactive. You are absolutely in the Position right now to Protect and to Prevent your Patients from going through unnecessary Procedures. So, they can Profit in the game of life. I think that's like six P's. I lost track. I don't know, I'm counting them off, but the "P's" just jumped out at me. Dr. John, what's so amazing about you, is that you are an expert. You became a "student of the game. I don't think it's ever been more appropriate to use those words then with you, Dr. John. You're an expert in sports medicine. You're an expert in biomechanics. You're an expert in kinesiology. You're really an expert in spinal structural dysfunction.

You're an expert in telling the story and you're really an expert on living the life experience to the fullest. I will tell you, if you are not one of Dr. John's social media friends, then you're really missing out. The reason you're missing out, is because he has an incredible talent to document his life in such an uplifting, such a positive way, that's seventh P, I think right here. We could just keep going with that, but the truth is, he has really positioned himself, his practice, his patients, and more for success. I would love for you, Dr. John to talk a little bit about why your facility has become such a game changer when it comes to patients, who fly in from all over the world to see you and why it's become such a game changer compared to everything that's out there?

Dr. John:

I think I respect the most about how I approach it. The way I go about things is I'm following the breadcrumbs, so to speak, that the patients are leaving behind. I respect and honor what we have within us and so much the simplicity in it. Like whenever things go haywire, ancient wisdom always prevailed and there's certain principles that are always going to be there, no matter what, they're always sitting there. I just incessantly, stubbornly will stay on it because I just don't ever really think we've mastered the basics. It's still hard for me to eat good foods. It's still hard for me to go get my nervous system checked. It's still hard for me to sleep at the right time. It's still hard for me to move and squat and lunge like I've never mastered those. It's hard for me to breathe properly and to choose better emotional outlets and make all these decisions which we will never master. We're never done with it.

I feel like when my patients come in, I'm always saying, "I'm right next to you". Like I'm not leading you, I'm right next to you. I always say, "we", for example here's what we're going to do. We're going to do this, we're going to get checked. They love how I say, "we", all the time because they're with me. So, absolutely to the point that I'm very blunt about this, "the only thing you NEED from me, is to check your spine and adjust you". That's what you can't do on your own but all these other things that I'm talking about, you've got, and I'll lay that out on day one. I'm just going to be a tutor or a helper, like I'm just the right facilitator in power and you're going to take the reign on your own life and lead this ahead because you're the one living. I can only release whatever has been blocked through an adjustment, if you need it, and then that's it.

There are no clocks in my office on purpose. There are salt lamps all over the place. There are ocean pictures on the wall and I always say that as soon as you walk in, you have no choice, you are going to start healing better than you ever have. It's an environment, as what we're about to do training wise, you've never experienced before. So that's what I'm kind of trying to bring people back to. In expressing that innate potential inside. It knows how to squat. It knows what it wants to eat, it knows when it needs to sleep, it knows who is going to attract the relationship, it knows its dreams. If we can just connect back to that, tomorrow is going to be better, the next minute it's going to be better. If we can keep building on that, who knows what level we can bring everybody to.

Dr. Bard:

You, Dr. John, are absolutely 100 percent above-down, inside-out. You lead by example. What you've done in your genius and in your magic is you really teach the game of life to your patients and everyone who's fortunate enough to know you. You do this leading by example. You lead a healthy lifestyle, you teach how to live a healthy lifestyle not just inside the lines, but more importantly outside the lines, and especially off the field, which everyone knows is really where the game of life is being played the majority of the time.

I loved your book, I really did, *"Minimize Injury, Maximize Performance"*. if you're reading this right now, don't, wait, don't walk, don't run. You need to fly to Amazon right now, get this book in your hands, because if there was a subtitle to this book, it's really "how to own your own life". That was my takeaway when I read your book. I said there's too much goodness in this book that the world doesn't know about, in terms of nutrition and how we eat, and you've got some incredible recipes. What I also love about the book is it's incredibly footnoted, it's incredibly researched, and you really take it back perfectly to the science. You, Dr. John are a "100 percent an all-in doctor". Dr. John, what is the easiest way to find out more about you?

Dr. John:

If you go to www.dontcutmykid.com that is a landing page for the book, and my practice website is also on there, all my social media connects are there and then through my practice website you got my email and even my cell phone, so do not hesitate for anything. Reach out to me, if you have a question about anything or just want to jam about something.

Dr. Bard:

This is the doctor's doctor, and he's "living the dream". He's lived the dream as he continues to reinvent himself, which I love because there's so many life lessons that he offers and more. Do yourself an incredible favor, get in touch and get him into your world in some which way, shape, or form. Dr. John, you are such a gift to chiropractic, you are such a gift to baseball, to parents, to families and to your patients as well.

HERE ARE THE BULLET-POINT TAKEAWAYS:

#1 - His father "Tommy John" became the namesake of the most common surgery for baseball players known as "The Tommy John Surgery" which is the surgical repair to the ulnar collateral ligament.

#2- His father "Tommy John" had 288 major league baseball career wins in 26 seasons with both the Los Angeles Dodgers and The New York Yankees putting him far in the top 1% all time. The surgery performed by the L.A. Dodgers physician, Dr. Frank Jobe was considered at that time purely experimental. If the procedure failed, Tommy John was preparing to learn to throw the knuckle ball from Hall of fame Pitcher Hoyt Wilhelm who had 21-year career in major league baseball.

#3 - Injuries and the need for the surgery has now reached epidemic proportions in youth sports. Concussions are up 500%. ACL surgeries in six to eighteen-year olds is up 60% in the last twenty years. Dr. James Andrews, a renowned Orthopedic surgeon now has over 40% of his practice geared towards children. Over 57% of the "Tommy John" Surgery takes place in 15-19-year-old athletes.

#4- Dr. John teaches in his book "Minimize Injury / Maximize Performance" that the power lies within the hands of the parents and how parents can take charge and control with respect to building a better and healthier child athlete.

#5 - The youth sports industry is over a 15 billion dollar a year industry and Dr. John advocates that education of proper and healthier choices begins in the home first.

#6 - Dr. John started as a multi-sport athlete himself and was given a Division 1 scholarship to Furman University in South Carolina. He later played in the Cape Cod league and as a pitcher too, signed a major league contract with the Los Angeles Dodgers.

#7- After a medical complication from an Arthrogram procedure for his shoulder, he stopped playing baseball and went full bore into studying to become a Chiropractor when he noted that all the athletes that he was personally training always healed better when they were receiving Chiropractic care and he then decided to make this his career as a Doctor of Chiropractic.

#8 - He advocates letting all of his patients know that he is right there with them every step of the way in their treatment, both inside and outside of his office. He wants his patients to know that he is intricately involved in their healing and serves as a role model for all his patients.

#9 - His office is an harmonious sanctuary for both his patients and himself with no clocks, salt lamps, special lighting and ocean pictures on the walls. He has created a true healing center.

#10 - His website is www.DontCutMyKid.com which serves as an educational tool for so many.

13

WELLNESS PRACTICE SUCCESS –
(DR. RAJ GUPTA)

Read about: DR. RAJ GUPTA & DISCOVER how he has created a 20,000 square foot GO-TO WELLNESS Practice and 1 of the PREMIER Wellness Centers in America. Learn how he has created a Health Care MALL of WELLNESS Services for a myriad of conditions successfully. The author of "The Wellness Solution" learn how he has positioned himself and his WELLNESS Practice to be at the FRONT of the PACK for years to come.

Dr. Bard:

We have somebody who I could say, he's very special. I could say, he's pretty incredible. I'll probably run out of superlatives on the show but I want to welcome our incredible guest, here today, joining us live on the Dr. Success Spotlight Show, the author of the *Wellness Center Solution* and more. Welcome to the show, Dr. Raj Gupta.

Dr. Gupta:

Hey doc, thanks you so much for having me. It's my honor, thank you very much; you're so kind.

Dr. Bard:

Not only are you the author of this incredible book, which we're going to dive right into but you're also the president and founder of an incredible company known as "Soul Focus". With soul being spelled S-O-U-L, which is really kind of a statement in and of itself. I think it's really interesting in the sense that if you look at the tagline for your book, the *Wellness Center Solution*, the tagline for your book is how physicians can transform their practices, their income and their lives. When we talk about chiropractic, we always talk about one key word that is parallel to chiropractic. That word is, "alignment". I will tell you that you will learn of an alignment between what Dr. Gupta's vision is and his business model, that really is in direct alignment with absolutely the theme of the Dr. Success Spotlight Show, which is how doctors are able to create profit, freedom and fun.

I don't know what came first when they say the chicken or the egg. I'm not going to tell you what came first. All I'm going to just tell you is that it is in complete harmony of what you've created for not just an alignment with the Dr. Success Spotlight Show but really in alignment for the entire profession of chiropractic. Now, right out of the gate in your book Dr. Gupta, you addressed the "perception versus the reality" of being a doctor. For those who don't know I can absolutely tell you that there is a difference. You nailed this perfectly, where you talk about the perception and the perception being obviously the prestige, higher income, serving countless multitudes of sick people versus the reality of a lack of referrals from medical professionals and student loan debt and business debt and lack of insurance reimbursement. You attacked this right from the beginning and the thing I think that set you apart above and beyond the call of duty is how you have defined wellness. Can you speak a little bit of your definition of wellness in the chiropractic model?

Dr. Gupta:

Well, that's awesome and thank you again and you're absolutely correct. Today, there's all kinds of glitz and glamour associated with being a physician. Unfortunately, physicians are one of the only professions or professionals that are making less money every year. Typically, during your career, each year you go on and the more proficient you become, you make more money. That's just not true in healthcare today. With insurance company reimbursements cut, it's difficult to survive. The glitz and the glamour that is portrayed through media just isn't true any longer. I believe there is a national trend towards wellness in our country. People are starting to get the big idea. What's most important to me is that people are starting to take accountability for their own health and I don't want to give Americans too much credit because they're doing due to the all mighty dollar. Insurance deductibles and out-of-pocket costs have gone up significantly for the average.

Now, the average Joe is starting to realize, I better take better care of myself to save myself money? Whatever the reason, now is the time. We've always had a foot in the door, but now as chiropractors, we are able to kick that door open for two reasons. One, the opioid epidemic is real. There are hundreds of thousands of people each day dealing with this. In fact, something that is really sad is this. I brought tears to the eyes of my staff this morning when I brought it to their attention but in my town here at New Jersey, outside of the municipal center, they have flags and a sign that said, 1,691 people have died this year in the state of New Jersey as a result of overdose to opioids or drug abuse. What's sad about that is forget about the number being shown. What is most sad about that is that I drove by that sign last week and it was 1,691.

When I drove by this week, it was 1,721. In one week, it went from 1,691 to 1,721. That's how many more people died in the state of New Jersey in one week. So, if the opioid epidemic isn't enough to bring in wellness. It is a national trend for people to want to get healthy. So now is the time for chiropractors to kicking in that door and say, we've been screaming this from the rooftops for hundreds of years, now is our time. I believe, wellness includes diet, rest, exercise, of course adjustments and mental attitude. By managing each one of those aspects equally, people can reach their ultimate productivity levels and energy levels. It's our time doc.

Dr. Bard:

So, in other words, it is okay to D-R-E-A-M and that is your acronym actually in your book. Now, what you will notice right away and it screams, not shouts, it screams out how profound, how simple and how easy you've taken the convoluted, the confused, the complicated and you've made it super simple. That is your magic, Dr. Gupta, in the sense that if you asked Chiropractors to speak of the word wellness, especially in chiropractic circles and you get 100 chiropractors in the room, you're going to get 100 different definitions. However, what you've captured, so perfectly is your ability to number one, package this. Number two, present it. Number three, to promote it. We're going to call those the three P's here today and number four, how to profit from it, which is the fourth P.

I think it's so interesting because right out of the gate in your book, if you look at the military as an example or even a sports example, it's often the case if you notice what they'll actually do is they'll break somebody down only to really build them back up. When they build them back up, they build them up bigger, they build them up stronger, they build them up faster and better. You do this very well in your book, whereby you actually go the illusion that doctors have when they get involved and say, gee, I think it's great to become a doctor to reality and then to victory. What I would love for you to do, is to share how you have created a wellness model that is an A to Z comprehensive approach that is the cleanest, simplest, most fun wellness model that I've seen to date.

Dr. Gupta:

Well, thank you. So, I started with the acronym D-R-E-A-M. I've been preaching about DREAM, ever since I graduated chiropractic school. I wanted to create a wellness center that fired in all cylinders on every letter of DREAM. So, for diet, we do functional medicine, we do nutritional counseling. We have to eat properly. We have you exercise properly. We get that stress off your nerves so you could sleep better. The greatest thing about DREAM is that each letter affects the other letter. If you're mental status is okay, you're going to sleep through the night. If you're a mental status is not okay, chances are you may wake up in the middle of the night and unable to sleep. So, to diet, rest, exercise, we have a full fitness facility, a full-service gym where we do personal training and group exercise classes. We have gym memberships, we have a eucalyptus steam room and infrared sauna in the locker rooms with Italian tile that we imported.

All for the experience, so you can enjoy your workout better and you're pampered. With adjustments, of course, that goes without saying is going to reduce the stress on your nervous system and allow you to function at a higher capacity. If you have a landline phone connection as opposed to a bad wireless connection. For "M", we have the spa as a mental attitude of getting a massage or a facial. We have a massage and facial club just like Massage Envy. In this spa, we offer MediSpa services, so it's a look good, feel good experience. Thus, we have everything in full focus in the wellness center. It's firing on all those cylinders. Again, you said it perfectly. Wellness is a buzzword in our profession but there's a guy that has a wellness center down the block from me that is just chiropractic and massage. That's not wellness to me. If you're going to have a full wellness center, you better fire on all cylinders. To take care of that person from head to toe and I believe it's us as chiropractors to have been put on this earth to do that.

Dr. Bard:

We are joined here on the live broadcast of the Dr. Success Spotlight Show with the amazing Dr. Raj Gupta, who is really, if you don't know about him, then get ready because this is truly one of the upcoming rising stars. He is to a degree the best-kept secret in the wellness business I have to share with you, Dr. Gupta that when I read your book, *The Wellness Center Solution*, I actually felt about a third of the way into your book, and I've never said this before that you wrote this book specifically for me, personally. The reason I felt that way was because you did something so incredibly powerful and that's you're genius.

My background actually happened to be in the health club business. I was a long time N.P.C. (National Physique Committee) state judge. I've been a bodybuilding judge for many years. I'm actually an IFBB professional judge with IFBB Physique America as well. This hit such a cord with me because of what you did. Dr. Gupta you took this model and you made a perfect collaboration, a perfect synergy between the health club model and the Soul Focus Model and you packaged it for chiropractors, which is your incredible genius. Can you share a little bit about how you've put this together?

Dr. Gupta:

Of course, and actually doc, I did really did write it to you as you're a chiropractor. I wrote it for our entire profession. We need as chiropractors to diversify. We can't be solely reliant on insurance company reimbursement because as I mentioned at the beginning of our discussion that is what is constantly being cut and reduced. So, if you're relying solely on insurance company reimbursement that means your income's going down every year. So, you need to diversify, and bringing in the best cash services that match what we do that is in alignment with what our purpose is, is diet and exercise. The spa really serves to just help people to relax. So, I thought of creating wellness centers where you walk in and the first thing is the trickling of water and spa music. I built the place so that people can get a one-hour vacation every time they walked through the door.

I'm happy to say, I have massage chairs throughout the waiting rooms, and entry ways and fountains everywhere. I am very happy to say that oftentimes I will walk into Sole Focus and there will be a person in a massage chair and I'll see the same person at the end of my work day, meaning that they were here the entire time I was in the office. People use the wellness center as their oasis, their escape, and that's why I built it. I want people to be able to distress, and come to the haven, where they feel that they are being pampered as it's all about them.

So, wellness and how chiropractors are able to dive into wellness is very simple. You don't have to have a 20,000 square foot facility like I have. You are very easily able to start doing some nutritional counseling. You can start offering protein shakes or protein bars leading your patients down the path of health and wellness when it comes to diet. The massage and facial club are something that you could do that off hours. Even if you don't have enough rooms in your practice. There are numerous different exercises that go hand in hand with PT. You can bring in personal trainers to use your facility, when you're not in it to do personal training. Specifically, on the weekends when most people have time to do so. So, wellness to me is something that I feel is the vehicle that our profession can use to become a household name. It's imperative to me to rewire the American mind out of this sick care model to a healthcare model. The way we do that, is to show them how to get healthy. No one has ever done it and I believe it's up to the chiropractors. It is our job to do it.

Dr. Bard:

I was really mesmerized and I was intrigued by how you put the entire Soul Focus Model together and again, emphasis on the word, S-O-U-L. One of the things, I think you've done incredibly well, is your ability to be able to change and your ability to adapt to the healthcare market as it exists. What we often talk about is something known as what we call the "mall of healthcare services", which is in essence really what you've put together but more than putting it together, you've really approached this from a five-star approach. You put together a five-star facility. You've attracted a five-star team. You're attracting patients both far and wide. I think it's interesting because if you look, for example, at the LA Fitness Model and if you look at the 24-hour fitness model, and the Gold Gym model and the lifetime fitness model, you start to see that the demand for these types of services has really never been better and it's never been higher.

Now, one of the things that I noticed that you do and I have a very strong feeling that nothing you do is by luck, nothing you do is by coincidence. Everything you do is by structure, is by focus, is by determination, is by clarity and it's based upon an end result. One of the things I think that is really powerful is how you've created value for what you term "your guests", not your patients. I think it's very interesting for the number of individuals that are exposed to your incredible five-star mall of healthcare. Can you elaborate a little bit more on the difference and the bridge from going from guest to patient?

Dr. Gupta:

When you use the word patient, you get the white coat vision. When you're talking about the word guest, you feel like a guest in a hotel and depending upon the environment of the hotel, which is five stars, being a guest has its privileges. So again, I want a patient or a guest to feel pampered when they come through the doors. I'm very happy to say that they do. I see guests here for longer periods of time that I come to work and that's how I know it's their hang out, it's their solitude and the place where they're able to get away.

So, what you have to do to create that environment or atmosphere is very simple. You want paint colors in the center that evokes relaxation, tones, and feelings. You want the spa music. You want people to have a juice bar or a a smoothie bar. We sell prepared foods, but you know what? It's not garbage. It's all great foods. They're mainly organic, they're gluten free. They have no preservatives. They only last a couple of days but people know now that they can come to Soul Focus and we have free Wi-Fi and high top end massage chairs.

We encourage them to come and make this their haven. We don't want people to come in and leave. I want them to fire in all cylinders. One of the happiest moments of my life was just recently, I was in on a Saturday treating patients, filling in for my associates as he was away for the weekend. I had a patient who ran over from the gym. She says, oh my gosh, I heard Dr. Raj is in the hallway. Am I able to get an adjustment? However, I've got to get an adjustment quickly because my 10:00 group class starts. I'm like, come on in, so she gets on the table. She's so happy to get adjusted from me. She's like, doc, I'll be back at 10:45 at the end of the class because I have acupuncture scheduled. I'm like, right on. She goes on and she has a massage and I'm having lunch at 1:00 here. I'm like, man, that's the big idea and why I built this place. She said to me with a tear in her eye, thank you for building it.

Dr. Bard:

What you'll notice is in Dr. Gupta is your ability to and this is what resonates about you that makes you so incredibly magnetic, so incredibly attractive, both inside and out, in the sense that you are a master, master communicator. What I love what you've done is how you really integrated and built your relationships with personal trainers, which I think is an incredible. It's really to some degree, almost like one of the great secrets in our profession and you've mastered this. I'll tell you that the integrated practice model is absolutely better than ever as you, Dr. Gupta have designed it and I think the key here is collaboration, as we talked about before. That collaboration is really the key. It is in your model, it is in your team approach. It is not an insurance-driven model, but much, much more of a cash-based model, where your guests and your patients definitely value your care on the highest level.

You put together this all-star team of nurse practitioners, chiropractors, physical therapists, medical doctors, nutritionists, acupuncturists and more. This is so good, man that I want to make an appointment at your center because it shines so bright. What I wanted to ask you is this as you are a torch carrier for the wellness model on the grand stage, the right way, the best way, the smartest way and the most profitable way. You've done this, so incredibly well, in your humble, in your modest genius. If I'm a doctor reading this and I'm saying, gee, he's answered so many questions, but I definitely am so curious, how can I get more information? How can I tap in to his neurology? How can I tap in and get a piece of Dr. Gupta in some which way, shape or form, either in a lecture, in a book? Personally, would you be so kind as to share your best contact information, and more importantly, how they can also get ahold of your book?

Dr. Gupta:

Of course, it's my pleasure. My website is www.drrajgupta.com Most importantly, if you're interested in implementing wellness services, go to the website. I have a free download with 10 secrets on how to implement wellness services in your office today. A very simple, very easy, very straightforward way so that you could start diversifying immediately and bringing cash services into your office. On my website, you'll be able to learn a whole lot more about me. Get some tips on how to implement wellness services and the biggest tip I can give you is as a chiropractor be on purpose, be genuine and you will attract not only the right team that follows you through the gates of hell but you will attract the right patients who want to take advice from you, and you too, will have a very successful, prosperous career, and be happy that you became a chiropractor, which I know that I was born to do.

Dr. Bard:

Dr. Raj Gupta, an incredible doctor, really an incredible family man. Let me tell you something, this guy is fun and I'm not kidding. When you see him, the first thing that's going to happen is your mouth is going to start to open up and the reason it's going to open, it's going to smile because this guy gives off a buzz, a vibe and energy because he's heart driven and I can't recommend getting this book strong enough, *The Wellness Center Solution*. One of the things that I was blown away by which is another little bonus is one of the things he does in his book, is he includes pictures in his book which shows his model. He is a pool of knowledge when it comes to helping chiropractors, educating chiropractors, motivating chiropractors, and delivering the goods on something that has been so evasive for so many chiropractors to try to capture correctly, which is the wellness model. He is such a Star. We're so lucky, so fortunate, so honored, so privileged to have had Dr. Gupta with us here today on the Dr. Success Spotlight Show.

HERE ARE THE BULLET-POINT TAKEAWAYS:

#1 - Based in New Jersey, Dr. Gupta is the author of the book, "The Wellness Solution".

#2 - He is the President of SOUL FOCUS which teaches Doctors "how-to" create a successful Wellness practice that is focused on service and maximum patient satisfaction.

#3 - He believes that the opioid epidemic has created a shift in the marketplace for patients seeking Wellness based services and taking accountability for their own health.

#4 - He provides everything from Chiropractic to Functional Medicine to Nutritional Counseling to a Full Fitness Facility as well as a Full Med-Spa including a Smoothie bar, a Prepared Foods section and a Yoga studio.

#5 - He believes that Chiropractors should diversify to position themselves at the front of the Wellness line and allow patients the opportunity to go from a Sick-care model to a Wellness-care model.

#6 - He introduces his Wellness practice and its related services to individuals that he terms initially as "Guests". From there, they then have the opportunity to transition into becoming a patient within his practice.

#7 - He believes that the practice aesthetics that include the colors, the tones, the music, etc. all contribute to a soothing, relaxing, inviting environment for his guests and patients.

#8 - He put together his All-Star team of Chiropractors, Nurse Practitioners, Medical Doctors, Physical Therapists, Nutritionists, Personal Trainers, Massage Therapist, Estheticians, Acupuncturists and more.

#9 - Patients often spend entire half-days and full-days taking part in a host of the different services Dr. Gupta provides in his Wellness practice.

#10 - Dr. Gupta has created a One-Stop shop of Wellness services, all under one roof and makes sure that his entire team have a "Soul-Focus" on maximizing the guest and patient experience for the best.

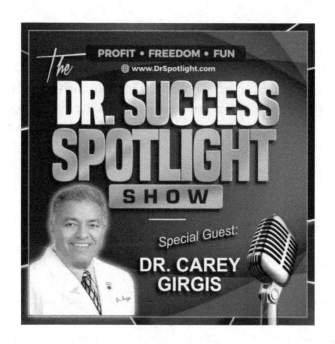

14

LASER PRACTICE SUCCESS – (DR. CAREY GIRGIS)

Read about: DR. CAREY GIRGIS & DISCOVER how he has created a GO-TO LASER THERAPY Practice and one of the PREMIER Laser Therapy Treatment Centers in America. Learn how he utilizes LASER THERAPY for a myriad of conditions successfully and how he has positioned himself and his Laser Treatment Center to be at the FRONT of the PACK for years to come.

Dr. Bard:

You are in for great opportunity here today to learn one of the real stars in the world of technology, specifically in the world of laser. We want to welcome, I'm not going to call him the laser king. I'm just going to call him the laser prince for today. Welcome to the show, Dr. Girgis.

Dr. Girgis:

Thank you. I'm honored to be on your show.

Dr. Bard:

This is really special for a lot of reasons. This is dedicated to the doctors who are very curious about the utilization of how to make laser successful in terms of results and successful in terms of profitability. Let me give you a little background, on who the prince and soon-to-be the king of laser is, and his name is Dr. Carey Girgis.

He has done something incredible and what he's done is he's utilized technology by bridging both the care of both disc and joint correctly, the right way. The simple fact is that he has not one, not two, not three, not four, but he actually has nine spinal decompression tables. As you know the only way you ever get to that is something called "supply and demand". In other words, you don't roll out of bed and get nine tables. What happens is you start with one table, you fill it up, you get a second table, you fill it up, you get a third table, you fill it up, and you see how the momentum of success really works.

What also happens though, is initially, he started with one laser. Then, "supply and demand", the same exact thing happened. He had to add a second, he had to add a third, he had to add a fourth and soon to even add more. So, the real magic here is learning how and why he has been so incredibly successful in laser. So, Dr. Girgis, there's a lot of different things I can ask you, but what I wanted to ask you, first and foremost is why you feel that laser has allowed you from a technology point of view to open up to a larger market?

Dr. Girgis:

Well, it's really simple. First of all, I just want to thank you and Dr. Kaplan for insisting on me to try the laser because I was a slow learner. When I was told about laser, I have had experience in the past, where a salesman would come to my office trying to sell me a laser and I looked at it and I treated the patients. It was like a flash light and it just didn't make any sense. I resisted having to try it. I wanted something with the results, something that produce results, that the patients can appreciate. I can see the evidence right there. Something that is evidence based and a scientific method that I could use to improve the quality of my care to the patients. Obviously, you and Dr. Kaplan have emphasized the fact that you want us to be better doctors, not just another clinic or another clinician but you have emphasized to be a better doctor.

By being a better doctor, we're able to produce better results from our patients to get greater benefits. So, I really thank you guys both for insisting that with me. Not all lasers are the same. I use the Microlight. The wavelength is the most important aspect of the laser as is the depth of penetration. The FDA classifies lasers into three categories. Class four which is the surgical laser. The ones that produce heat, evaporates the skin and actually coagulates the soft tissue and that's used in surgery. That laser is not the most effective in my opinion. That's because of the danger that it could cause to the patients. There are two classes, Class A & Class B. The class A is the low-level laser, but it's only use is for surface types of penetration on the skin.

The class 3B, which is the Microlight 830 has 830 nanometers. It has a depth of penetration for up to a five to seven centimeters into the body. So, it's able to reach great depth than the average laser and that's why it has the greatest benefit in it. So, laser in my practice has been a tremendous expansion. I felt so bad that I didn't use it initially. I didn't listen to you sooner because some of the patients had not appreciated the benefits that today would have if I'd had a done it before. Laser has been a tremendous addition to my practice because of the depth of penetration.

The Laser reduces the amount of time for healing and for redness and inflammation, accelerating the mitochondrial effect of the cells to regenerate and heal tissue. It's an incredible piece of equipment. I utilize it with just about every condition that comes in. When a patient has pain, cuts, bruises, whether it be shingles or it would be cold sores. I've treated patients with shingles, and the condition lasted less than 10 visits, and it went away including blisters, including pain, burning sensation, all of it gone. It's incredible.

We had a patient who fell on her face, riding a bike, busted two teeth and broke the tooth and busted her lip. I treated her with a laser. The symptoms disappeared and when she went back to the dentist. He said, "What happened to your hematoma?" She said, "I used laser." He said, "You're using what?" She told him, the cold laser treatment that I used on her that got rid of the hematoma immediately. Within three visits actually, it was gone. Although, there was scar, the contusion that was on her face disappeared and I have pictures. I took pictures before and after. I have done this, case after case. I've learned now to take pictures before, during and after a condition. I've treated tons of them. It's incredible. I really thank you guys for helping me focused on that technology.

Dr. Bard:

It is incredible, Dr. Girgis, and what really is incredible is you. You are incredible. I'm going to tell you why. The reason why is because these are my takeaways from what you just shared with our readers. My takeaway right from the beginning is really three things. Number one as the saying goes, "when the student is ready, the teacher will appear". For so many patients, who go to a doctor's office, go to a chiropractor's office the fact of the matter is, they're a little unsure, they're a little reserved, they may be a little bit scared. The reason why is because they're not 100 percent sure that the treatment may be effective because as you know, when you're talking about a class 3 or class 3B laser that this is a non-thermal laser. So, in essence, we know obviously that you can get treatment with a host of other medical procedures and case in point, an X-ray. Obviously, we know that you can take an X-ray and you don't feel that. There are so many things you don't necessarily have to feel, but you know how effective it is based upon one word. That word is results. So, what I love, right at the top of the list for me, personally is how you went really from a skeptic in laser to an incredible student in laser to an incredible specialist in laser. My second takeaway is It's no coincidence that all three of those words begin with the letter "S." You went from skeptic to student to specialist. What made you a specialist in laser is obvious. What made you a specialist is your desire to help sick people get better naturally, noninvasively, cost effectively and successfully by utilizing technology to the best degree.

My third takeaway was I loved when you said that you actually now instead of just opening up to the musculoskeletal world, you've really found success in opening up to potentially based upon medical necessity opening up to larger market share by what would be considered potentially non-musculoskeletal conditions through the utilization of laser. You take pictures. You do pre and post. So, the reality is this. If I'm a patient and I'm a skeptical patient and I'm not sure and I see your degree of specificity, I see your diagnostic ability, I see the fact that you're measuring things in the beginning because you're going to measure things at the end, well that's what a great doctor does. You my friend, are a great doctor and we love that about you. So, my question to you is this. Now, one of the things you've done so instinctively well, is you've been able to conjoin the utilization of laser therapy with the treatment of spinal disc conditions. Can you share or talk a little bit about that with our readers with respect to how you utilize laser to effectively assist the healing of spinal discs from spinal decompression and more?

Dr. Girgis:

Absolutely. That's how it really started when I was introduced to the Laser and began to use it. The effect is incredible on self-healing and reducing inflammation. I thought we're just going to help the patient feel better.

I then realized that because of the depth of penetration of that, because Microlight is the deepest penetrating cold laser in the market that we know of, because of that, it is able to reach the disc because in spinal decompression therapy we are doing it non-surgically. We are trying to speed up healing. Not just only reducing the bulging material but decompression brings in the nutrients and the oxygen and fluid back into the disc and rehydrates it and restores as much as possible to the health of the disc. There could be micro tears in the annular fiber, the annulus in the disc itself. The wall where they have the micro tears needs to be closed up. The laser has been tremendous in their ability to be able to close up those micro tears to heal the walls from the damage that it has time. So, because of that, it has produced an incredible and better effect as it speeds up the healing and closing of these wounds. In addition to that, that's when I ran into the other conditions when patients would come in and say, "I have shoulder pain, elbow pain, wrist pain, knee pain". I began to implement and if I was able to help the disc to improve the condition, why wouldn't that take place at other joints? I began to study, and I began to research. I didn't stop right there as I wanted to learn more about it because I want to be as knowledgeable as possible and to be able to teach this stuff instead of just learning it for myself.

It's incredible because I wanted to absorb that knowledge to know that I'm doing the right thing for our patients. As a result, we're getting to see all these different conditions. There's a myriad of research that's being done with a major university, which is Harvard University, New England. Research has been done in cold laser therapy for a myriad of other conditions. This is going to be within the next 5 to 10 years. There is going to be Lasers for use in all clinics, from medical clinics to chiropractic clinics because of the amazing effects with no side effects ever to speak about. It manages pain, reduces pain and it accelerates the healing. It increases the cellular metabolism. Cell repair is what we want to repair the disc and other soft tissue. It reduces inflammation and edema. It helps reduce the healing time instead of spending weeks and months to heal. It reduces the amount of time and it doesn't interfere with patient's daily activities.

I love the hands-free applications of the Laser. You don't have to spend the time to hold the laser or monitor it because it's a cold laser. You just place it, then you walk away. So, it's limited as far as the time that is spent on the condition. So, it's better efficiency for our staff and our office as we're not using any medication. We are able to conduct that activity on a daily basis without any problem.

The cold laser is amazing because it's not a lot of expense. When I bought that first laser, I was very reluctant. I didn't know how to manage to pay the cost when I first started. I paid for my first laser within three weeks. It was paid off. That's why I have four lasers. As a matter of fact, I have the fifth in the mail because I need a fifth one, so we we're working on it. It is very safe with no side effects to speak of at all. It is amazing, and I love it. I thank you for introducing it to me and giving me the courage to go ahead and start using it.

Dr. Bard:

I love it and what I love about it is, number one, your enthusiasm for the technology of laser. At the end of the day, this will always come down to one simple thing and what it comes down to was one word, RESULTS! It's always been about results and I think that's one of the incredible things here that you've been able to generate, as you're adding even more lasers, which I think is incredible. One of the things that we've discussed privately, and now to be able to share with our reader, which is one for doctors that are in the business of laser to also be in the business of disc. It's amazing how the two kind of work together.

One of the things that you've shared with me before is the simple fact that when you're treating a patient, often you will use the verbiage of two simple words. Those words are when you're treating a patient who has a disc with laser that you like to use, the verbiage of what is known as "heal and seal," which really is a great explanation in terms of what light therapy is doing. How it's affecting the mitochondria, how that's affecting red blood cells, how that's affecting oxygen, how that's affecting better healing and creating healthier cells. We know that healthy cells will equal healthy tissue. When you have healthy tissue, especially in avascular areas like spinal discs, then anything you can do to bring in more blood flow, more oxygen and more healing in terms of the good stuff, that's the beauty of laser. I know that there's readers here in abundance at this moment, and a number of them may have had, for lack of a better way to say it, Dr. Girgis, a challenge and when I say a challenge, what I really mean is maybe they didn't get out of the gate as quick as they wanted in practice. Maybe they opened the practice and they got beat up along the way. Maybe they had a bad business situation. Maybe they didn't have their marketing dialed in. Maybe, maybe, maybe and at the end of the day, they feel like they're behind the eight ball. You, my friend, came from the most incredible background and that was from driving an ambulance in New York to the incredible, incredible success that you've had.

So, in closing, is there anything that you can share with our readers in terms of where you personally were able to dig deep and to be able to really reinvent yourself, to create momentum correctly, to move into the most profitable business model? By utilizing obviously laser, but more importantly, how were you able to overcome the challenges that you had when you first got started to the incredible success that you're having now, can you share that?

Dr. Girgis:

Absolutely. And you know, I thought it would have been a monumental task to do this because really our colleges have failed in teaching this and that is the business aspect. Most colleges have really produced excellent technicians and clinicians and diagnosticians. They're able to do the therapy and do the best job possible to produce the best result as technicians, but they failed to teach us the business aspect. Some people have said to have an office, it's 50 percent the skill of the doctor and 50 percent business. I say, it's 100 percent, either one. You have 100 percent business skills as far as success and being able to be successful Chiropractor and to help your patients. There's also a 100 percent business aspect and that is the part that is missing from clinicians. I knew I was going to be a good doctor and started my office, but soon, I had no real deep knowledge at all of how to run a practice. You know, as a matter of fact, all athletes that are successful, they all have coaches. So why would they have coaches if they're at the pinnacle of their athletic skill? It's because the coach is able to see things from a different point of view and able to point you to the right direction. I have tried over the years, multiples coaches, I could name them. However, practice management groups that I joined and I tried them all, it was just a pay monthly and get a bunch of raw stuff but, no real substantial benefit that I could have until I met you and Dr. Kaplan.

You guys have changed our lives because I was able to get the real practice that I always wanted. You held our hands. You took us right under your wing, so to speak, and with your coaching you got us through the difficult times. I was almost ready to quit chiropractic practice because I thought chiropractic is wonderful and really good, but if it was that good, why aren't people flooding our offices? Why aren't they coming? We do such a good job and it's really because of lack of knowing how to approach the patients correctly. You taught us that step exactly and that exploded our practice and it's incredible. You gave us a new breath to breathe and you gave a new vision and new excitement. Now, I can't wait to go to the office to see the patients and see the results. The most incredible part is the fact the patients keep coming back and they keep referring patients to us.

Much of our practice comes now from word of mouth. The people are telling others to send this patient to us because of the business principles that you've taught us and showed us how to do it really practically. I can pick up the phone and call you any time. You answer a phone, even if you're on a golf course. It's incredible to know that we have the coaches that have always held our hands with this. They care about us. They require us to do things the tough way. You crack the whip when it's necessary, and you mend our wound when we are hurting. It's really amazing how you're so sensitive to our needs, and you've been a great help and you're stuck with me forever. You know, so here it is. I'm really grateful to you. That's how we were successful because we needed the right coaches to help us get through previous tough times. You're teaching us the things that the colleges have not been able to produce. You guys had the experience, you've been there, you've been very successful yourselves. You're able to take that and transfer your success and to show us exactly what to do. The questions that I would be baffled about and not knowing what to do, we simply call you up and you have the answer at the tip of your tongue where you saved us a ton of time and effort and I'm so very grateful to you.

Dr. Bard:

Well, both Dr. Kaplan and I always say that "we are the lucky ones". The reason we're the lucky ones is because of you, Dr. Girgis, and your incredible wife Sally, and it really is the highest calling. Listen, it's fun to win, it is about winning, and doctors are in competition with nobody but themselves. There's an old saying per Dr. Kaplan which is, "When you can see the invisible, you can do the impossible." I think when you surround yourself with people that are helping you see the invisible, then you could do things that have never been done before. Set new practice records, reach a whole new audience, love life. You have a very crystallized, very focused dedication to one thing and that is helping sick people get better the right way. That is the magic of sharing that together as a whole as we do with all our incredible family of doctors. These are the best of the best in the country and it's such an honor to have you on this show.

If you're curious and you want to meet Dr. Girgis, live and in person, the easiest place to find him, believe it or not, is at the National Spinal Decompression Certification Program at Parker University. He doesn't miss any of these. He is a student of the game. He comes to every single one of them. He is really such a giver, such a great teacher, such a lover of life and we just love having him there.

HERE ARE THE BULLET-POINT TAKEAWAYS:

#1 - Based in Westerville, Ohio he uses Laser Therapy to bridge the care between Spinal Disc patients and Joint patients correctly. He was initially resistant to getting started with Laser Therapy as he wanted something for his patients based upon science and results and he found that in Laser Therapy.

#2 - Not all Lasers are the same. The wavelength and depth of penetration is the key.

#3 - He explains the differences between Class 1 thru Class 4 Lasers. He prefers the Class 3.

#4 - He utilizes Laser Therapy for a host of other conditions outside the conventional musculoskeletal applications and is amazed at the results for tissue healing.

#5 - He takes pictures of before, during and after of his Laser patients to demonstrate his results more effectively.

#6 - He prefers utilizing Laser Therapy with his Spinal Disc patients. Based upon the depth of penetration by bringing in nutrients, oxygen and fluid back into the disc.

#7 - He is contributing to Laser Research Studies for a myriad of conditions based upon the science, the safety and the fact that there are no side effects.

#8 - He prefers the "hands-free" option that some Lasers provide which is much more efficient for his patients and staff.

#9 - By using the proper Laser verbiage with his patients he can educate them on the highest level. When it comes to Spinal Disc care with Laser, he routinely talks about the "HEAL & SEAL" benefit of Laser Light Therapy.

#10 - Prior to becoming a Doctor, he was a former ambulance driver in New York City. He found success in practice by not approaching it as a 50-50 balance between clinical care and business but instead approaches it from a 100% "ALL-IN" approach to both. He believes in finding the right Coach that believes and teaches that same concept and striving to become the BEST!!!

15

CONVERSION SUCCESS –
(DR. CHRIS LAURIA)

Read about: DR. CHRIS LAURIA & DISCOVER how he has mastered PATIENT CONVERSION Success. He has simplified the process and shares how he handles the process of Patient Lead to Patient Conversion to Patient Success. He shares how he handles Facebook Patient Leads and gives insight as to how he has set records in this amazing interview.

Dr. Bard:

Welcome everybody to the Dr. Success Spotlight Show. I want to welcome you. We have such a special doctor with us today. He is the one, the only, Dr. Chris Lauria from Roanoke, Virginia. Welcome to the show Dr. Lauria.

Dr. Lauria:

Hi, Dr. Bard. Thank you very much. I'm excited to be on, I'm excited for the opportunity to be a part of this.

Dr. Bard:

I'm going to share with our readers a little bit about your background. You are from Roanoke, Virginia. You are really onto something very powerful and something very special. You've done something very unique in this profession and you've gone from obviously the pinnacle in sports on a collegiate level to really reaching the pinnacle in practice right now. We're going to dive into one of the things that you are really doing some groundbreaking work with in terms of conversions of what we would call the successful transition of a patient lead to an actual patient. But first things first, I was very curious, you could have practiced anywhere in the country. Why did you end up practicing in Roanoke, Virginia?

Dr. Lauria:

Well, I had to follow my wife on that one. So, I graduated in Atlanta, but I met my wife when I played baseball at the University of North Carolina. She's a North Carolina Grad, also from the state of North Carolina. So, I went back up to New Jersey after that. I'm second generation. I practiced up there for about three and a half years and then after spending eight years in the south and undergrad then in chiropractic school, my wife wanted to get back to the south, it was tough for her to be up in the Jersey attitude. We ended up in Roanoke, which at that time was about halfway in between both sets of parents. So, that's what drove me down here and pulled into Roanoke. Here I am now 21 years later.

Dr. Bard:

This is really a magical thing because as I've gotten to know you, and I am so really, really blessed and fortunate to have watched this evolution of how you started in practice and you sent me the coolest thing a couple of weeks ago. You sent me a message that said, I've been doing this for 25 years. The first 23 have been, a challenge like most, if not all. However, the past two years have really been fantastic and it wasn't always like that. So, in essence, share with a little bit about, what some of the challenges were for you initially when you got started up to the past two years where there has been a real shift in your success?

Dr. Lauria:

Yes, 23 years of trying to find my niche so to speak. I did a lot of high-volume family chiropractic stuff, which was high stress. A lot of people were really not getting paid for the amount of people I was seeing because of the discounts and things like that. I've always been looking for a way to find new patients to build the volume. It was a very stressful time and I was trying to do that continually. Then, with the insurance, just writing notes and upon notes and trying to get accepted for a minimal fee per visit with that part of it, kind of really wore me out. I think a lot of it was identity too.

I was trying to be something that really, really, I wasn't. So, what this has allowed me to do with my new brands and specialty marketing is I've found my niche. Treating people with chronic pain, treating disc problems, learning and having my purpose changed into accepting that that's what I am. The freedom of looking at these people in the eye and knowing that I can help with the various techniques that I have here for them to get out of pain, which ultimately, we worked years thinking about correction, not talking about the pain they're in, with all the subluxation and all that, which was all great.

The bottom line is people want to feel better and if we can help them somehow and, in some way, to improve their quality of life, then we've done well. I have freedom now because people come here and it fills up my office with patients that are happy because of that. I'm having a ton of fun too doing it. It's just been a freeing, freeing feeling the last two years for me. Based on all of that and because I'm so free, I'm making a lot of money without the stress of having the big insurance companies too.

Dr. Bard:

One of the things I love about you, is that you've been able to take your success as an athlete at a very high level at the University of North Carolina, which is a high-level Division One school and as good as it gets as a baseball player. What you've done consciously or subconsciously is you've turned this now into a game and you've turned it into the game of success and the game of winning. I think the key here is your timing. I think your timing is so uncanny in the sense that you are such a great listener, but you're also a great communicator. One of the things, you've done so well in terms of communication is to take what so many doctors have had issues and concerns and problems with, which is handling the new patient lead. In other words, a patient that may have expressed an interest in coming to see you, but now for some reason life got in the way and they didn't show. You my friend have done something special, especially in the world of social media. If you could share a little bit about why you've been able to have such an incredible success with taking the lead and getting that lead to the point where they're excited to show up and they do show up in your reception area. How are you doing that?

Dr. Lauria:

I decided to start this process two to three years ago, when my practice was suffering. I had gotten leads before. I tried everything to try to get patients in but I decided that when I was going to get a lead that I was going to try to minimize my chances of not showing up. So, what happened was with any lead in my office, especially decompression leads through Facebook. Any patient that calls is I handle the new patient call.

196

I don't have my staff do that. I tell the patient, this is Dr. Lauria, you've called our office to sign up for a consultation to see if you're a candidate for our program. I wanted to personally call you because a lot of people have a lot of questions at this point, about our care program and that type of thing. So, you know, then, I follow a certain script to make sure that doesn't get too long. But the personal call from me to the patients has been a game changer. I'll never give that up and it does take time. Every day at 9:00 AM, I've set a timeframe where I'm calling leads every day at 11:00. I'm calling the leads that I get throughout the day. Yeah, some of it is lengthy and that's fine but when these people have spoken to the doctor personally, it makes a difference. Then, when they come through the door, the relationship is already built. Simply because they're wowed that a doctor would call them, on an initial consultation. Plus, I can answer any questions they might have. They're all worried it's from Facebook. Is this a real thing? Are you going to charge me, what is the trick here? However, when I call and have that conversation, I'm able to dispel a lot of those things that are in their mind.

Dr. Bard:

One of the great things you've obviously done so well, is you literally have flipped the script. The reason that I say you flipped the script is, because I know when I started, holy cow, 31 years ago, that it was standard policy on day one. In other words, after the patient was adjusted the first time, what would we do? We would always call them up and explain that better, same or worse is all normal. These were just simple one-minute conversations. Often, they would even go to a recorder, but I've got to tell you, I noticed the difference as probably so many that did it noted that the compliance of these patients was better. We used to talk about what we would always call the P.V.A., the patient visit average. I, like many found that the patient visit average was higher on the patients that I called day one and as time went on, as we've learned. I think, one of the things Dr. Kaplan has done so in his genius, is he took the P.V.A. and instead of patient visit average, it is now officially, "patient value average". That's one of the things, I wanted to talk to you about. If you'd be so kind to share in the sense that what you said before was spot on. The fact that you are a specialist now, if you can talk a little bit of how you've been able to connect the dots between now, disc treatment and nerve treatment that would be awesome. How are you doing it so well now?

Dr. Lauria:

Well, first of all, to back up I'd still call after the first treatment when they get decompression. So, I'm calling them again and then, at this point if someone's struggling after seven visits I'll give them a call on the weekend too. We all know with disc cases and decompression, it can be tough with some people. If I have to make a couple of calls to ensure them that we're moving in the right direction and it might just be, like you said, leaving a message, so when they come in next time that makes a huge difference for me, in compliance and people following through on the program. So, I'm not just calling them once. Some people I'm calling a few times just to reassure them and I don't have the staff do it. As far as going from subluxation or nerve treatment to disc treatment, the brand is the key. I tell everybody that I speak to the minute I became a Disc Centers of America, and I turned my practice signage over, with all my paperwork, thus there's not chiropractic stuff anymore. They know when they walk through the door that I'm a specialist in treating, disc problems, or early disc or whatever it might be.

My entire consultation, I emphasize that this is not chiropractic. You've got to be a candidate for our program, and we're working on herniated to degenerative and bulging discs in the spine. So, everything that they get, everything that I say immediately, brands me as I'm doing something different and that I specialize in disc problems. Then, I have patients that ask me, if we used to be a chiropractic office. Yes, but I've done training. I don't do chiropractic. We specialize in spinal disc problems, so it's the entire brand. Everything I say, everything we do, when they walk in the door, they know that's what they're coming for.

Dr. Bard:

It is so seamless and it is so powerful. To me, the biggest takeaway that I'm getting from you, the real golden nugget here is that you, my friend, are an amazing relationship builder. You build relationships, which is probably the oldest cliché in the business, but at the same time, so few do it well. The real secret to doing it well is crossing the t's and dotting the i's. In other words, a lot of people could be good on a first date. A lot of people could have a good second date. However, after a while, what happens is they get in their comfort zone. They get a little bit lazy. I got to tell you in Chicago, when we got a chance to see you at the National Spinal Decompression Certification and you're sitting there front and center. The real highlight of that whole weekend was having dinner with you, Friday night, and we got a chance to really spend quality time. I'm so excited to see you next time because there's so much that you've got going on that is so positive, so much with your family, so great with your son. You're such an amazing family man, and you just the best part, man, you're so much fun.

Dr. Lauria:

Well, I'm having fun. It wasn't just two and a half to three years ago that it was not fun. It was, simply stress. Where am I going to go? I'm grasping just to make ends meet and trying to get loans to keep things going. It wasn't fun. The certainty now that this has given me, the freedom that it's given me is great. It's been a complete turnaround. It's always been fun but there was a lot of underlying stress behind it, not too long ago. Now, I told someone the other day, I feel like I can take this model if I wanted to open clinics anywhere else in a month and have a booming practice wherever I would want to do it just following this model with what I'm doing now.

Dr. Bard:

Number one, I think you hit it right on the head. The fact is that you're very entrepreneurial. Number two, you think differently than most doctors. You act differently than most doctors. You practice differently than most doctors, and the best part to me about you, Dr. Lauria is you are smelling the roses. You are enjoying your P.T.C., Your "present time consciousness". You're enjoying this part of your life right now, so well deserved, so well earned, and you are the best of the best.

Dr. Lauria:

You can say that. The National Spinal Decompression Certification made me understand what I'm doing well but I've got a lot to learn. Dr. Kaplan always stresses that we want to strive to be the best doctors. I wrote five or six things, then after that last certification that I know I need to do to continue to try to become the best so I'm not resting on anything right now. I've got a way to go.

Dr. Bard:

You're incredibly humble and that's exactly right because you've got your eye on the prize. You've got your calendar time-lined this year that there is another certification in November at Parker University in Dallas. You get a chance to hang out with the guys, with the team, with the Disc Centers of America family and the Concierge Coaches doctors. For us, that's such a highlight and obviously the www.chiro-event.com, which is really my favorite event that we do all year long that's open to every Chiropractor fortunate enough to secure a seat.

We just did one this weekend, and there were doctors from 10 different states in attendance and the amount of emails and texts and phone calls that I've gotten from this past weekend is so over the top. They loved it and it's a similar story. It follows a certain path of similar to your success when you first came the first time to www.TheChiroEvent.com. That's how it started for us is because you came to the Chiro Event in Florida and that was when I had the pleasure to meet you for the first time.

What a great, great story you are Dr. Lauria. If you want to make your life better, I promise you, put yourself in his circle. If you get a chance to meet Dr. Chris Lauria down the line, you'll be better off. I guarantee it. There're not too many things in life that I can guarantee, but I'll guarantee that.

HERE ARE THE BULLET-POINT TAKEAWAYS:

#1 - Based in Roanoke Virginia, he was a former high-level collegiate athlete and Division1 baseball player as pitcher for North Carolina.

#2 - He went from being a family Chiropractor with discounted family plans he then found his stride when he went to a specialty-based practice as a Disc specialist.

#3 - He found freedom in running a true cash-based practice that showcased his technology.

#4 - He found that by handling the New Patient phone call himself by calling back all leads generated he discovered that there was a much higher show rate and conversion rate.

#5 - He found that Facebook leads are a bit skeptical "upfront" so he addresses that in his script and in his initial New Patient phone call.

#6 - He still to this day even calls the patient often after their 1st visit and found that this also increased is patient visit average tremendously as well as their compliance.

#7 - He found that by branding his clinic as a DISC Centers of America that his ability to project as a "back pain" specialist and as a Spinal Disc specialist radically improved. This has served to position him as separate and distinct from all other Chiropractors in his demographic.

#8 - He found that by building stronger relationships with his patients by communicating with them at times that they may not expect via a simple patient phone call has been very key.

#9 - He feels that his practice model today as a DISC Centers of America branded center is so successful that if he decides to open other locations outside of Roanoke, he would be able to easily duplicate his results anywhere he chose to go.

#10 - He found that by attending the National Spinal Decompression Certification (at Parker University & National University) he has raised his success on all levels as his conviction, his certainty and his confidence as well as his clinical mastery has improved tremendously from this event.

16

NEW PRACTICE SUCCESS – (DR. JASON KAPLAN)

Read about: DR. JASON KAPLAN & DISCOVER how he SKYROCKETED his BRAND-NEW practice. Learn how he was able to "hit the ground running" by implementing some very SPECIFIC tips, tools, strategies and secrets that positioned both him and his wife as "SPECIALISTS" in his demographic. A MUST-LISTEN interview for any doctor who wants to get into MAJOR Positive Cash Flow as soon as the doors of a new practice are opened.

Dr. Bard:

Whether you are in practice for 50 years, or whether you are just getting ready to open a brand new, kick butt practice you want to read this. The reason why is because of our incredible guest here today. Somebody who walks the walk, talks the talk, but more importantly, has proven it and has opened one of the most incredible practices in the country in the shortest possible time. We want to welcome Dr. Jason Kaplan.

Dr. Kaplan:

Thank you, thank you very, very much. I appreciate it.

Dr. Bard:

What a treat! This is for a host of different reasons and the real reason here is because of the simple fact that if "success leaves clues", then there will be plenty of them, here shared today, because of one simple reason and that one reason is you have done something very, very powerful including your wife, Dr. Stephanie. What Dr. Jason Kaplan has done is really nothing short of remarkable. He has created a multi-million-dollar practice, and if that makes your jaw drop a little bit, it should, but if you're really wanted it to drop a little bit lower the thing that makes it so powerful, so incredible, so unique, so distinct, and so different is the amount of time that he has done this in.

Now, if you're not familiar with Dr. Jason Kaplan. I will share with you a few simple things. If the name happens to sound familiar, I will tell you that it is. The reason that it is familiar is because yes, it is true. He is the son of Dr. Eric Kaplan. He is his youngest born son, and what's so incredible about that is not only is he his son but once you get a chance to meet Dr. Jason Kaplan, you really get a feeling that he absolutely marches to his own beat. So, I actually thought of an incredible thing that I wanted to share with our readers. We've never done this before but I thought of 10 simple words that describe Dr. Jason Kaplan perfectly.

They are the following: Number one, resilient. Number two, persistent. Number three, disciplined. Number four, focused. Number five, opinionated. Number six, engaging. Number seven, magnetic. Number eight, dedicated. Number nine, thankful and number 10, three simple letters, one word, F-U-N. He is so much fun and if you had the pleasure of knowing him, you'll know why we're jumping into the deep end of the pool here. What I wanted to ask you right out of the gate, Dr. Kaplan is you didn't just come right out of school and open a practice. There was I would say, a journey, a path to get to the point, where you opened this incredible practice in Wellington, Florida. How did that journey begin and where did it bring you to the point of opening your practice from the day you graduated?

Dr. Kaplan:

Yes. When I first got out of school, I knew I wanted to be great, and I wanted to be the best and I knew that the one thing you cannot learn in school is experience. So, I wanted to work for the greatest, I wanted to work for the best. So out of school, I worked for several brilliant doctors, who did all types of treatments and modalities and I learned so much and I was actually learning from all those amazing doctors along the way. I picked up all this knowledge and experience and it really, really helped me in the practice I'm in now, treating patients with spinal decompression and laser. A lot of things that you don't really learn in school to this day. So, to get all that hands-on experience I went to work with some brilliant doctors that spent the time with me, and coached me, and guided me and really shaped me into the doctor I am today, which made me have this office that I have now.

Dr. Bard:

If there was a word that I left out, there really should have been at 11th word on the list, and the 11th word, is that you're incredibly humble. So, my question to you is you could have practiced anywhere in the country. There was a lot of opportunities to practice in other states. I remember even during your journey of wanting to even practice, believe it or not, in the state of Colorado. I remember that when you were a student and its funny how life takes certain twists and certain turns, and brought you to this incredible right place, right time, right location, right doctor, right marketing and right vision. That's a lot of rights, but the reality is you ended up practicing in Wellington, Florida. Why did you choose there?

Dr. Kaplan:

At the time, I was currently practicing up in Orlando, Florida and I wanted to come back to South Florida because of my mom and dad. There was a brilliant, brilliant doctor here, who was getting ready to retire. When I started I was seeing less than 20 patients a day. In less than two years, I'm over 95 patients a day now. We have three spinal decompression machines. We can consistently see over 70, 80 patients a day, even in the summer in the office. So, it's actually an amazing opportunity that I had to just jump on. That's why I'm in the horse capital of the entire world in the beautiful West Palm Beach, area of Wellington.

Dr. Bard:

So, believe it or not, there was a TV show many years ago that many of readers are familiar with and the name of the show was called "*Extreme Makeover*". What you did with your incredible wife, Dr. Stephanie Kaplan, is you basically turned this practice on its heels. It was good to begin with, but it was really in a certain area, or a certain demographic, or a certain dimension of practice and then what you did was really dramatic. One of the things you did right out of the gate that I would love for you to share is you changed the demographic with respect to what type of patient you were attracting, number one, and number two, how those patients paid for their care. Can you share a little bit as to the pendulum swing as to the percentage of when you took the practice over being an insurance-based practice to where you are now in a substantially driven cash-based model?

Dr. Kaplan:

So initially, it was an old-school chiropractic office. It was almost 100 percent insurance based. They only treated in insurance, nothing else. It was very, very little cash. It was a very old office with carpet and wallpaper and pink walls and green walls. So, the first thing I did was I came in, and I redid the whole look of this office. I ripped out that old carpet, put beautiful hardwood floors in and painted the entire walls and did chair rails in every single room. I put more concealed lighting, trying to get this place looking as professional as possible. Then I brought in the spinal decompression and marketing.

I didn't want that high-volume insurance-based chiropractic practice only. I wanted to bring in the cash patients that actually value their care, value their treatment, that have these issues that are not getting results anywhere and I wanted to give those actual results. So, by bringing the spinal decompression in, and since it's a cash process, it really turned this office a whole 180. I mean, we've gone completely in the opposite direction from an old-school, paper-based, insurance-based office to now almost 100 percent cash. I see less than 20 percent in insurance. I'm almost 90 percent all cash and that is probably the greatest thing in the entire world.

Dr. Bard:

You are such a one-of-a kind doctor a one-of-a kind heart, a one-of-a kind role model and here's where the story starts to get really interesting. The reason it gets interesting is because what Dr. Kaplan did, and he did it so well, in his genius and so smart, is that he decided that he just didn't want to run a conventional chiropractic-only practice. He looked at his practice as a specialty-based practice, and became not just one of the leaders in Florida, in the world of spinal decompression but became a national leader because yes, this is the same doctor, if the name sounds familiar, that teaches the actual hands-on part of the clinical applications for the National Spinal Decompression Certification Program, which happens to be coming up in November at Parker and you can contact them to try to secure a seat. It is the most popular single weekend CEU course that's given. As you'll see, when you get a chance to learn more about, Dr. Jason Kaplan is that he is without any shadow of a doubt an "all in" type of doctor. So, my question to you, Dr. Kaplan is this, why did you feel there was such a need for being a disc doctor and a disc specialist at this point in time?

Dr. Kaplan:

I was trained in school that 99 percent of all pain most likely comes from the actual disc and from pressure on the nerve root, and I was tired of patients coming in a thousand times, and still having the same problems over and over again. If they have a bad disc, they get tired and they get frustrated with chiropractic, and go right into surgery. I want patients to know that there's another answer. I want patients to know that there's another fix without having the metal put in their back. So, patients who have been frustrated with chiropractic care in the past come in here and I show them the difference. I show them how we can actually treat these disc problems, disc bulges and herniations with the radiating pain, the numbness and tingling. All these issues that affect their entire lives that we can treat, and often get them completely pain free, set them free, numbness free without any drugs, without any surgery, without any long-lasting alterations to their life.

I cannot tell you the sad thing of my practice is in fixing failed surgeries. I've got one patient that's had eight back surgeries, yes eight. His quality of life now is horrible and I wish he would've come to me first. So that's truly why I really wanted to do this because I wanted to help people. I wanted to actually treat patients and get them better without having to refer them out. I did not want to be the chiropractor that treats them and says, I'm sorry, we went as far as we can. You have to go with surgery now. I want to really get them feeling better in house without the drugs and without the surgery. I've found if you truly care, if you truly treat people the way you yourself would like to be treated, the business comes, the patients come and they get better. You truly got to give them your all, give them your love and make them feel better, and they can feel that. They can really, really tell.

Dr. Bard:

So yes, it is 100 percent true that your marketing is dialed in, that you've got multiple, what we call "portals of entry" into your practice but the reality is simply this. You have captured market share in your demographic above and beyond even the wildest imagination because you are seeing the patients that were going for epidural injections. You are seeing the patients that are dependent or were dependent upon narcotics and opioids. You're seeing the patients that we're going for microdiscectomies, laminectomies, spinal fusions, foraminotomies and more and inclusive of metal in their back, which is a whole other litany of concerns, issues, problems and more. You are literally like the Robin Hood of chiropractic in the city of Wellington.

Dr. Kaplan:

I cannot tell you how many patients come into this office with surgery scheduled. The surgery is already on the books scheduled and they try spinal decompression as the last resort. I tell them, you're not going to try it. You're going to do it. Every single patient halfway through canceled their surgery. They all canceled it halfway through our treatment. It's truly incredible. With the whole marketing side, I'm very fortunate because I have a marketing genius. I had this amazing doctor named, "Dr. Perry Bard", who is the marketing guru of gurus and he has gotten me through my website, through my Facebook, through my television ads. If it wasn't for you Dr. Bard, and all the marketing expertise that you taught me. Doc, I owe you everything because the marketing is all because of you.

Dr. Bard:

I've heard some good things about this "Bard guy" that's all I can tell you.

Dr. Kaplan:

He's an amazing doctor.

Dr. Bard:

Thank you for that but I've also heard some great things about this guy named "Dr. Eric Kaplan", and for those of you, who don't know the story. There is obviously something that we are "tongue and cheek" about. It is definitely behind the curtain, and for a lot of readers who are not privy to—well, it's been considered and what we've been told is the "greatest story in chiropractic" in terms of passing a torch over 31 years ago. I was so blessed to become an associate of Dr. Jason Kaplan's father. Little did I know that would be the greatest gift that would just keep giving, and to this day, still more fun than ever before.

When you know the timing of this, being so prophetic, in the sense that this past Tuesday we dropped our son off at Chiropractic College. The same school that Dr. Jason Kaplan attended to start his journey, his life, his career, and our son Devin couldn't be more excited. He's gotten so much of that from you Dr. Jason Kaplan, who has been really a mentor, a coach, really an incredible role model, who's done it right, done it smart and doing it better than any of your peers. So, if we're going to talk about percentages, let's talk about one of the greatest percentages that exist today in practice, which happens to be your conversion rate. Meaning, one of the things that you're known for is your ability and you touched upon it just briefly, which I love is the simple fact it's 100 percent. Every patient that's been scheduled for surgery that came in to see you, did not have to have a surgery. I think this is beyond a hall of fame type of approach to practice. Share with our readers a little bit, on why you feel your conversion rate has been so powerful?

Dr. Kaplan:

Because you can pretty much classify every patient into two areas, either cervical decompression of their neck or lumbar decompression of their back. If a patient comes into you with headaches, neck pain, shoulder pain, arm pain, pain around the shoulder blade, mid back pain that is cervical decompression. If they come into you with low back pain, hip pain, sciatica, pain in the knee, pain down the ankle, pain in the foot, numbness, tingling, that's lumbar decompression.

No matter any symptom that you have, you can classify that into two areas and you could just about always get them feeling better. You can take them part of the way with chiropractic, but you can take them all the way with the decompression. When the patients get better and when they come in pain free, they tell their friends, and they tell their friends and it just snowballs. So that's why I take these ordinary chiropractic patients, I show them, it's the disc that's causing the pain. It's the nerve root that's under pressure, and whether the cause is a cervical disc or a lumbar disc. Once you get them on the decompression machine, they start feeling better. The proof is in the pudding.

Dr. Bard:

We learned so much here. We learned that it didn't necessarily come easy to Dr. Jason Kaplan. He got out of school and he basically paid the price almost back to, I guess you would say "basic training" if I can make a military analogy. He could have come right out, and opened the practice, but what he did with his incredible wife, who he happened to meet in Chiropractic College is a story unto itself because what you'll learn in this dynamic is that both doctors share incredible things in common. Which is their commitment to excellence, their commitment to detail, their focus on saving patients from terrible outcomes with epidural injections and spinal surgeries. Yet, at the same time, they each are unique, separate, and distinct in their treatment approach in terms of how they handle the practice, which is so incredibly powerful, and really remarkable.

One of the things I'm really curious about is because this often about habits and often about neurology. Why do so many chiropractors, graduate Chiropractic College and have a difficult time finding their path, finding their mode of operation, their MO, finding their special sauce. Well, what we've learned from Dr. Jason Kaplan, is he decided to become a specialist which is part and parcel of what we do, in that we take care of the motor unit. When we talk about the motor unit, we're talking about a bone, we're talking about a nerve, we're talking about a disc. So yes, you can go off into left field if you want, and you can do a host of other things.

Dr. Kaplan:

But "All Roads Lead to Disc". I'm telling you, that's the most important thing I've ever learned in my entire life, "All Roads Lead to Disc". You must be a disc specialist to be a pain specialist, to be a health specialist.

Dr. Bard:

I love those words.

Dr. Kaplan:

Thank you. I appreciate it. Do you know where I got them from?

Dr. Bard:

I'll tell you something. If you're reading this, and you say, gee, this is starting to make sense. He comes out of school. He takes an existing practice. He revamps it.

He invests him and his wife both invest in the practice. Yes, he could have went out and bought stocks. Yes, he could have went out and bought mutual funds. Yes, he could've bought real estate—He put everything back into his business and he kept sharpening the saw, basically shining the diamond and making this, what we would call a "D.D.G." practice shine. If you don't know what D.D. G. stands for, it stands for drop dead gorgeous. You shot this practice out of a cannon to bring it to the level, dollars and cents wise, to make this a practice that is unlike any with numbers seven digit plus numbers to back this up. If I was reading this I would love to meet you.

Dr. Jason Kaplan is one of the keys, and I call him the most popular instructor at the National Spinal Decompression Certification Program. If you don't believe that, just watch some of the videos of how all the doctors formed a circle around him when he starts going into his tips, his tools, his strategies and his inner secrets to patient management at the National Spinal Decompression Certification

Program, which is coming up in November at Parker University. Dr. Kaplan please share why this is such a game changer for so many doctors in a single weekend?

Dr. Kaplan:

It's the only weekend course where they actually teach you, not only the science and the application, but really the hands-on training. It's the only thing that will give you all the resources you'll ever need, all the science behind it, all the medical studies and all the documentation. They go into not just the decompression but the laser, and all the treatments that we do with it. Then they go into actual hands-on questions, so patients with disc issues and how you treat this patient with disc problems and how you treat that. Truly, it's the only way we get a full-blown manual, an instruction manual on how to actually explain it, how to actually market it, how to actually sell it, how to actually use it and treat with it. It's really a one-stop shop because it goes over every single aspect of what you need to be a disc specialist and a spinal decompression doctor.

Dr. Bard:

If I'm reading this, my head is exploding right now with wanting to know more about what you just said. So, I will share a phone number. It is (888) 990-9660. If you call that number, you will learn more about this incredible program that is coming up. The 10X anniversary program. It's going to be a celebration, it's going to be a gathering, it's going to be an event and it's going to be really something that doctors get an opportunity to come away, and come Monday, hit the ground running because not only did they get a chance to meet you, Dr. Jason Kaplan, not only do they get a chance to meet your incredible wife, Dr. Stephanie Kaplan, not only do they meet the creator of this program, Dr. Eric Kaplan but they also get a chance to meet absolutely some of the most successful spinal decompression doctors in the country in one weekend, one event, one opportunity. All it takes is one phone call. Once again, it's 888-990-9660. Call today.

HERE ARE THE BULLET-POINT TAKEAWAYS:

#1 - A graduate of Parker University he met his wife Stephanie in the registration line day one at Parker. He is the youngest son of Dr. Eric Kaplan and practices in Wellington, Florida.

#2 - He and his wife purchased an existing practice in Wellington Florida that primarily was a 90% insurance driven practice. They eventually converted it to a 90%+ cash driven practice.

#3 - He worked as an associate doctor in 3 different practices prior to opening up his own.

#4 - He only presents "cash-based packages" to patients requiring Spinal Decompression and or Laser Therapy.

He is getting ready to expand into the Peripheral Neuropathy area of practice and will follow the same cash package model.

#5 - He routinely sees over 95 patients a day less than 2 years in practice that overwhelmingly have secured financing or prepaid their individual treatment.

#6 - He continues to re-invest in the practice as it is 180 degrees different from when he started as he made it look beautiful and resemble a 5-star professional clinic as beautiful as any orthopedic surgeon's office or any plastic surgeon's office.

#7 - He became a DISC specialist and captures the majority of his market who have been prescribed injections or surgery for degenerative, bulging and herniated discs.

#8 - He classifies the strong majority of his patients either into a cervical Spinal Disc Decompression Patient or a Lumbar Spinal Disc Decompression Patient.

#9 - Upwards of 30% of his New Patients are considering spinal surgery or are already scheduled for spinal surgery prior to meeting him.

#10 - The combination of the DISC centers of America ads, inserts, flyers, postcards, social media, website & TV commercials have made Dr. Jason Kaplan a local celebrity and the GO-TO doctor in his market. He also teaches the clinical portion of Spinal Decompression patient management to rave reviews at the National Spinal Decompression Certifications at both Parker University and National University of Health Sciences.

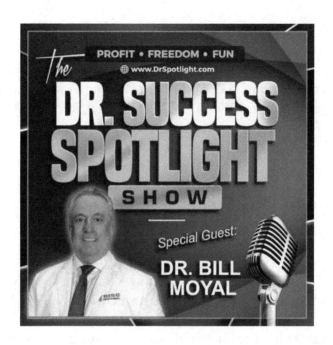

17

BRANDING SUCCESS – (DR. WILLIAM MOYAL)

Read about: DR. WILLIAM MOYAL & DISCOVER how he has utilized the POWER of BRANDING to SUPERCHARGE his practice. Learn how he has utilized the National Chain of Spinal Decompression Centers and BRAND known as DISC Centers of America to position himself and his practice as a "GO-TO" center for excellence in Spinal Disc Care with over 5100+ professional, Olympic and world class athletes **treated from all over the world to his credit.**

Dr. Bard:

We have somebody that has been in my life for, believe it or not, 35 years. I am your host, Dr. Perry Bard. I want to welcome our very special guest here today, Dr. William Moyal from Miami Beach, Florida. Welcome to the show Dr. Moyal.

Dr. Moyal:

Well, thank you, Perry for having me and I'm glad to be here.

Dr. Bard:

You have done something very unique. What you've done is you've really moved to the front of the line when it comes to something that many people look at as something generic. What you've done is you've been able to really brand yourself, your business model and your identity in a very powerful and a very, very unique way. For those who don't know, I will tell you this, Dr. Bill Moyal, is known really what we call a "doctor's doctor". In other words, he's the doctor that all of us seek out because of his knowledge base, his attention to detail and his incredible skill when it comes to the art of adjusting. His real strength now, is the art of branding. So right out of the gate, Dr. Moyal, how did you figure out how to brand yourself, your business model, your identity in such a powerful and such a successful way?

Dr. Moyal:

I would have to say that before you can brand or before you can advertise or do any of those things. You have to have a very strong product. So, I was very fortunate to surround myself as you have with more than 30 of the best doctors in medicine, chiropractic and osteopathy over the years while I was a student. Unfortunately, many of them have passed, but it's my honor and I think my duty as well to continue their work. Over the years, what I've done is to synthesize all the things that I've learned that was either from osteopathy, medicine, physical medicine and chiropractic and I created a system that is reproducible and predictable.

218

As a result of that, I was able to get to athletes and it started with one guy, Mark Clayton wide receiver of the Miami Dolphins. Then, he brought in others and over the years, the last count is something like 5,115 professional Olympic and world-class athletes from around the world. I think getting back to the question is you have to have the product. My product was the skills of making changes and figuring out chronic and physical cases or problems or injuries that other people couldn't figure out and getting results. As a result of that, having other athletes say, "Hey, I'm sending you my buddy."

A good example, is Dr. Rich Lohr who had a massive shoulder problem for more than 20 years. Went to Dr. Jobe, went to all kinds of people, a long time with his chiropractor and so on and so forth. Spend a ton of money, I think he told me like $100,000 trying to fix his shoulder and nothing helped him and he thought he was going to be out of practice. Then funny enough, we met in 2012, at where? The National Certification for Decompression in Dallas. We talked, I adjusted him, one adjustment cleaned out his whole shoulder, never had a problem since. He's been able to work out, go back to working out, exercising and practicing without any problem. So, it's having the level of skills and confidence to be able to do what you need to do and deliver a product, not just talk it, but actually deliver the goods and get results.

Dr. Bard:

My question to you, Dr. Moyal is simple and that is there are a number of doctors out there that may be up to speed, not your speed, of course, but maybe up to speed in terms of their level of adjusting skill, their knowledge base, their diagnostic attributes, all of that. These are solid and good doctors. The difference though in your world is your ability to really surround yourself, to really envelop yourself, to really embrace the brand, case in point as a disc doctor, specifically the world known as Disc Centers of America. If you'd be so kind to share how you've made Disc Centers of America yours? How you've really moved to the front of the line with respect to leading the charge as a representative of Disc Centers of America, can you share that?

Dr. Moyal:

Absolutely. I think you just kind of hit it on the head of the nail when you said, that I've been known throughout for this and that. I was always branded as to the guy that was good and that if you have a problem and that's where you need to go but I never had any branding. So, when you and I, we met again in 2012 in the very forefront of teaching spinal decompression at the National Certification Class in Dallas, I was just happy to share my knowledge and happy to share whatever I knew and to take it to another step. It kind of reminds me when I was in school where you learned motion palpation. I was very frustrated and I just wasn't getting it and I took a break, walked away for about six months and when I came back I owned it. It just made sense all of a sudden. I think that's the same thing when you and I got back again, and Dr. Kaplan got back together in early January. It was coming back to the family and something just clicked. It's like embrace the brand because the brand is power. Look at McDonald's, look at these other companies. They have a brand, they stick to it. Everybody knows it. That's when I understood that I looked at what the brand meant.

I saw the changes that in those two to three years that I was gone and watched you go from a few offices to now over 100's. In really seeing that, you have to have a certain level of quality, a certain level of systems and that all those things fall under our brand so that people know that there's a certain expectation and quality when you go to a Disc Centers of America clinic. I looked at all that. I looked at the branding, I looked at what I was doing. I had multiple names and decided, you know what, you can't be three different names. You have to either jump in or as they say, you know, do a number two or get off the pot. I just jumped in and as a result of that and going to the boot camps and going to the trainings and listening to what Dr. Kaplan says, in that we're the "gold standard". It is then when it clicked. I took the logo and changed the logo to gold. To me, it represented a step higher, a step above because if we're the gold standard and let's represent that not by words but just by pictures because we know pictures speak a thousand words.

Then, you and I had some other conversations and all of a sudden, we decide, hey, how about ID badges? We were just looking at all those things to complement. Then, I was at the last masterclass at Dr. Lohr's office, I had been approached by someone that sold floormats, so I asked, "can you do this logo and this thing on the floor"? Yeah, absolutely. So, at masterclass, one of the things that made me really happy was to present Dr. Rich with a floor mat with his logo of Disc Centers of America-Decatur. So, all those are little steps to complete the brand, to complete the image that we're trying to project, and embrace it at the same time because you're either all in or you are just plain. I don't want to be plain anymore.

At 60 years old, I'm complete, again. I was always the guy that was here and there, but I never knew how to brand myself. I never knew how to market myself correctly. When this came about, and especially in January after spending a couple of years dabbling here and trying to learn this and that, it just all made sense. It was like, wait a second, it's all here in one package. You provide all that. You provide the guidance, you provide the tools. All we have to do is embrace them and utilize them, and yeah, I want to be creative. I like to take it in, a step above and transform it, but to the benefit of everybody, not just for myself, it's for everybody. We all have the ability to be creative. Sometimes, we just don't give ourselves permission to do that. So, from the moment somebody walks in, the floor mat is there. Something on your walls is there, your business cards, your scrubs, having the logo on it, your doctor's jacket, the ID badge, etc. Even when someone comes in, if they're going home after the first day and they just signed up for a package in your office, give them something. I just finished ordering some really nice backpacks with the DISC Centers of America logo and those are going to be the bags that contain an ice pack and some vitamins or supplements or whatever else I can think of that's going to be in there.

One of the things that we tell people is to drink a lot of water. They need to hydrate. Well, I just got these alkaline sticks that makes any bottle of water into alkaline water that's going to be in there. So, everything was going to be towards giving them something extra and special. Then, if it costs me $15, $20, $30 bucks for the bag with all the goodies in it, big deal. Especially, if I just go over the case, but it could be worth $3,000,

$4,000, $5,000 or $6,000. It's just another way of saying, we have a brand. We have a high-quality brand. We provide a high-quality service and that's what you need to expect and that's what you're going to get out of this office.

Dr. Bard:

You have an amazing attention to detail on the front end. You never, never get a second chance to make a great first impression. So, what you've done so well Dr. Moyal, is you're paying attention to a lot of the things that really most chiropractors are overlooking, not finding important. I'm going to say this and I'm really going to piss some people off when I say this, but I'm going to say, maybe too lazy to do.

Dr. Moyal, is fun with a capital F. One of the things I dig about him, is that he is really a gifted teacher. One of the things that I really dig about him, is his willingness and his openness and really his ability to help other chiropractors who have had challenges. Other chiropractors that have had challenges in the business, challenges in the art, in the skill, but especially, now, in the branding and in sharing that right now. What I'm very curious about is Dr. Moyal is right now in terms of how you see your brand, specifically your Disc Centers of America brand. Disc Centers of America websites now takes up the most real estate on the internet in the disc world. In other words, when you do a search for disc-related problems, all you see is, Disc Centers of America Clinics and it is you, Dr. Moyal that is really leading the charge in that. Where do you see the brand going and that includes yourself in the next six months to a year?

Dr. Moyal:

I see it exploding. I think the big thing is that whoever comes on board needs to embrace it completely and don't play. I'll give you a great example. You know, we talked about doing the commercials, talked about doing Facebook. It took me six months to get started. Now, I kick myself for not doing it sooner because just today alone, we had somebody from Facebook and somebody booked an appointment from watching the commercials.

I can't wait to start setting up the second series of commercials and to brand new ones because that thing is exciting as heck. The other thing, we talked about the frontend, but on the backend, just because somebody signed up and paid you and they come in, it doesn't mean that you forget them either.

The new drip email educational system that's coming out with that has just come up and is going to be phenomenal. Following up, even though, the patients are ready and they're getting results, continuing to educate them, sending text messages, sending videos, sending emails, sending postcards, letters, may be a little unexpected package in the mail. Just to stay on top of mind consciousness to let them know that we are different. You didn't just come in and pay us and thank you very much and that's it. No, it's going to continue because those patients, if we really understand the disc, after the age of 35 are losing hydration. So, we also know that 80 percent plus of the population have back problems sometimes in their life and everyone that stays alive is getting older.

So, we have three strikes against us, which really means that in one sense we have a patient for life, but unlike pharmaceuticals, unlike hospitals that kind of depend on those people that keep the doors open at the cost of someone's health. We actually improve the quality of their health, the quality of their function, the quality of their movement and allow them and allow ourselves to age gracefully with movement instead of being stiff and dehydrated and unable to even just go walk the dog or play with the kids.

So, when you truly understand that you have a patient for life, all you have to do is gently and simply explain to them, this is a natural process that up to now has been natural because it's been accepted and there is really nothing you can do about it. You're just getting older. Kind of like the joke about the patient that goes to the orthopedist and he says, Doc, my right knee hurts. Well, you have arthritis in your knee, because you're old. Well, but the other leg doesn't have a problem. So, it's not that it has to do with age. Some of it does, obviously in genetics, but sometimes there's an injury that's the predisposing factor. There may be some trauma that happened in the structure, and as a result of it, is now developing into a bigger problem. So, if we understand that and we realize what we can do, and even do a better job as a chiropractor is to allow increased spacing between the joints and in the vertebrae. You allow those vertebrae in that person's spine to deteriorate at a lesser rate, or at a slower rate while improving the quality of movement and function. So, it's not just about the branding. It's also you can't brand if you don't have the product and understand the product of what you're providing the patient.

Dr. Bard:

Dr. Moyal, you have been able to really marry the brand with a heightened level of skill and it's been great to really watch the progression of how you've been able to put this together. So, I'm going to do with your approval, a quick ten second commercial for you, Dr. Moyal, in the sense that you're a blast. You're such a cool guy. You're really an awesome, awesome doctor. If you really want to meet, Dr. Moyal you have the opportunities at three places: Number one, a place called, www.thechiroevent.com. Number two, the masterclass, which is known as the National Spinal Decompression Masterclass or the Peripheral Neuropathy Masterclass, which is coming up. But, if you're really want to see him in his glory because it is a party, it is fun, it is really like a family reunion and that is the National Spinal Decompression Certification Program, which is exclusively taught through Parker University and National University. It is a CEU program, and the magic, and the beauty of that is you get to meet Dr. Moyal in person, live, large and in charge. An abundant heart and an abundant giver. The best of Miami Beach, the best of Florida, and really the best in chiropractic, it is such an honor.

HERE ARE THE BULLET-POINT TAKEAWAYS:

#1 - He started as a student surrounding himself with 30 of the top doctors in the country in Medicine, Osteopathy and Chiropractic as the basis of his education.

#2 - Located in Miami Beach Florida, he started in practice treating a number of the Miami Dolphins. From there the word spread and he became known as a sports medicine specialist.

#3 - He believes at the core of Branding, that you must 1st start with a very strong product. His product then became "Reproducible and Predictable."

#4 - He embraced the fact that DISC Centers of America is known for quality, consistency, reputation and training. Thus, he decided that he wanted to envelope those attributes within his own practice and build it up from there.

#5 - He decided that he wanted to go "ALL-IN" and thus decided he would attend all Bootcamps, Workshops, Seminars and Masterclasses that were given by DISC Centers of America to continue his ascent in practice.

#6 - From his embroidered Doctors clinic jackets to his embroidered Doctors scrubs (which he made himself) to the floor mats, to his signage, to his patient carry-all bags to his clinic badges and I.D.'s and more, he wanted to showcase the DISC Centers of America Brand to all and he found that the return on investment is powerful.

#7 - He has had every Spinal Decompression table that has ever been made and feels that the Acu-Spina is the one that is able to produce the most consistent results as it has the most medical research behind it.

#8 - He contributes at both the National Spinal Decompression Certification at Parker University as well as the National Spinal Decompression Certification at National University of Health Sciences.

#9 - He has developed his own Psoas Major Muscle Relief Technique that has been tremendously helpful to his patients suffering from Disc disease and often teaches this technique to other Chiropractors.

#10 - He feels that there is strength in numbers and as a Doctor practicing under the DISC Centers of America brand, he comes up more in internet searches and then prides himself in educating his patients why DISC centers of America set's the gold standard in Spinal Disc treatment.

18

MED-LEGAL SUCCESS –
(DR. JORDAN H. JORDAN, D.C., J.D.)

Read about: DR. JORDAN H. JORDAN & DISCOVER how he has re-defined the BEST of two worlds. An ultra-successful Chiropractor, he now conjoins both CHIROPRACTIC and the PRACTICE of LAW seamlessly. Learn HOW he positioned himself for SUCCESS in practice, in business and in LIFE, artfully, masterfully and strategically. A GIFTED orator and storyteller, Dr. Jordan H. Jordan shares how he EXCELS in the MED-LEGAL world.

Dr. Bard:

What makes our featured guest so incredible is, he has a very, very rare, and he has a very, very unique distinction. I don't know whether I should address him as doctor or I should address him as counselor. I want to welcome to the show, the one and only, Dr. Jordan Howard Jordan. Welcome to the show, Dr. Jordan.

Dr. Jordan:

Oh, thank you so much. I appreciate that introduction.

Dr. Bard:

Dr. Jordan Howard Jordan has such a unique distinction as he not only is a Doctor of Chiropractic and a great one at that, but he also has a very unique distinction of having another two letters after his name. Those letters are D.C. followed by J.D. Dr. Jordan is not only a Doctor of Chiropractic, but he's also an Attorney at Law, which has given him such a platform unlike no other, and a level of esteem, a level of certainty, a level of comprehension and a major level of success in coupling both chiropractic and the practice of law.

It's interesting because if you think that you can navigate the laws of the universe with respect to practice success, I can emphatically tell you that you'll never do this alone. One of the things that if you've been around long enough, and you've been in the world of business and you've been in the world of entrepreneurship and you've been in the world of success, that you know that basically, you're going to deal often on a day-to-day level in the course of doing business, you're going to be dealing with contracts, you're going to be dealing with mergers, you're going to be dealing with acquisitions, you may be dealing with real estate, commercial dealings and obviously, medical-legal proceedings, which would definitely include the area of personal injury. I can tell you that very, very simply that the way the world of practice success works is you don't do this alone and that's why Dr. Jordan Howard Jordan is amazing.

I will tell you that for the record, Dr. Jordan has had a thriving chiropractic practice for years. A waiting list practice in his own private building for many, many years. Now if you learn about what makes him so unique and what makes him so special is you will learn that this is a guy that never rest on his laurels and regardless of his previous success in the chiropractic world, when he decided to pursue the lofty goal of being a doctor and an attorney, he really brought something to the table. I would like to, right out of the gate Dr. Jordan, know where was your motivation, after a very lucrative, very successful chiropractic career to want to become, a Jurisprudence Doctor, a J.D., an attorney at law?

Dr. Jordan:

Well, one thing that happened to me was I had a very bad accident. I had an accident on a bridge. I actually flew off the end of the bridge and almost killed myself like Evel Knievel, except that it didn't break every single bone of my body. I hired an attorney, who happened to be a fraternity brother of mine at the time and he said, he knew a lot about personal injury. What he failed to tell me is that he never had a personal injury trial. I found out after I graduated, there's a major distinction between understanding personal injury law and being a personal injury trial lawyer, which he wasn't, and eventually, I lost my case. I wound up having to pay attorney's fees to the other side. It wasn't pretty.

So then, I began to think about the law, and how interesting it was that I was almost killed by a negligent driver and I suffered the ultimate price, that was one thing. The other thing is I want to touch upon what you said before, when you were in chiropractic practice or you're in a medical practice, you're subject to so many laws and they don't discuss that in chiropractic college. You're subject to Medicaid law, you're doing a Medicaid practice, Medicare, worker's compensation, personal injury, etc. If you have a multidisciplinary practice, it could be Stark Laws, it could be the Self-Referral Act. There are so many different rules. There's the Board of Chiropractic Medicine Rules and Laws. There's other statutes, and if you don't know what's out there and you don't have a coach constantly guiding you through it, to make sure you have the right contracts that are in your favor, you're going to wind up in a lot of trouble. I realized that very quickly when I became a Doctor of Chiropractic, and that was most of my motivation on wanting to become a lawyer.

Dr. Bard:

What you've been able to do here is really reinvent yourself and reinvent yourself on a level that is unmatched in our profession because you are definitely in stratified air, Dr. Jordan, with respect to what you have accomplished and what you have done. Can you talk a little bit about when you were in an active, full blown, 100 percent practice, where your focus was at that time, and then we'll talk about how you've been able to bridge that in a way that nobody else has? Can you talk a little bit about your prior practice?

Dr. Jordan:

Yes, I was one of the few people that never went to a chiropractor before I went to chiropractic college. My mother told me that instead of going to physical therapy college, if I was going to spend a lot of time in school, I should take the extra step and be a doctor and that interested me and piqued my interest. We'd talk about what type of doctor would be best for my personality. She said, you're very coordinated, you have great hands, you love to work with athletes, you should be a Doctor of Chiropractic. Now, the way that she found out about chiropractic was in the 1950s, when nobody was seeing a chiropractor. My mother lived in Brooklyn, and she had migraine headaches, and she had really bad stomach problems. So, she went to all these different doctors, nobody helped. A chiropractor from Palmer, moved to Brooklyn, next door to where she went to school in Lafayette High School, and her friends started to go to the chiropractor for various ailments.

While my grandmother found out that the chiropractor was helping people in the neighborhood and she thought, you know what, I have nothing to lose, my daughter is suffering. Let me take her to see the chiropractor. She had one visit with the chiropractor. The migraines went away, the stomach problems cleared up, the digestion improved. My mother said, a great chiropractor helped me, with great hands like you, you should become a chiropractor. So, I thought, okay, I'm not doing anything else really that positive with my life at this time. Let me try it, let me learn about it. I went up to, thank G-d, the greatest chiropractic college in the world, where you and I met, and I had the privilege of being your first clinician in the school. Even more significantly is that you and I got to meet, what I consider and you probably consider as well, one of the greatest chiropractors who ever lived, Dr. Sid Williams.

Now, I didn't know anything about chiropractic, and when I went up to chiropractic college, believe it or not, this may seem a little bit naive, but it's true. I was asking the chiropractors, the clinicians, what type of treatment they gave to the patients in a student clinic, and they said they used chiropractic adjustments. Well, I never had a chiropractic adjustment. So, I said, well, do you have medication? And they were laughing at me, and I said, well, do you do surgery there? They were laughing at me, and I didn't understand why, until I was about one month into the school program when I met Dr. Sid Williams. I'll never forget this. I was sitting in the third-row front at the center in front of the greatest chiropractor who ever lived, sort of like what I would consider a chiropractic evangelist, somebody as huge as Billy Graham.

He began to talk about the discovery that DD Palmer made that he gave to BJ Palmer and that had BJ Palmer in the school teaching the students that when it comes to disease, he said, "There's one cause, one correction, one cure for all disease." That's just the way he said it. When he said it, I think I must have jumped three feet in the air and when I came back down, I think my hair was standing straight up. I got the big picture at that point that he began to discuss innate intelligence and I thought this is what I've been looking for.

He's talking about that G-d made the universe, and G-d heals the body, when the chiropractor removes the interference. With that principle, that's the principle that I applied every day in school. That's the principle I apply to my practice for over 20 years. That's the principle that got people well. That's where my passion is with chiropractic to this day. That when I make a chiropractic adjustment, I know that the patient is going to get

231

better and how do I know so surely is because for the last 33 years of giving great patient chiropractic adjustments, they almost always get better. Very few people, unless they are very stressed, and maybe have a negative block in their own mind, don't get better. With that mindset, knowing that the patients are going to get well. That when I make the right adjustments, my belief transfers to them and that's my power between my patients and me. I know that they're going to get well and then they do.

Dr. Bard:

In hearing that at this very exacting moment, I wish you were able to actually see the smile on my face from ear to ear. I can without a doubt, tell you that I am overjoyed, and that is an understatement to have with us, the incredible Dr. Jordan Howard Jordan with us, D.C., J. D. and master of his professions. When I first went to chiropractic school, it was an eye-opening experience. It was an awakening and I was in the largest class in the history of any chiropractic college ever at that time.

When I went to school day one, there was a large assembly and I will never forget stepping out of the assembly and what you saw you never forgot. What you saw were clinicians and the clinicians were actually, believe it or not, lined up in their blue clinic jackets. They were lined up trying to procure, trying to create relationships, trying to get new students for clinical visits in the student clinic because the precursor to going into the outpatient clinic is to be able to do student visits. So, you needed enough student visits to get to the next level and beyond. I know this is going to sound absolutely crazy. I believe, out of my entire class, 360 students at that time. I believe I was actually the last student in my class to take a clinician. I actually said at that point that I just didn't want anybody working on me. I was holding out. I guess you would say, it was a "chiropractic student virgin", if you will, to the point where I said, if I'm going to hold out, I want the best, and believe it or not, it took a year and a half later but I got the best.

I was in a gym on a Sunday afternoon. I'll never forget it. The name of the gym was called Coffee's Gym in Marietta, Georgia. I knew exactly who, Dr. Jordan was because he happened to be training at the same time and he always sat in the first row at every assembly. That's how he was. He's always going to be right up front, I'll never forget it. He was two years ahead of me and I'll never forget that day, on a Sunday afternoon, when he came up to me, and he asked me very simply "who my clinician was", and when I said, "I didn't have one". I'll never forget his words. He said to me, "great, I'll be your clinician". That's when this whole journey started with respect to understanding that he was always an "all-in" type of doctor and what I would love for you to do, Dr. Jordan, is to share with our readers about how in the jurisprudence world, how upon practicing law now, how you've been able to make that transition so successfully, and where your area of specialty lies in the practice of law.

Dr. Jordan:

Well, after being in practice for a couple of decades, I found myself doing a lot of personal injury work. I knew the business very, very well. I related to the law very, very well. I was very, very good at doing depositions. I had no fear at all going to the courtroom and testifying. I've testified in dozens and dozens of cases as a medical expert before I became a lawyer and I had a lot of friends that were lawyers when I had my practice. They taught me all about personal injury and I was very, very involved in the personal injury cases in terms of coding and billing, in terms of documenting every soap note near perfectly. Every note in a personal injury case has to be near perfect and every report has to be near perfect. So, I was practicing and practicing and practicing that as a Doctor of Chiropractic.

So, when I went to law school, I had the privilege of going to Nova Southeastern University Law School. Most people when they graduated law school could not hit the ground running because they really don't teach you in law school how to be a lawyer. They teach you how to research, they teach you research and writing but they really don't teach you procedural steps that you need, but because I was a Doctor of Chiropractic for so many years, and I had done the depositions, and I had been to trial, and I had documented the cases, and I spoke with so many different attorneys, I was able to practice personal injury law from day one. It just came very naturally. I'd been in the courtroom for many, many years. So, it was just a very natural, easy transition for me.

Dr. Bard:

You have always not just been in the practice of healthcare, and then obviously now, so successfully, in the practice of law concurrently, but you've really always been in the business of relationships. You have always been such an amazing relationship builder. You're such a modest doctor. You're such a modest attorney and at the same time, you have such a big personality. I think that's one of the things that so many people are attracted to you by. I remember when you were practicing, I stopped by right when I came back to Florida and you had this gorgeous building. This private building which you owned at the time, which was fantastic. I'll never forget, I remember walking in and you gave me a book

You gave me a book at that point, and it was called "Unlimited Power". It was written by Anthony Robbins. I think it's interesting because you were always ahead of the curve. You were always, on the cutting edge. You were always, a student of success. You have always been so driven. When you're not in the practice of health care, and you're not in the practice of law, what do you, Dr. Jordan, like to do for fun now?

Dr. Jordan:

I've always been involved with sports. My father wanted to be a pro baseball player. His brother was a fantastic ballplayer and probably would have been a professional ballplayer, but he had to go to work to support my grandmother during the Great Depression. The first gift my father ever gave me was a ball. He wanted me to be a pro baseball player. So, I've been involved in athletics since I was little kid. I played baseball, I played college tennis, I played college baseball, I played college softball, I played competitive hockey. I've been a soccer coach for 10 years. Presently, I'm a United States Soccer Federation Referee and I do soccer games all over the state, big tournaments with my son. I've been involved on the tennis team at Broward College. My life is sports and athletics and fitness and getting adjusted and doing long distance bicycling and trying to complement that with some really great nutrition with many fruits, vegetables and as much clean water as I can put down, that's my passion. My passion is athletics. When I'm not working, that's what I love to do most.

Dr. Bard:

You've done nothing in your life casually. Everything you do is really full tilt and if you have an interest in something, as long as I've known you, you always, always are "all in". I love that you share that with our readers. What I would love for you to do, is if you could so kindly share with our readers your contact information, and the reason that I would love for you to do this, is because I can guarantee, there's not too many things in life I can guarantee, but I can guarantee that there are doctors that are reading this right now, and they have chiropractic questions, they have legal questions. There's an old proverb that says, "that you never know what someone is actually going through until you walked a mile in their shoes". I think the unique foundation that you've created, and the unique position that you've created as an expert in both fields, puts you in such a very unique position to address any of the medical, legal concerns that so many chiropractors have. You are without question, in my mind, the best point person to go to. If somebody has a question how they can get in touch with you directly?

Dr. Jordan:

Yes, but just quickly, I just want to respond to something that you said that I think is very, very important is that yes, you've noticed that when I'm in and I've made any decision, I'm never half-in, I'm not half- baked. I'm running full tilt. The reason that I do that is, I noticed that when I became a bodybuilder and I started to bench press, my average bench press because of athletics, right off the bat, I was already bench pressing my weight of 160 but after one year of lifting weights when I was 18 or 19 years old, I took like bench press from 160 to 300 and people want to know how I did that. The way I did that was going full tilt. I didn't have an average workout. I didn't have an above average workout. Every single workout I ever had, especially at Coffee's Gym, working out with you and other great people like you in the gym.

My philosophy was don't look back, leave it all on the track because if you're going to get better, you've got to push, you've got to push no matter what you're doing, whether you're a doctor or whether you're an engineer or whether you're a scientist or whether you're a bodybuilder. If you want to get better, you can't go in there at 70 percent because then your max is at 70 percent. If you want to get better at anything, you got to take it all the way and then some and drive it through. That's the only way to improve. My phone number is: (954) 415-8253. I love to help my brothers and sisters in chiropractic, especially, if they have a legal question. There are so many issues. There's malpractice unfortunately, there is asset protection, there is Medicaid Law, personal injury law, Worker's Compensation Law and more. There are so many things that I would love to share, so that would be my pleasure.

Dr. Bard:

You have such an amazing skillset. For our readers, who are fortunate enough to read this today, they got a small taste of the magic that I've experienced by having Dr. Jordan Howard Jordan in my life for, believe it or not, 34 years. That doesn't happen by chance, that doesn't happen by luck. That happens by a very specific design. If you want to make your life doctor radically better, then my highest suggestion to you is figure out a way to get Dr. Jordan, Doctor of Chiropractic, Counselor-At-Law in your world, in your universe, in some which way, shape or form. The quality of my life has been radically better because of the simple fact that I've always been lucky enough to have him in my life and it's been the ultimate, ultimate gift.

HERE ARE THE BULLET-POINT TAKEAWAYS:

#1 - He had a thriving practice as a Chiropractor for years. He then incurred a series bike injury breaking multiple bones which forced him to retain a Personal Injury Attorney where he learned the hard way the difference between a Personal Injury Attorney and a Personal Injury Trial Lawyer.

#2 - He saw a major void for Chiropractors who were trying to navigate Personal Injury Law, Medicare/Medicaid Law, Multi-Disciplinary Law, Workers Comp. Law, Stark Law and more. He felt by becoming an attorney, he brings such a unique skill set to the table that would thus allow other Chiropractors to not have to deal with legal issues alone.

#3 - He actually never went to a Chiropractor before attending Chiropractic school. Upon arriving he threw himself completely into every aspect of the Philosophy Art & Science of Chiropractic.

#4 - He embraced the one cause, one correction, one cure foundation of Chiropractic and used this as a driving force to build a wildly successful practice.

#5 - He practiced in his own stand-alone building of which he owned the real estate in Broward County, Florida.

#6 - He experienced tremendous success as a Chiropractor in the Personal Injury world as a treating doctor. He was always very comfortable when it came to giving depositions and making court appearances which started fueling his drive to also pursue the practice of law with a focal point on Personal Injury.

#7 - He feels the strength of any case in Personal Injury comes down to the documentation and doctors that are able to excel in this area will often prevail on behalf of their patients.

#8 - He was always heavily involved in sports. From baseball, to softball, to tennis, to soccer. He has also been a United States Soccer

Federation referee for the past ten years. This competitive spirit has allowed Dr. Jordan to WIN.

#9 - His philosophy was don't look back, leave it all on the track because if you're going to get better, you've got to push, you've got to push no matter what you're doing. Whether you're a doctor or an engineer or a scientist or a bodybuilder. If you want to get better, you can't go in there at 70 percent because then your max is at 70 percent. If you want to get better at anything, you've got to take it all the way and then some and drive it through.

#10 - He now counsels Chiropractors on utilizing specific legal strategies to protect their practices and to protect their assets and does so from a position so unique as he continues to walk in the shoes of both a Chiropractor and an Attorney at Law.

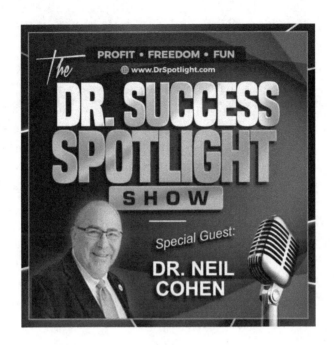

19

CHIROPRACTIC SUCCESS – (DR. NEIL COHEN)

Read about: DR. NEIL COHEN & DISCOVER how he has taken the CORE Philosophy of CHIROPRACTIC to a NEW level. As Vice-President of Sherman College of Chiropractic, Dr. Cohen leads CHIROPRACTORS in defining WHO they are & WHAT they must do NOW to become the Chiropractor of their dreams. A MUST-LISTEN interview for any doctor who wants to get to the ROOT of what makes Chiropractic the #1 Natural Health Care Profession in the World & HOW Chiropractors can LOOK INSIDE to find their hidden POWER.

Dr. Bard:

Do you believe in miracles? Today, by so many measures is a miracle. A miracle in the sense that some shows that we do on the Dr. Success Spotlight Radio Show take literally, 37 minutes and we can put the show together. Some shows actually, believe it or not, take about 37 days for us to put together. What if I told you, that today's show, actually has taken 37 years to put together. It is such a distinct honor to have with us, the one and only, vice president of Sherman College of Chiropractic, Dr. Neil Cohen. Welcome to the show, Dr. Cohen.

Dr. Cohen:

Well, thank you Dr. Bard. What a great introduction! I truly appreciate that and I appreciate our longtime friendship of over 37 years.

Dr. Bard:

Well, as they say, "what a long, strange trip it's been". The reason for that is the timing of the show is really simple, in the fact that as a chiropractor, you know the truth. The truth is you must always know where you've been, to know where you're going, but the emphasis really should be on the now. So very simply doctor, if I ask you, doctor, what are you doing right now to make your life, to make your world, to make your practice, to make your universe better? That's a very, very heavy-duty question that starts with you Doctor. It begins with the truth and with absolutely being truthful to yourself.

First and foremost, Dr. Cohen is, one of the most magnetic doctors, one of the most magnetic souls you will ever meet, really in the purest sense of the word. He has become the torch carrier for what it means to be a chiropractor. You may ask, why is that so important right now? Well, I guess you would say, almost in the words of the great, Paul Simon, who said "that the answer is simple, if you take it logically, I'd like to help you in your struggle to be free". That comes from a song, called "50 Ways to Leave Your Lover". The reason I said that is because Paul Simon is at the root, a Queens, NY. boy and Dr. Cohen is a Queens, NY boy.

So, we all start the same way with the differences defining what you are as a chiropractor. The good news is Dr. Neil Cohen, spends his time now helping chiropractors define who they are as chiropractors. What I would love to ask you, Dr. Cohen, is your story, which took 37 years in the making for this to happen. I would love for you to share your personal story from student to associate to owner to entrepreneur, and now, to vice president. Can you share a little bit in terms of the evolution as to how you started and to where you are right now?

Dr. Cohen:

Yes. What a great question. I'd like to even go back just a little bit further to how I became interested in becoming a chiropractor. I've said for many, many years that chiropractic is a calling, it's not a career. I believe with all my heart that I was called into this profession by a much higher power, much greater than I, and it happened this way. I was really searching for a purpose in my life and I had been searching for a purpose in my life for my entire life. I knew a few things. I knew I loved people, I knew I wanted to help people, I knew that I enjoyed serving people. And I actually went to college for two years and I dropped out because I could not find my purpose. I started in the entrepreneurial area and then something happened. I met my beautiful, gorgeous wife, who at that time was going to a chiropractor and we started going out and she was telling me about this chiropractor, and I really was a naysayer at the time. I said," listen, I don't know anything about that". She said, "why don't you just come in with me on one of my visits and meet him"? I said, "yeah, I can do that".

I was young, and I was strong, and I was not quite as professional and a bit less mature. I went in there pretty much ready to read him the Riot Act about what he did as a chiropractor. He took one look at me, and he said something to me that changed my life. He said, "you have a bad neck". I said, "what do you mean"? While he was saying that I did have a bad neck, I had missed so many days of school with a bad neck. I had grown up with stiff necks, tonsillitis, all these different things. He said, "I really like your girlfriend, I really like Randi and I want to give you some X-rays. I want to give you an adjustment and I'm going to do that all for free". And I was about 20, 21 years old and I got to tell you, free was a really good work back then. So, I took him up on his offer and he took an X-ray of my neck. I had a reverse curve, he showed me that. He said, "this can be corrected with chiropractic". He gave me an adjustment and literally that first adjustment changed the course of my life.

I knew right away that I wanted to be a chiropractor. It was perfect timing. I had two years of college. I said to him, "where the heck have they been keeping this stuff"? This is amazing. I felt like I walked in with a suitcase on my back, and now, I'm free. As Paul Simon said, "that was my struggle to get free", and I got free from that first adjustment and it literally caused me to pause and to think, what is this? Where have they been keeping it? So, I asked him and he couldn't tell me. He couldn't communicate the chiropractic message. The only thing he was able to do was hand me a list of chiropractic colleges throughout the country and he said, "you should be a chiropractor". So, I wrote away to all the colleges, and what had had happened was, I decided on the college for the worst reason in the world, and this is why students even today, decide on college based only on geographical location. Me, being in Florida, I picked the closest college to where I was in Florida and that was Georgia. So, I went up to Georgia, and little did I know, as I went up to Georgia. You and I did this almost simultaneously, Dr. Bard. We went up almost together. I got up to Georgia and I met a guy named Dr. Sid Williams. At the time I met him, I thought he was off his rocker, but this was a guy, who was so committed to teaching the world about the profound negative effects of vertebral subluxation and teaching the world about the profound positive effects of a chiropractic checkup and an adjustment, that it literally got implanted deeply into my soul. Thus, I became this stalwart, steadfast warrior for this principle, we call Chiropractic, which really is very, very simple.

It teaches us that the body is self-healing and that the nervous system does everything within the body. If the nervous system has interference that's not good and only the chiropractor can remove nerve interference, and

I bought this thing, hook, line and sinker, and I have to tell you, you said something wonderful. It's important that we know ourselves. The greatest gift we can give to yourself is to know ourselves and the greatest gift we can give to ourselves, is to walk in the truth and this became my truth and this is the way I walked. Now, I've walked this way until the present day. I had a practice, a very successful high-volume practice in South Florida for many years, a family practice, and my practice was based on success from telling the chiropractic story.

I believe in one thing. That your practice grows proportionate to the amount of people that you tell the story of chiropractic to. So, I became this individual that had a wonderful gift for articulating the message, telling as many people as I possibly could about this, wonderful, wonderful gift called chiropractic. It eventually led to me being the executive vice president of Sherman College. So that's sort of the cliff notes.

Dr. Bard:

Well, not only is it a great story, but it happens to be one of my truly favorite stories, and the reason it's one of my truly favorite stories is because I've actually for 37 years had a front row seat to be able to watch the evolution of success through "Dr. Neil Cohen". He didn't just roll out of bed, it didn't just start this way. It was a maturation, it was an evolution and it was something that I always referred to by this great movie years ago. One of my favorite movies of all time and one of the reasons, it was one of my favorite movies is because it had a message. It also had the greatest title in the world, and it was called "Awakening". The reason I loved it, is it was a Robert De Niro and Robin Williams' movie. Thus, I got a chance to sit court side to have a front row seat to watch the "Awakening" of Dr. Neil Cohen to go from student to clinician to healer to doctor to vice president. And guess what? He is just getting started.

Dr. Cohen and I actually went to school, in what Dr. Cohen and I always referred to in Chiropractic as "the golden era". Now, if you're curious why we called it "the golden era" is when you look back, some may define the 1980s, as the "lofty 80s". Whereby 80 percent, of the populace had 80 percent insurance coverage. So, when we came out into this brave new world, and hit the streets running, it was a different playing field. it really was. As they say, "times are never good, times and times are never bad, they're just different". So, I also with Dr. Cohen defined it as "the golden era" because of what we termed at that time, was "the giants of the profession" the leaders of chiropractic at that time, the college presidents and the creators of all these great techniques and really some of the most engaging teachers and lecturers in the country were always at "arm's length". So, what I would love for you, Dr. Cohen to share is how the playing field has changed, and how in many ways it's gotten even better?

Dr. Cohen:

That's a very astute understanding that you have Dr. Bard. What we used to have is the leaders. We used to have BJ, and then we had Dr. Sid, and then we had Dr. Parker, and we had Dr. Sigafoose, and all the different greats, Dr. Bard, and all the ones that I'm leaving out. Unfortunately, we don't have those singular leaders anymore. What we have is we have a much more collaborative effort on the part of chiropractic leadership to get this message to the world in the past. Yes, we still have a lot of ego in chiropractic today. We still have a lot of separation in chiropractic today, a lot of division. What we do know is that we are one profession and that one profession is going to succeed only with collaboration, only with a cohesive, strategic plan to set forth what it is we do and what it is people can expect from a chiropractor. In the past, back in the 80s and earlier, Chiropractic was really fighting for its literal life.

People may not remember, but in 1988, there was a largest antitrust lawsuit against chiropractic, I mean, from the AMA because the AMA was trying to eliminate and contain the profession of chiropractic with propaganda. Four chiropractors sued the AMA and believe it or not, we won, and we beat the giant and that ended in the AMA's inability to propagandize against chiropractic and that was only in 1988. In 1972, the last chiropractor that we know of, was jailed for practicing chiropractic without a license. This is not long ago. Chiropractic was literally fighting for its life. Now, people have become much more aware of the dangers of allopathic intervention, at least at a higher level. So, people are seeking more natural means. This was the goal of the leaders back then. Many of them are gone, if not most of them but have succeeded in bringing chiropractic to the forefront as an alternative to getting sick people well versus the allopathic philosophy and model, which is really the treatment of an illness.

At Sherman College, we're very proud of our Salutogenic Model. Salutogenic is much different than pathogenic. Pathogenic is they're looking for the treatment of disease or why disease happens. In the Salutogenic Model, we want to know why health happens and that's with chiropractic why health happens. So, we need to get together and begin to teach people this great secret. The great secret is that they have the power of the universe within themselves and it's a power so great that science has never been able to quantify it and they won't be able to. The unfortunate thing is people have been robbed of the belief that the body actually can heal itself and so we need like they did in the "Wizard of Oz" to convince those characters that they already have everything that it takes to be healthy. When patients walk in your door, they know they have everything that it takes to be healthy, you just flip the switch and we need to get together as leaders in this profession and share this message and do this with humanity, for humanity to reshape humanity. We need to know what we believe, and why we believe it, so we can do that.

Dr. Bard:

Doctors, are you feeling the passion? Are you feeling the energy? Are you feeling what I've been feeling for 37 years? Are you feeling the love? Are you feeling the heart? You see, Dr. Cohen speaks from his heart and it is so deep rooted. In chiropractic, we always, always talk about something known as "the ties that bind us". Chiropractic has always been rooted as a profession in "the ties that bind us". In other words, we all started the same way, what direction we go in, well, that's a very individualistic thing but the magic and the real juice behind success is how you can define it for your patients, how you could define it for yourself.

So, I think it's so exciting because of the simple fact that what you've done, Dr. Cohen is in your genius, you've made this very simple and the most beautiful things in life are simple. So, you've been able to simplify how doctors communicate chiropractic better, more efficiently and it starts with themselves. So, what I'm curious about right now is this, as I love your evolution. If your life was a movie, I'm going to tell you, I'd be sitting front row, major popcorn, stuff in my hand, major *Goobers and Raisinets*. I'd be on the edge of my seat because it wasn't easy for you. I would love for you to talk a little bit about how some of the challenges in your process were turned from lemons into lemonade and how you were able to overcome those personal challenges I have a feeling, a very strong feeling that there are chiropractors in abundance reading this that will see a very similar path. Can you share that personally?

Dr. Cohen:

Yes, and I'm really happy to do that, and thank you for mentioning that. This is wonderful way to be able to share this with who knows how many hundreds or thousands of people or maybe even more that are out there. I believe that some of the things that we have to overcome is we have to be very, very honest with ourselves. We can't kid ourselves, that's number one. We have to own who we are. We also need a support system. For me, I've always had a tremendous support system. Not only did my wife turn me onto chiropractic, but she has been there every step of the way, supporting me and this is absolutely crucial that you have people in your life that are devoted to what it is that you're doing.

If you have any folks that are in opposition to what you're doing that are close to you, that can become a strong distraction, they can cause you to drift. We have to anchor and being anchored is the most important thing. There are two things we do. We anchor and when we anchor, we know where we are and then we go. Once we take the anchor up, then we're going to another destination. So, we always know where we are, and we always know where we're going. The problem is, the drifting and many people in the chiropractic world are drifting and they're drifting because they are either not solid in their communication, they're not solid in their

246

technique, they're not solid in their certainty, they're not solid in their support system, and it could be even their marriage.

We have this incredible philosophy that teaches people to depend on that which created them, and we are the only ones that are able to share this philosophy, and yet, it's not just in our office. Chiropractic and its philosophy, and what it teaches transcends chiropractic. It's about your life and what does your life look like. What does your life look like with your kids, with your wife? In other words, are you teaching people to be the best version of themselves through chiropractic, but yet, you yourself don't have the best version of a marriage or the best version of a relationship with your children. These are the most important things. Chiropractic is a way to help people understand how to express life better. Life doesn't end with your health. Life expression is about your life. I've often said, that chiropractic is really not about health, it's about life because health is a subset of life because without life you have no health. This is very important to understand that when we look at our 33 principles, which is something else that we have to depend on, and if you don't depend on them, it's like not depending on gravity, it's not depending on what is really out there. Our 33 principles never mentioned the word health, but they mentioned the word life over 12 times, life or living. So, chiropractic is about life, it's about expression, it's about living, it's about restoration, it's about connection and being the best person that you could be throughout your life, not just in your office. So, what I would say to those folks out there that are struggling is you've got to have a support system. You can't rely on your ego, you can't rely on your own self, what you have to rely on is the power that is being given to you and you also have to rely on your maturity. You have to grow in this understanding of what chiropractic is.

You'll never arrive, I'll just tell you. You will never arrive because chiropractic is a bottomless well. We'll never fully get it but we have an obligation and a responsibility to learn as much about it as we can. We always are saying the same thing, but we're just learning to do it in different ways and it's important that we know how to give this message out in 50 ways. It's like you brought up that song, and I always think about that song in chiropractic, "50 ways to leave your lover". There's 50 ways you can be a chiropractor and there's 50 ways you can tell the chiropractic story. If you don't know 50 ways to tell the story or you just don't know how to be a chiropractor because being a chiropractor isn't about pushing on high spots, it's about relationships, it's about intimacy, it's about loving your patients in a way that they understand that you love them, you care for them and you care for them not just in their body, but their mind and their spirit as well. You never know who that guy is or that gal is that's walking into your office that's thinking about buying that shotgun or thinking about taking their own life or thinking about doing something really, really serious.

You could be the difference between them and an incredibly bad decision. So, take what you do very seriously, no drifting, know where you are, and know where you're going. Get that support system in place and make sure your marriage is strong, make sure your relationships are strong. You've got to do the right thing because at the end of the day, it's all about doing the right thing because if you're not doing the right thing, you have an opportunity to get in trouble. Then, what good are you, if you're a chiropractor in trouble. What good are you if you are a chiropractor who is not be able to practice chiropractic because you're not doing the things that are necessary to be compliant within this great profession? I think that for me, it's just a question of being balanced and grounded in all of those things.

Dr. Bard:

I love your analogies, I love your examples, I love the way you're able to really pull it together for so many chiropractors, who are looking to raise their game one more degree. I love how you also too, quote the Paul Simon's song, and I promise you I've never shared that with anyone. I waited 37 years to share the lyrics from that song because I just thought it was just "apropos". I thought it was just "spot on" for a kid from Corona, Queens and a kid from Flushing, Queens. I knew you had more in common with him. I just knew it and I love that. I love the simple fact that I think the greatest testament to your commitment to the profession is how you've been able to pass this on. So right now, Dr. Cohen and myself are really walking on hallowed ground, because of the simple fact, that if you would've told me 37 years ago that our children would have chosen this career path, I would have said, "you better pinch me, this isn't a dream, this has got to be a fantasy" because this is the coolest thing going. For Dr. Neil Cohen's family, with Dr. Sara Cohen, and soon to be doctor, Dr. Michael Cohen in the process as well. As many of you know, our son also, just started, holy cow, chiropractic college. How exciting is this?

What I would love Dr. Cohen is if you would be so kind, I know for a fact, that there are doctors reading this that have questions, that need a higher sense of purpose, a higher sense of understanding, a higher sense of comprehension and they just want to be able to tell the story a little bit better. They want to be able to dial in one degree more and that's your magic. It's always been your magic and the best part is it continues to get better. What's the easiest way to get in touch with you, if they have a question, and want to reach out to you for a one-to-one conversation or the possibility and probability of having you lecture to a much bigger audience for their state or their convention or their association because you're the best at that. Can you share that?

Dr. Cohen:

I'm happy to do that. My phone number at the college is (864) 578-8770 and my extension is 222. That's probably not the easiest way to get ahold of me because I'm always out and about running like crazy all over the world. If you follow me on Facebook, you know that I'm in multiple cities, multiple times a month, sharing this message and showcasing Sherman College. The best way to reach me, however, would be my email address, which is that's ncohen@sherman.edu. That's the best way to reach me.

The other thing that I would encourage folks to do is come to visit Sherman College. We're in the midst of a $20 million-dollar capital campaign. We're building on our beautiful 90 acres brand new building and we're transforming the campus. It's absolutely amazing. If you've never been to Sherman, please come and see it. If you have been, you won't recognize it. We have our Lyceum Program this year. You can get your continuing education credits. I will be there along with Dr. Cordero.

Dr. Bard:

Dr. Neil Cohen. He is abundant in his love for this profession, he is abundant in his commitment to this profession and he is abundant in all things that are good. Make your life better, I guarantee you by putting him in your universe. I have for 37 years. In baseball there's a saying that they have. If you ever talk to a ballplayer, they'll tell you that they are "living the dream". I can honestly and emphatically tell you doctors that for 37 years, I have been living the dream as a chiropractor because I had one person by my side as a brother in chiropractic, his name is Dr. Neil Cohen, and as we said, were just getting started.

HERE ARE THE BULLET-POINT TAKEAWAYS:

#1 - He grew up in Queens, New York. Moved to Florida and went with his future wife Randi to visit her Chiropractor. Upon receiving his 1st Adjustment, he knew right then he wanted to become a Chiropractor.

#2 - He attended Life College in Marietta, Georgia and was mesmerized in the Conviction of Chiropractic that Dr. Sid Williams had as the President of the school. He now carries on those same Dynamic Essential principles.

#3 - Over time he became the steady, stalwart, steadfast warrior of the Principal of Chiropractic.

#4 - After running a high-volume, family practice in South Florida, he found that his true gift was articulating the core principles of Chiropractic and was given the invitation to sell his practice and move to Spartanburg, South Carolina where he became the Executive, Vice-President of Sherman College of Chiropractic.

#5 - He vividly recalls the time that we went to school together where the giants of the profession from Dr. Sid Williams to Dr. James Sigafoose to Dr. James Parker helped carve the path of success for so many Chiropractors.

#6 - He feels now that with collaboration and a cohesive strategic plan of action for Chiropractic, that Chiropractors can reach new heights.

#7 - He feels that the key to his success has been his support system that starts with his wife and children. Two of his children had decided to follow the same career path and also become Chiropractors.

#8 - Our 33 principles never mentioned the word health, but they mentioned the word life over 12 times, life or living. So, chiropractic is about life, it's about expression, it's about living, it's about restoration, it's about connection, and being the best person that you could be throughout your life, not just in your office.

#9 - There's 50 ways you can be a chiropractor, and there's 50 ways you can tell the chiropractic story. Being a chiropractor isn't about pushing on high spots, it's about relationships, it's about intimacy, it's about loving your patients in a way that they understand that you love them, you care for them and you care for them not just in their body, but their mind and their spirit as well.

#10 - He now spends the majority of his time educating, teaching, traveling and making sure that the next generation of Chiropractors understand that the profession was built on the dreams of Giants, who had the courage to tell the Chiropractic story to everybody and thus to be relentless in the pursuit of our own inner truth.

20

SHARK TANK SUCCESS – (DR. KENGEE EHRLICH)

Read about: DR. KENGEE EHRLICH & DISCOVER how he has set the HOME CARE product world ablaze with the creation of "THE GOOD ROLL" pillow. Learn HOW he has combined the BEST of CHIROPRACTIC and the BEST Branding/Identity in the country as "THE GOOD CHIROPRACTOR". His "SHARK TANK" approach to creating better lives for his patients and the profession at-large is UNMATCHED. Listen to this EXCITING interview of one of the TRUE Superstars of the profession.

Dr. Bard:

I can't tell you how revved up I am today to share with you doctors, a special guest to the Dr. Success Spotlight Radio Show today that is so uplifting, so unique, so good at what he does, and really so much fun in terms of how distinct he is in our profession. It is such an honor to have with us someone who, in my opinion, a doctor that has no equal in our profession. It is such a true honor to welcome the incredible birthday boy himself, Dr. KenGee Ehrlich. Happy birthday and welcome to the show Dr. KenGee Ehrlich.

Dr. KenGee:

Nice one on the birthday thing. Very nice. Thanks for having me, brother.

Dr. Bard:

Well, you my friend are getting better, like fine wine in California. You are getting better with age, so today, we get really a rare chance to pull back the curtains, and to reveal what has made you, Dr. KenGee, the doctor to so many families, the doctor to so many athletes, the doctor to so many celebrities, and really so many patients that are sick and tired of simply being sick and tired. We are in such stratified air here today with Dr. KenGee Ehrlich. One of the greatest gifts in being a chiropractor is that we each individually, personally and definitely professionally get to define who we are. That's one of the magic things about being a chiropractor.

Dr. KenGee Ehrlich, you have done such an amazing job in that direction, and that now you, doctors, really get a chance to get an up close, and really a very personal inside look as to how exactly, Dr. KenGee became known as "The Good Chiropractor", which is his brand. It's really his identity. It is his platform for a host of very creative and very exciting gifts that he's created for his patients. It's really remarkable in that sense. This includes for the first time ever on the Dr. Success Spotlight Show, a very rare opportunity to be able to have in your possession at the end of this show, one of Dr.

KenGee's gifts in your hands by the end of this show, which we've never ever done before. It's really incredible. So besides being known nationally and internationally as "The Good Chiropractor", Dr. KenGee has also defined, himself and I love this verbiage because it is so profound, and it is so unique to him as a "master chiropractor". I can emphatically tell you that he lives up to every definition of that word and that he is a master, and I mean a master adjuster. He is also a master diagnostician.

My favorite is that he is actually a master entrepreneur. If you asked him, I bet you he'll tell you also he's a master husband and he's a master father, which to me shines so brightly here, in terms of what, Dr. KenGee is all about. This is not by chance, this is not by luck, this happens by design. So, what I would love to ask you, Dr. KenGee coming right out of the gate here today on Dr. Success Spotlight Show, is how you my friend got started as a chiropractor and why? What I'm curious about is why you chose Southern California I always called Southern California, where you practice the heart of the action, specifically Los Angeles. Can you share how you got started and why you practice in Los Angeles?

Dr. KenGee:

Sure. I went to school at UC Santa Barbara, which is basically just a party school. I was a music major and I was going to make beats for rap songs. Then one day, we're driving down to TJ or coming back from TJ after a big night of drinking. There were six of us stuffed in the Volkswagen Bug and the girl driving, going about 70, rolled the car about six times off the side of the freeway. I got out and I was like, "I'm good". The guy behind me, his ear was cut off, the girl driving shattered both of her legs and I got out and I was like, oh, I'm okay but when I went back up to Santa Barbara, I played the drums and I put this pair of drums on something called the quaint, which weighed like 50 pounds and right when I put those drums on, my legs went out. I'm like, "oh, that's weird". I didn't have any pain, just my legs went out, and so it started happening more frequently, where I would like step up on a curb and my legs would go out. Then the thing that made me investigate this further is I was at

Wiener Schnitzel, which obviously we don't eat anymore, but I went to throw my trash away and my legs buckled, and I was laying on the ground for like four or five minutes. I was like, "okay, something was wrong".

My buddy referred me to this chiropractor. He saw that I was subluxated at L5 and within 12 weeks it never happened again. This dude had a plane, had a Benz, had the hottest girl in the gym. I'm like, "this is for me". I asked him what his major was in school and he said he was a football player first and I said, "I can do that". So that's when I decided I'd be a chiropractor. So, I finished school in 1990, over 20 years ago. I grew up in Lancaster, California, and going to school in Santa Barbara, got a little taste of LA and my school was in LA. I went Cleveland Chiropractic School in LA and I lived in Santa Monica, so I just opened this spot. For the first few years I practiced under someone else and then in 2001, I opened my own spot on Santa Monica Boulevard. So that's how I came up and landed in LA and I just haven't left yet, no reason to.

Dr. Bard:

Now, I don't know if you can tell doctors in Dr. but obviously, his mojo, which I think is so refreshing, so unique, so powerful, absolutely mimics the core of this show. Which is uncut, unrehearsed, unfiltered, unplanned. That is part of the magic of Dr. KenGee. I think what's interesting, what's shines about you, Dr. KenGee is really so many things and I've watched you adjust. I've actually watched a lot of video with you most recently adjusting all patients, all shapes, all sizes, including some very, very challenging patient presentations that probably needed you, Dr. KenGee, probably more than anyone. Your dexterity, your kinesthetic touch, your ability to, as we would always say in chiropractic "to find it, to fix it and to leave it alone" is in part training, it's experience, it's innate. At the end of the day, your hands, Dr. KenGee are without question, pure magic. Share with our readers a bit as to how that skillset has defined you and how that came about?

Dr. KenGee:

Well, wow, thanks for the kind words. I guess I never really thought about it, but I trained and make it a point for me, to get my hands on as many people as possible and that's why they call it "a practice". I just practice on people all day long, and I try something new, see how it goes or didn't go and that's the art. I've been training to make it a point to do something in chiropractic every month, whether it's a seminar or a mastermind call or going to my local CCA meeting or whatever. I just try to surround myself with people at least once a month to keep my excitement up, my mojo up, learning new techniques from my friends, getting adjusted and just practice what I preach. Then just really care about what the people want and get in there and do it and educate them on, what the hell is going on and now we're going to fix it.

This is my life in chiropractic and I'm in, so anything I can do to get smarter, to get better, to see more patients, to get more new patients, to streamline my procedures, to make it time efficient for my patients and get them in and get them out as fast as possible, so we don't waste their day, and just keep learning.

I mean, I do mostly prone cervical adjustments and I remember first starting those in 2003. I don't know how many people that got adjusted but with repetition, everything gets smoothed after time. But you've got to start somewhere and just go to get your hands on as many people as possible. In the beginning, I'm trying to build my practice, I gave it away for the sake of getting practice. Now, I can afford the luxury of charging. So that's part of why I get my hands on it and the technical aspect that we also do. I'm also doing the motion study X-rays. That's something I just learned a few years ago. That's great for analysis and an amazing tool that I've never had before. Being able to show the patient exactly where the subluxation is really validates what we do, especially when we do post X-rays and afterward. So that's a little glimpse and how we get these hands to do it up.

257

Dr. Bard:

That is so refreshing, so unique, so distinct and so different is the simple fact that you, Dr. KenGee really are a "student of the game". I think when people meet you, they know about you, they understand what your purpose, what your mission is, and what you do on a day-to-day basis. You, my friend, are absolutely "ALL-IN", it is that simple. There's an old saying which is "why blend in with the rest, when you can have such a great opportunity here to stand out and be different".

Being successful in practice absolutely mirrors being successful in life. What we would say is "this not a dress rehearsal". You get one chance to do this right doctors, you really do. You get one chance to do this. Now, when I use the term "dress rehearsal", what I would love to ask you about is this Dr. KenGee and that is regarding dress. Let's talk a little bit about how you Dr. KenGee, dress in your office. Which I think is the perfect synergy between professional and tailored and fun and colorful. It's an experience. I mean, it is expressive. I think it definitely matches your attitude, I think it matches your energy, I think it matches your personality. Definitely, it raises the bar for all doctors, who really want to make the best first impression and the best lasting impression on their patients. Can you talk a little bit about the official, I guess I would call it, the "official good chiropractor game or clinic uniform"?

Dr. KenGee:

Sure. It evolved into what it is now. In the beginning, when I first started, I would wear a white clinic jacket. I was trying to actually comb my hair like superman, so I would look super clean cut. My wife was like, "what are you doing"? I was like, "I need to be myself". Right when I started being myself, oh man, it exploded. I would show up to practice with a purple spiked Mohawk. I would wear glittering pants. I always wear a clinic jacket though and always a tie. I think Dr. Fred Schofield always told me, always look better than your best dressed patient. So, I'd always have to make sure I look tight. I like to dress like I like to feel.

258

So nowadays, I still wear a clinic jacket, but it's black, like Johnny Cash and then I'll just wear whatever crazy pants. I mean, I couldn't imagine going to the chiropractor and see them wearing the same pants over and over, It's gross. They're not washed all the time. I rotate through 50, 60 shirts and ties. I got a couple of hundred ties. I just make them crazy. When you're looking styling, the female patients notice it and when you look crazy, the guy patients notice it. I just like to keep it fresh. I wear maybe one outfit every six weeks. I just got a huge rotation and I got pants with crazy prints on it. I don't wear socks or shoes now in the office and I got a better grip on the ground. When they come in, they think it's interesting but always black jacket, tie, no matter what. I just keep it tight and look good.

Dr. Bard:

It's so visual. What you're doing is so visual. There's an old saying that "we eat with our eyes first" and because your ability to grab your patients from above-down, inside-out to change them in a course of a better quality of life. It starts with them getting exposed to your universe, your practice, your vibe, your direction and your mission to be able to show them a beginning, a middle and an end after their treatment, which I think is so unique because I think you've been able to tie this all together so well. That's part of the magic, again, visually as to be able to show your patients some of their curve changes, show them biomechanically what's going on and there's some very specific things that you've done which is really a gift to our profession.

One of the things, I wanted to ask you was this and that is the uniqueness of you, Dr. KenGee with respect to your practice, is that it actually caters to a host of different actors, actresses, athletes, celebrities, families with a very unique passion that you also have. For something that's been so dear to our hearts, from a very, very early age, which happens to be, believe it or not, your connection to professional wrestling, which I think is amazing. Can you share the alignment that you've had as a chiropractor with professional wrestling?

Dr. KenGee:

It's funny because when I met my wife, she was a model from LA. So, she ended up getting into the WWE after we were engaged. She would go on the road with them and then once in a while I would go on a week-long tour with them and I would just bring my portable table and I would just get in there and I would set up my table. I wouldn't set up with the trainers where they would go to get taped or get their medications as often they take so many pills, they take antacids and all kinds of stuff to wash it down I would set my table up, right in the middle of where they all hang out and there'd be like 50/60 wrestlers and I would just flop open my table and I say "who's up" and once I start adjusting one person and they just get in line and they love getting adjusted. I'd adjust them before the match and after the match. It got to be a joke to whether I would go on the road or my wife would go on the road.

Eventually, she became the WWE champion, the Diva champion. All the wrestlers would always ask her where I was. They are happy to see her because they just want to get adjusted. So, they appreciate getting taken care of by somebody that can actually adjust. I actually met up with one of our buddies. He actually did the east coast WWE shows and I would do all the west coast WWE shows. His name was Craig Banks. I just met up with him last week to get adjusted in Ohio. Every single wrestler gets adjusted no matter what. Some of them have had fractured necks and they still want me to adjust them above and below the fractured segment or they'd have fusions or shoulder issues. I mean, they're a wreck. It's like they're getting in a 30 mile an hour car accident every time they get thrown down on the mat. So, imagine what they feel like after a match where they get tossed down 10, 15 times. They need us still to this day and a bunch of them still come to the office. I work out with a lot of them, a couple of days a week. They need us, every sport needs us like desperately.

Dr. Bard:

Well you hit it on the head, and I think the reason being is the simple fact that there's so many bumps, there's so much stress biomechanically, and also, I believe, as you know so well, the lifestyle being on the road. It's like being a combination of a rock star, a high-level athlete and a stunt person. With the things that they have to put their bodies through and to be "always on" as it relates to the cameras, it's not the easiest thing to be able to do things in one take and that's the magic of what they do. If you can handle those patients, which you've done so incredibly successfully for so many years, in every worst case scenario of how they present with every bad disc, every bulging disk, herniated discs and more and to be able to provide the degree of relief that you do and do with such passion and do with such flair and really do it with such lasting benefits, that is one of the things that have made you so unique and so distinct and so different.

What I wanted to talk to you about, Dr. KenGee is something that I think is the greatest thing since sliced bread. I'm not kidding. If you've heard me before and doctors you know me, after 32 years in this business, I've never gotten behind any single product ever on the Dr. Success Spotlight Radio Show. I want to talk about something that you've created. It serves multiple, multiple uses for every chiropractor and their patient base. It's called "The Good Roll". What I love about this, is it's a combination of a number of different things with respect to it being not just a cervical spinal support but it's also a sleeping pillow and it's a travel pillow. It's amazing and this is what caught my attention right out of the gate in terms of how you also use it. With it also being an adjusting support pillow and more. What I would love to ask you, Dr. KenGee is where did the idea for the Good Roll Pillow come from?

Dr. KenGee:

Well, great question. For years, I've always encouraged cervical rolls to sleep on the back and I had such a hard time finding one that fits for everybody. Those one from Meijer and Script are just terrible and they don't work. Then finally, I found this pillow from that guy on TV with a bad mustache. He developed the cervical roll and I loved it initially. So, I was selling like 50 of these things a month to all my new patients for like a year or two. Then finally, one of my friends who is also a PI attorney got one. I sold him one of the pillows, so he starts lying on his

261

back for 20 minutes, as I tell all my patients and that week he went to the hospital two times for a lung infection and he couldn't breathe, and it was so bad and then he got out. Then two days later, he went back again, and they put him on all kinds of steroids and all kinds of stuff to get better. Then he got off the pillow and that completely went away So I started looking into it and apparently, the pillow foam they use is all made with a chemical called "methyl isocyanate", which is a chemical that was actually released in India in the 80s and it killed 6,000 people. I said, "we can't be sleeping on foam". So, in making my pillow the right way is I had this old Japanese buckwheat pillow that I used to love when I slept on my side and it was always cool and we got rid of the foam pillows and I actually cut the pillow open and took all the foam out and I stuffed it with buckwheat from my Japanese pillow.

I started sleeping on it and it was amazing. The next day, both of our sinuses were completely clear. Every morning we're waking up with sinus issue and we just thought it was like allergies or whatever and we haven't had any sinus issues since sleeping on the buckwheat pillow. Then, both of us, were like, "we need to make these". There wasn't any kind of circular buckwheat pillows on the market. So, I said "okay, I'll just make it myself" and so we just invested a lot of time and a lot of money. I'm still developing it and figuring out ways to improve it, but when it first came out, it was such a pain in the ass because I had to open it and take the buckwheat out and give it to each patient. Now, we figured out a way where there's a button on the side where you can actually adjust it to firm, medium or soft. It fits every patient. So, we figured out how to get these pillows to fit properly. I'm training patients on how to use them, so they get a good night sleep.

It's like riding a bike or brushing your teeth. Someone's taught us how to do that stuff. Not one person I ever asked has been taught how to sleep properly. So, I teach them how to sleep and we do sleep training, like we do as a little baby. So that's kind of the story of how "The Good Roll" came along. It's my baby. It's all non-toxic buckwheat we use from an organic farm in North Dakota. The covers are made in India from raw, organic cotton. So, it's the best because I sleep on it. My kids sleep on it and I'm sharing it with my patients and eventually, the world. We're going to get everybody on a roll.

Dr. Bard:

It fills such a void in lifestyle management. It is such a unique product that I am so in love with that I guarantee every one of my patients will be on this. I'm buying them as gifts for the holidays. They don't know it yet. Everybody's going to get one. First of all, that's one of your surprises right there. I'm buying it for a host of different people because to me, this is the gift that keeps giving. This is the real, real deal. I love the fact that it was an evolution of your success. In other words, it didn't start out that way. That it actually was basically you having to go back to the laboratory. You had to keep working it, refining it, changing it, and making it the product that it is today, which I think is unlike anything, and I mean anything that I've ever seen in terms of how to manage stress.

The reality is, if you could sleep better, you will heal better. If you can heal better, you'll function better. If you can function better than I guarantee your quality of life for your patients, doctors will go up radically. What I would love for you, Dr. KenGee if you would be so kind, is to actually share your contact information with our readers, as well as, information on how they can get their hands on the single greatest gift, the single greatest product that I have ever seen for patient management. That's a big statement. You guys know me 32 years in this business. You know what I've done. I've never gotten behind anything like this and I will tell you for the record, this is a 100 percent unsolicited testimonial here for Dr. KenGee. I promise you that this product is that good. Do me a favor, Dr. KenGee, share with our readers right now, how they can get their hands on this.

Dr. KenGee:

All of my personal chiropractic contact stuff is The Good Chiropractor Facebook, Instagram, YouTube, www.thegoodchiropractor.com. The pillow website is www.thegoodrollpillow.com. I got a gift for your readers If they enter the code "spotlight", they'll get half price off of one.

Dr. Bard:

You are the gift that keeps giving. I'll tell you something, Dr. KenGee, if I make one suggestion to you. The only thing that I would change is that instead of being known as what you and everybody know you as in "The Good Chiropractor". To me, you are really the "The Great Chiropractor". If you watch a TV show called "The Good Doctor", which is the highest-rated drama right now on ABC, I promise you, "The Good Chiropractor" existed a lot longer than "The Good Doctor" and is in the process of being the "Great Chiropractor". If I asked any of your patients, I can guarantee that they probably wouldn't say that you're "The Good Chiropractor". They probably wouldn't even say that you're "The Great Chiropractor". What they would probably tell me and everybody else is that you, Dr. KenGee, are "The Best Chiropractor" and I can't thank you enough for being our most, most special guest on the Dr. Success Spotlight Radio Show.

We gave a lecture in November to 150 doctors in an audience in Dallas, Texas and I showed one movie clip and the movie clip that I showed I had never showed it before. I never shared with anyone, but it really kind of sums up Dr. KenGee. What I showed was an excerpt from a movie and it was a movie called "The Karate Kid".

In the Karate Kid, there's a scene, where Mr. Miyagi is talking to Daniel-son, and he tells him these words. He tells him that you can walk on the left side of the road, you can walk on the right side of the road, just don't walk in the middle. That is the gift that Dr. KenGee shares. He absolutely walks the talk, he lives the lifestyle that we have exemplified on this show of profit, freedom and fun. He is so much fun. He really is the epitome of what makes our profession great. We are so thankful, so honored to have had him on our show.

HERE ARE THE BULLET-POINT TAKEAWAYS:

#1 - Based in Southern California, (Los Angeles) he started as a music major at University of California-Santa Barbara. After a serious automobile accident and suffering serious neurological deficits, he decided to go to Cleveland Chiropractic school in Los Angeles.

#2 - He became a Master adjuster and a Master Chiropractor by making it his mission to put his hands on as many people as possible or as he says, "To Practice". Over time his skill set became unmatched.

#3 - His purpose now is he feels anything he can do to get smarter, to get better, to see more patients, to get more new patients, to streamline his procedures, to make it time efficient for his patients to get treatment is where is emphasis is right now.

#4 - He utilizes motion x-rays with pre and post studies to objectively measure and validate all of his patients care programs.

#5 - He like to dress in the clinic how he feels yet always wears a clinic jacket, often black. Bright colors and combinations he rotates about 60 different outfits, which is an extension of his personality.

#6 - As his wife was a Professional Wrestling Champion with the WWE, he was introduced to the world of professional wrestling and became the Chiropractor to wrestlers, athletes, celebrities and entertainers from all over the world. He also sees them for care when they attend the ESPN award show known as the ESPY's.

#7 - He looked at the entire pillow market and found that they were all sub-standard in terms of what they offer.

He created the "GOOD ROLL PILLOW" which is a circular buckwheat pillow and is unmatched in design and details and cost.

#8 - The packaging of the GOOD ROLL PILLOW is remarkable. Bright green neon logo and wrapping. Beige covering with bronze and gold designs that is completely adjustable in terms of comfort.

#9 - His videos of his adjusting expertise as well as utilizing THE GOOD ROLL PILLOW are all over YouTube, Facebook, Instagram.

#10 - The Good Roll Pillow utilizes non-toxic buckwheat from an organic farm in North Dakota. The covers are made in India from raw, organic cotton. His kids sleep on it as well as all of his patients. Eventually, everyone will be as he says, "On A Roll".

IN CLOSING....

It's been said that, *"The Journey of 1000 Miles Begins With The 1st Step"*.

You've taken the 1st step by reading this book.
Now the work begins.

Just like in the movie THE UNTOUCHABLES, when Sean Connery is about to take his last breaths and then grabs Kevin Costner by the collar and asks him these most important and final last words,

"What Are You Prepared To Do"?

I must ask you the same question......

As you read, each chapter was summarized with a **Top 10** list of takeaways from each Doctor featured.

SO, to help you along your own personal pursuit of squeezing more juice out of life, setting & reaching goals & living a life of no regrets, then as my final gift to you, I will share my personal **TOP 10 Tips, Tools, Strategies & Secrets to "Living The Dream"**.

1. Money is replaceable, time is not. Whether you realize it or not, you are "on the clock".

2. Keep a legal pad and write down everything you want to get done TODAY. I usually keep my list between 10-20 busy deeds.

Cross it off as it gets completed. Carry over to the next new page what has not been completed today. If you get tired of looking at the same busy deed, ask yourself "is it that important" or are you simply procrastinating. If it's the later, wake-up and work.

3. Put yourself in an environment that brings out the best in you to learn, to grow, to be, to do, to have, to create, to give, to love.

   A beach, a hotel, a library, a coffee shop, a mountain, a city, etc.

   Come away different than when you arrived and dial-it in.

4. Take time to move/exercise. Movement creates energy and energy "Feeds the Machine".

5. I use a Blackberry Flip Phone. Not because I'm retro but because I'm not here to play games on my phone. My phone is a communication tool and a business tool.

   It thus allows me to G.S.D., (Get S*** Done). Short, direct, to the point. If you are using your phone for anything else, wake-up.

6. Music. Music is a feeling, a mood, an emotion, a tool. Music allows you to go back to place that creates meaning. Allowing you to put a soundtrack to your own journey.

   Use Spotify to create playlists. Use it to bring out the best in you. Then most importantly, balance it with extended periods of silence. That's how you "Pump the Well".

7. Your purpose here is to simply understand yourself better. To be 100% honest with yourself. To get more out of the life experience. Just like a deck of 52 cards, every day you're dealt a different hand.

   How you played the hand yesterday may not be how you play the hand today. Okay to take 1 step backwards to then take 100 steps forward.

8. Get up earlier and understand that it is always about 1 word. "Momentum". YES, and Coffee because I like the taste. You create your own balance.

   Surround yourself with hungry, brilliant people who share your vision and go to work.

9. Everyone in my Life has 1 thing in common. They make me Laugh. That's my "Inner Circle".

   The more you Laugh, the more you become. Find people/ experiences that do that for you.

10. Don't take any S*** from anyone.

Now, here is your 1st busy deed.
Tell me what you enjoyed the most about this book.
Could be 1 thing, could be 10 things.

There is a reason you must do this. Do it now.
Send me an email at: DrPerryBard@aol.com

Share the Love,
Dr. B

For Information on Dr. Perry Bard's Lectures, Seminars, Trainings, Workshops, Bootcamps, Certifications & Masterminds,

Contact: 888-990-9660
www.ConciergeCoaches.com

For Information on Seating to the #1 Rated Event of Entrepreneurial Doctors,

Visit: www.TheChiroEvent.com

CPSIA information can be obtained
at www.ICGtesting.com
Printed in the USA
JSHW031642210121
11138JS00001B/1